THE SONNETS, SONGS AND POEMS

OF SHAKESPEARE

THE SONNETS
SONGS & POEMS OF
SHAKESPEARE

EDITED WITH INTRODUCTION, RUNNING
COMMENTARY, GLOSSES AND NOTES BY

OSCAR JAMES CAMPBELL

ILLUSTRATED WITH 25 WOODCUTS

SCHOCKEN BOOKS · NEW YORK

The illustrations in this volume first appeared in the *Hypnerotomachia Poliphili,* of Francesco Colonna, Venice, 1499, treasured by bibliophiles as the most beautiful production of the Aldus press. Giovanni Bellini is supposed to have been the artist, but there is no adequate evidence to confirm this supposition. A translation by Sir Robert Dallington, *The Strife of Love in a Dream,* with some of the 170 woodcuts of the original, appeared in London in 1592, about the time that Shakespeare was beginning to write his sonnets. The drawings are chosen for background and tone, not as illustrations of specific poems.

CONTENTS

ACKNOWLEDGMENTS

Like everyone else who has written on Shakespeare's sonnets since 1944, the date of the appearance of the indispensable *A Variorum Edition of Shakespeare: The Sonnets,* I am greatly indebted to the scholarship of its brilliant editor, Hyder Rollins. To an unpublished manuscript of the late John Corbin I owe even more. During the later stages of his study of the sonnets I was closely associated with his work. After his death I revised and partly rewrote his manuscript in preparation for its publication. Although the form in which his ideas are expressed in this work is mine, I have adopted many of his critical opinions. However, I have rejected so many parts of his design and modified so many others that I must take full responsibility for all the ideas expressed in this edition of the sonnets and also for the language in which they have been clothed.

My most immediate indebtedness is to Mr. Alfred Rothschild, co-editor of the Bantam Shakespeare. He has read all the proof of this volume with devoted care, detected infelicities in the style, some inaccuracy in the glosses, and a few errors. Many of his suggestions for improvement I have adopted with gratitude for his indispensable aid in helping to make the book a little more worthy of its subject.

O.J.C.

THE SONNETS

1. THE KEY

This edition of Shakespeare's sonnets is designed not so much for scholars as for general readers, most of whom now give sustained attention to only a few of the poems. They linger over those lyrics that are appealing for their beauty and eloquence, without bothering about any relationship between individual sonnets or about each poem's contribution to a story. Even scholars often find their interests waning before they have read all of the sonnets.

One reason for this fitful attention is that few readers hold a key that will unlock in each sonnet a significance of larger import than its marking a "moment's monument" in the career of an intense emotional experience. The present editor seeks to provide such a key. He will try to show that, if the poems are read in the order in which they appear in Thomas Thorpe's 1609 quarto, with a few displacements, they tell a coherent story of Shakespeare's relationships with a young aristocrat, who becomes his dear Friend, and with the Dark Lady, a seductive girl who served at the same time as the mistress of both men. The sonnets are not a narrative of events, but, like most other sequences of the age, lyrical expressions of moods, emotions, and ideas. They are verse letters sent in groups of two or more either to the Friend or to the mistress.

The sequence is divided into two parts. The first 126 sonnets are addressed to the Friend; sonnets 127–152 to the Dark Lady. Both parts were written at approximately the same time and should, therefore, be read collaterally.

Some commentators add a fourth character to the dramatis personae—a so-called rival poet. But it will later appear that there was more than one literary rival for the favor of the Friend.

Our search for the identity of the Friend and the lady must begin with an examination of the dedication to the first publication of the sonnets, in the 1609 quarto issued by Thomas Thorpe, their printer:

TO • THE • ONLIE • BEGETTER • OF •
THESE • INSVING • SONNETS •
Mr W. H. ALL • HAPPINESSE •
AND • THAT • ETERNITIE •
PROMISED
BY •
OVR • EVER-LIVING • POET •
WISHETH •
THE • WELL-WISHING •
ADVENTVRER • IN •
SETTING •
FORTH •

T.T.

Put into the normal word order of an English sentence, Thorpe's dedication reads as follows: "To the only begetter of these ensuing sonnets, Mr. W. H., the well-wishing adventurer in setting forth wisheth all happiness and that eternity promised by our ever-living poet, [signed] T. T." (i.e., Thomas Thorpe).

The dedication is written in Thorpe's usual bombastic style and is deliberately obscure. The most crucial of his ambiguities is the phrase "onlie begetter." Sir Sidney Lee took the word "begetter" to mean "procurer" or "obtainer," and thought it referred to one of Thorpe's agents, William Hall, who had got hold of author's copies of the sonnets, which he delivered to Thorpe. Francis Meres' *Palladis Tamia (Wits' Treasury)*, published in 1598, contains a list of works Shakespeare had written up to that year, and includes his "sugred sonnets [circulating] among his private friends." In the following year, 1599, William Jaggard, a not very honest printer, issued a volume called *The Passionate Pilgrim*. In it he published sonnets 138 and 144 in forms slightly different from those of Thorpe's quarto. These publications may have whetted Thorpe's appetite for a manuscript of all the "sugred sonnets." So he alerted William Hall to be on the lookout for a copy. Hall was successful and delivered the prize to Thorpe, who issued it in 1609. Sir Sidney's guess is now accepted by few if any scholars.

A. L. Rowse in his recent *William Shakespeare, A Biography* (1963), revives a theory first propounded in an article published in *The Athenaeum* of April 27, 1867, that Mr. W. H. is Master William Hervey, the third husband of Southampton's mother. He goes on to explain that the manuscript of the sonnets was stored away in Southampton House and came to light only at the dowager Countess' death. Professor Rowse, like Sir Sidney, accepts "begetter" in the meaning of "procurer" —a definition the word assumes in no other instance in Elizabethan literature.

The two most popular choices for the role of Mr. W. H. as "begetter" in the sense of "creator" or "inspirer" are Henry Wriothesley, the third Earl of Southampton (1573–1620) and William Herbert, the third Earl of Pembroke (1580–1630).

To Southampton Shakespeare dedicated his early erotic poems *Venus and Adonis* and *The Rape of Lucrece* in terms that reveal a growing intimacy between the poet and his patron. To Pembroke and his brother Philip, the Earl of Montgomery, the editors of the first folio edition of the plays dedicated their volume. They explain their choice as follows: "But since your Lordships have been pleased to think these trifles something, heretofore; and have prosecuted both them and their author living with so much favor. . . For so much were your likings of the several parts, when they were acted, as before they were published, the volume asked to be yours." I am aware that any use of these great Lords' names without adding all their formal titles was a star-chamber offense. However, Thorpe was bold and unscrupulous enough to risk prosecution if he thought, in his illegal fashion, that he could thus effectively conceal the identity of Mr. W. H. Considering the part that the Friend plays in the sonnet story, Thorpe would have felt that the concealment of the Friend's identity was a crucial matter. In spite of these obstacles to identification, most scholars now believe that many details of the sequence are meaningless unless they concern real men and one very real woman.

In assuming that the sonnets are essentially autobiographical I differ from a school of interpretation that believes them to be, like the poems in the Greek Anthology, a purely literary exercise. Sir Sidney Lee became the leader of this school after reversing his early opinion. His first view was that though Shakespeare's phraseology is often cryptic, the experiences recorded "are those of Shakespeare's own heart." But in an essay entitled "The Vogue of the Elizabethan Sonnets," affixed to an enlarged edition of his *Life of Shakespeare* (1917), Sir Sidney abruptly, and without explanation, confesses that he has changed his mind. When he compares, with great learning, the mass of sonnets that issued from the presses

of Italy and France in the sixteenth century, he finds most
of Shakespeare's poems imitations of the works of his Con-
tinental predecessors, and therefore mere trials of literary
skill.

It is true that the style Shakespeare adopted for his sonnets
is a compound of rhetorical artifice, conventional in design,
technique, and conception. Yet he has transformed these conventions into expressions of originality and in the process
made the spirit of the sonnets definitely realistic. In this respect they differ from those of the English Platonic School,
whose chief ornaments were Spenser and Sidney. The characters in their poems tend to have more symbolic than personal
significance; but Shakespeare's are real men and women.

The second group with which I am in conflict is composed
of many contemporary critics, who believe the poems to be
Shakespeare's collected sonnets, written on many different occasions for many different purposes. Buried in this mass, they
admit, is the autobiographical drama of three characters.

There is, however, an equally strong tradition for the belief
that the sonnets are entirely autobiographical. Wordsworth's
famous statement, contained in his "Scorn Not the Sonnet," can
serve as a touchstone for the many members of this school of
interpretation: "With this key Shakespeare unlocked his
heart." By the middle of the century, David Masson (1822–
1907), best known as author of the great biography of Milton,
was able to write, "Criticism seems now pretty conclusively to
have determined that the sonnets of Shakespeare are, and can
possibly be nothing else than a poetical record of his own
feelings and experiences. They are autobiographic, distinctly,
intensely, painfully autobiographic." Poets and men of letters
have been prone to adopt this view. For example, the American poet, Sidney Lanier (1842–1881) writes, in 1879, "The sonnets told a shocking story of a faithless friend and a fickle
mistress." The famous scholar F. J. Furnivall (1825–1910) took
an extreme view of the question. "No one," he emphasizes,
"can understand Shakespeare who does not hold that his sonnets are autobiographical and that they explain the depths of
the soul of Shakespeare who wrote the plays." To this literary
and scholarly tradition I attach my interpretation.

Between Southampton and Pembroke, the best modern critical opinion is on the side of the latter. Whatever Thorpe's
dedication may mean, Mr. W. H. cannot possibly stand for
Mr. Henry Wriothesley. The lack of any record of his friendship with the poet after 1594 makes him an unlikely candidate

for the Friend. Moreover, the absence of his name from the Heming and Condell dedication of the *First Folio* shows that the noble Lord had evinced little interest in Shakespeare's career as a playwright. Even more significant is the fact that there are in the sonnets no references to Southampton's later stormy career. A minor but significant piece of evidence against Southampton's candidacy is the fact that the sonnets' punning on the word "will" is pointless unless the Friend's name, like the poet's, was William.

This leaves us with William Herbert as possessing the strongest claim to being Mr. W. H. On the death of his father in January, 1601, he became the Third Earl of Pembroke. Shakespeare's relationship to the Pembroke family must have been established early in his career. His first plays, those written between 1589 and 1592, were acted by a company called Pembroke's Men. This organization appears first in the record during 1592 and was disbanded in September, 1593. The actor's patron was the Third Earl's father, and his mother was the famous Countess of Pembroke (for whom her elder brother, Sir Philip Sidney, wrote *The Countesse of Pembroke's Arcadia*). The relation of actor-servant to the families of their patrons was often close. And, between an already renowned poet and the cultured Earl and his Countess, it was probably sympathetic and intimate. In 1592 their son and heir was 12 years old, a "lovely boy" in Shakespeare's view, even before he had occasion to address the youth directly. Shakespeare's frequent tribute to his beauty shows that he was a handsome youth. If this child were father to the man, he already possessed qualities that would make him congenial to the poet.

Dover Wilson in his recent *An Introduction to Shakespeare's Sonnets* calls attention to a portrait of Pembroke drawn by the Earl of Clarendon (1609–1674) in his *The History of the Rebellion and Civil War in Ireland* and to John Aubrey's *Brief Lives*. We learn from these sources that Pembroke was an ideal man of the Renaissance, dedicated to learning, a patron of poets, a minor poet himself and of an "affable, generous and magnificent disposition." He was unfortunately "given to women," and his "licentious grace" made him irresistible. These qualities must have existed *in petto* in the boy to whom Shakespeare was immediately attracted and later became utterly devoted. Dover Wilson's reasoned interpretation of the evidence leads him to the same conclusion as that of the late Hyder Rollins, the learned editor of the massive two-volume *A Variorum Edition of Shakespeare: The Sonnets* (1944). After long study of all the evidence, Rollins believed that the case for Pembroke was stronger than that for Southampton.

Therefore, following an approved method of scientific investigation, I have adopted as a working hypothesis—and when everything is "clouded with a doubt" it can be no more than that—the assumption that Pembroke was the man to whom most of the sonnets were addressed. The conclusions I draw from this tentative theory form the basis of my interpretation of individual sonnets and their sequence. This method brings order to a tangled situation and thus fulfills the editor's main purpose. It enables the reader to follow without confusion the story of the poet's way of meeting an intellectual and moral crisis of his middle years.

2. THE DATE

The most widely held view is that Shakespeare began to compose the sonnets during the years 1593–94 and that he continued writing them occasionally up to the end of Queen Elizabeth's reign in 1603. These were the years in which the vogue of the sonnet reached its height in England. There is no external evidence extant to establish the truth of these assumed dates.

If Shakespeare did write his first sonnets in 1593 and if they were addressed to William Herbert, later the Earl of Pembroke, the youth, who was born in 1580, would have been only thirteen years old when he received his first poetic letter. At that age he could have grown into a "lovely boy." But to urge a thirteen- or fourteen-year-old adolescent to marry so that he could perpetuate his beauty seems faintly ridiculous to us. (It is true, however, that the Elizabethan gentry arranged marriages for their children at what seems to us a scandalously early age.) We do know that in 1595, when Herbert was fifteen years old, his parents were trying to induce him to marry Elizabeth Carey, but he would have none of it. At this time the poet probably had come into close enough touch with Herbert's parents to become aware of the problem of their son's marriage and to give them such help as he could in solving it.

Shakespeare's response to their proposal was successful in a way they could not have anticipated. He not only wrote seventeen ornate sonnets on the subject they had asked him to develop, but in the process he also became a close friend of the young man and his kindly mentor. Shakespeare's insistence on Herbert's beauty shows that the youth was susceptible to what seems to us exaggerated flattery. This family situation forms so natural a reason for the poet's turning from dramatic composition to the writing of sonnets that it seems likely that Shakespeare did not begin his sonnet story until the year 1595; therefore it was not the popularity of the vogue that induced him to write his own sort of sugared sonnets, but his response to external prodding.

The question of how long Shakespeare continued to write poems for his sonnet story can be partially answered by the proper interpretation of sonnet 107, the so-called "dated sonnet."

> Not mine own fears, nor the prophetic soul
> Of the wide world dreaming on things to come,
> Can yet the lease of my true love control,
> Supposed as forfeit to a confined doom.
> The mortal moon hath her eclipse endured,
> And the sad augurs mock their own presage;
> Incertainties now crown themselves assured,
> And peace proclaims olives of endless age.
> Now with the drops of this most balmy time
> My love looks fresh, and Death to me subscribes,
> Since, spite of him, I'll live in this poor rhyme,
> While he insults o'er dull and speechless tribes:
>   And thou in this shalt find thy monument,
>   When tyrants' crests and tombs of brass are spent.

The critics all agree that the sonnet contains a reference to important political events. The interpretation most widely accepted is that the poem is Shakespeare's public congratulation to the Earl of Southampton on his release from prison ("confined doom") where he had languished since 1601 for his involvement in Essex's rebellion. King James, upon coming to the throne in 1603, ordered him released. Since the editor of the present volume believes that Pembroke and not Southampton was the Friend, he cannot accept this explanation. Moreover, there are more cogent reasons for rejecting this interpretation. "The mortal moon hath her eclipse endured" would have to mean Queen Elizabeth has died. This would be an offhand, almost insulting way of referring to an event of such national and world importance. Nor would the poet have been likely to herald the advent of a new monarch in so casual a fashion.

Other scholars have found the year 1596 a more likely date. That was the Queen's climacteric year, her sixty-third; from its widely apprehended dangers she emerged unscathed on

September 6, 1596. This would have been an appropriate moment for the poet's congratulation. Moreover, occultists believed that great and notable changes in the state frequently occurred in September, the month in which God began his creation of the world.

John Corbin, in his manuscript already referred to, offered a third solution, which we adopt, with a tribute to his insight, and now proceed to develop. Corbin began his scrutiny with the phrase "not mine own fears," which, taken with the triumphant "Death to me subscribes" (yields), makes the meaning of the sonnet emphatically personal. It announces that fears of his own death and imprisonment have been dispelled along with similar fears for the safety of the Queen. His release from an intimately personal anxiety coincided with the nation's release from its anxiety. This widespread relief produced a state of universal euphoria that Shakespeare shared with peculiar intensity.

The only time at this period of Shakespeare's life when he might have thought himself in danger was during a few days after the outbreak of Essex's "rebellion" on February 8, 1601. Shakespeare and his fellow actors had played a perilous role in that uprising. Although from the vantage point of the present the *putsch* seems to have been hare-brained in conception and insanely rash in execution, at the time it carried the threat of Civil War and bloodshed.

Shakespeare's Company was indirectly involved in the "rebellion." A group among the conspirators induced Shakespeare's Company to produce *Richard II* at the Globe Theatre on the Saturday before the fatal Sunday. They were persuaded to do so with difficulty. The Company, when approached, objected that the play was so "out of use" that they would have "small or no Company at it." But the conspirators met these objections by paying forty shillings more than the usual fee of ten pounds for a command performance. That in itself was then a considerable sum. The Globe Company, thus bribed, did stage the play, including the offensive scene of the King's deposition. The Queen, though frightened, took the necessary measures for her protection. When the unarmed band entered the city to find the streets empty and no signs of popular support, they retreated to Essex's Castle, barricaded it, and, after a token resistance, surrendered. The management of the Globe, though closely examined, was exonerated. Essex and most of his fellow conspirators were executed and their property was confiscated.

Biographers of Shakespeare have made light of his involvement in these events. But to present on the stage the dethronement of a king, and Richard II in particular, would seem to the Queen a very serious offense. For Richard II was widely regarded as her historical symbol, as the following anecdote shows. The Keeper of the Tower, William Lambarde, records a conversation with her shortly after Essex's beheading. Lambarde and the Queen were going over the pandects (legal records) of her predecessors on the English throne; when they reached the name of Richard II, she said "I am Richard, know ye not that?" Hence a dramatization of his deposition would be an inescapable suggestion that she too could easily be dethroned and possibly, like him, killed. Essex's crime was thus not only treason to her personal affection for him, but also to the "divinity that doth hedge a King."

There is no record of any other performances of the tragedy during the political crisis. In spite of the Queen's angry assertion that it "was played forty times in open streets and houses," "forty" still is a byword for a great many and the Queen was in a mood to exaggerate. In any case, the temper of her assertion is of more importance in this context than its accuracy.

However, the Queen showed her forgiveness of the actors in a manner extraordinary even for her. She ordered the Company to play a command performance at court on the evening before the day on which Essex was beheaded. That must have been a gruesome occasion for both the Queen and the actors. Shakespeare, in particular, must have shuddered at the thought of how narrowly he had escaped the punishment she had meted out to the principal conspirators, and rejoiced that Death had "subscribed" to him and that the Queen by escaping the plot had "her eclipse endured." In this time, his love, like everything else, takes on a fresh glow and makes him anew convinced that his poetry will erect for his Friend the monument that will outlast the tombs and crests of Kings and tyrants.

From the evidence presented in this chapter, we can safely conclude that Shakespeare began to write the first part of his sonnet story no later than 1595 and that he continued composing poems for the sequence at least as late as 1601.

3. THE SONNET VOGUE

Petrarch (1304–1374), the first great writer of a sonnet sequence, established the conventions that dominated the vogue
in the literature of Europe for nearly three hundred years.
Almost all of his 317 sonnets, now called *Il Canzoniere,* were
addressed to a lady, half real and half ideal, whom Petrarch
calls Laura. All expressed in one way or another the grief and
despair that the lady's inaccessibility provoked. There is some
doubt as to whether Petrarch's passion was real or merely a
form of literary devotion conforming to the ideals of chivalric
love. The sonnet vogue passed from Italy to France, where
some of the greatest poets, such as Ronsard, DuBellay, and
Desportes, assiduously cultivated the art. Desportes' volume,
entitled *Premières Oeuvres* (1575), contained more than three
hundred sonnets addressed to three different ladies. The collection was very popular in England, where it exerted a great
influence.

The two English collections which did most to establish the
conventions of the form when Shakespeare adopted it were
Thomas Watson's *A Passionate Centurie of Love* (1582), addressed to his patron the Earl of Oxford, and Sir Philip Sidney's *Astrophel and Stella.* Watson takes professional pride in
showing that his work is not original, for he meticulously gives
the source of every one of the ideas and conceits that he has
borrowed from his Italian and French predecessors. Sidney
takes the name Astrophel, lover of the star, to address the
beautiful Stella. The lady was really Penelope Devereux,
Lady Rich, with whom Sidney had an unfortunate love affair.
But only part of the sequence concerns the romance. The rest
of the poems are conventional, and imitative of earlier models.
When the poet began to compose his sonnets, three varieties
had been definitely established: (1.) love sonnets, (2.) sonnèts
to a patron, (3.) religious and philosophical sonnets. Shakespeare wrote examples of each type and often combined all
three in a single sonnet.

Shakespeare, moreover, exploits one or another of the many
conventions developed by the fashionable sonneteers. For example, Petrarch and nearly all his imitators wrote poems on
the so-called eternizing theme—the idea that poetical en-
comium is the most effective way to confer earthly immortality upon a patron. Thirteen of Shakespeare's sonnets celebrate this idea. It is announced in stately fashion in the first
lines of the 55th sonnet:

> Not marble, nor the gilded monuments
> Of princes, shall outlive this powerful rhyme . . .

A subject closely associated with the eternizing theme is The Triumph of Time. The title suggests the Roman custom of celebrating military victories with magnificent processions through the city streets. Petrarch created visionary and symbolical imitations of these Roman pageants in a series of poems called Triumphs—first of Love over Life; then, in ceremonious procession, of Chastity, of Death, of Fame, of Time, and finally of Eternity. Shakespeare celebrates only the Triumph of Time, a subject to which he devotes some of his most eloquent sonnets, for example his 60th, in which

> Time doth transfix the flourish set on youth
> And delves the parallels in beauty's brow,
> Feeds on the rarities of nature's truth,
> And nothing stands but for his scythe to mow . . .

Mark Van Doren suggests that "as far as the sequence has unity, it is organized about the theme of Time's decay." The leitmotif of the series is the ravages of time—"Time swift-footed, terrible Time."

Though Shakespeare uses many of the less significant Petrarchan conventions, he mercifully spares us the one in which the sonneteer laments his failure to win the lady. Shakespeare's lover does not luxuriate in the woes of a rejected suitor. We are spared the description of sleepless nights and long-drawn-out despair; he does not even praise his unattainable lady in overwrought poetical conceits. On the contrary, in sonnet 21 he ridicules the conventional far-fetched comparisons between the adored one and objects in Nature:

> With sun and moon, with earth and sea's rich gems,
> With April's first-born flowers, and all things rare . . .

And again in sonnet 130 he belittles the same convention when he exclaims

> My mistress' eyes are nothing like the sun;
> Coral is far more red than her lips' red:
>
> .   .   .   .
>
> And yet, by heaven, I think my love as rare
> As any she belied with false compare.

More than half Shakespeare's sonnets have emancipated themselves from the tyranny of Petrarchan conventions and sound new notes in the lyric chorus of the age. He finds, for example, other causes for grief than the disappointments of romantic love. In sonnet 30 his tears flow: "For precious friends hid in death's dateless night . . ." And in sonnet 29 it is his lack of "this man's art and that man's scope" that renders him melancholy. Sonnet 66 shows him sunk in Hamlet's mood, distressed by the triumph of folly and evil over wisdom and virtue: "And captive good attending captain ill . . ." In one sonnet (111) the poet admits that he suffers humiliation at life's casting him in the role of an actor. He chides Fortune,

> That did not better for my life provide
> Than public means which public manners breeds . . .

Another striking innovation is the expression, half rueful, half revolted, of his feeling toward the brunette, the so-called Dark Lady. Most of the sonnets from 127 to 152 inclusive describe the tortures with which her disdain and infidelity afflict him, for he knows that her attraction is merely sensual and therefore destructive of his better nature. Some of the most telling of the poems attack her deceit, which the lover recognizes but is loath to believe.

> When my love swears that she is made of truth
> I do believe her, though I know she lies.

Other sonnets betray his abject slavery to her whims, as when in sonnet 143 he makes an appeal for mere kindness and begs her to ". . . turn back to me / And play the mother's part, kiss me, be kind. . . ." At one of the rare moments when the lover escapes from the spell cast upon him by her physical charms (sonnet 129) he can execrate the lust which holds him captive, recognizing it to be "The expense of spirit in a waste of shame . . ." And in a deeper searching of his soul he can cry out, as in sonnet 146, against the rebel powers that betray his spirit, and beg his soul to "Buy terms divine in selling hours of dross . . ."

But having remarked all this, the reader must realize that the true subject of the sonnets is neither love nor friendship, nor yet the triumph of the poet's devotion to his patron over the lure of an unworthy passion. Rather, these poems celebrate the variety and fullness of the world in which every human drama must be played. Shakespeare's interests range from the humorous to the ineffable. He can envisage the situation of the careful housewife who, while chasing a chicken, leaves her crying child in the lurch, and in the next moment echo the cosmic surge of waves on the pebbled shore. He is as sensitive to the exquisite tracery of the choir of a ruined monastery as to the "wide world dreaming on things to come." Above all, he is concerned with inevitable death and the decay of all man's proud achievements.

The form Shakespeare adopted for his sonnets—three quatrains and a couplet—was the same one employed by all important Elizabethan sonneteers, except Sidney and Spenser. Shakespeare ordinarily places a strong pause in sense and in rhythm at the close of each quatrain, and often the strongest pause of all falls at the end of the eighth line. He manages the form with ease and grace, evoking from it a great variety of music. In these artfully composed sonnets, the couplet sums up the true essence of the poem or, more often, introduces what Tucker Brooke calls a "surprising negative." This furnishes a dramatic reversal of the point of view developed or stated anew in each quatrain. But in most of the sonnets the last two lines bring the poem swiftly to earth. Like the songs scattered through the plays, the sonnets, to borrow a phrase from Mark Van Doren, are likely to be "brightest at the beginning and often burn out before the end."

4. THE CULT OF FRIENDSHIP

Throughout the sonnets Shakespeare addresses Pembroke as a beloved in the language adopted by Petrarch and his followers for the adoration of a woman. On the surface many of the sonnets written to the youth appear to be orthodox love poems. This fact has influenced many readers to suspect that they betray homosexual impulses. However, many English gentlemen in Elizabethan England paid enthusiastic allegiance to the Renaissance cult of friendship between two men. This type of relationship had scriptural warrant in the love of David and Jonathan, which "surpassed the love of women." In spite of the adulation the Virgin Queen expected from her courtiers, two of her favorites among them extolled male friendship. Richard Edwards in a moving play, *Damon and Pythias* (1571), made the ideal proverbial. And John Lyly in his *Euphues,* or *The Anatomy of Wit* (1579), paid extravagant tribute to such friendship, ranking it far above love between the sexes in nobility and fidelity. Lyly wrote, "The love of men to women is a thing common and of course; the friend ship of man is infinite and immortal. Love is but an eye-worm, which only tickleth the head with hopes and wishes; friend-ship the image of eternity, in which there is nothing move-able, nothing mischievous . . . Friendship standeth stiffly in storms. Time draweth wrinkles in a fair face, but addeth fresh colours to a fast friend, which neither heat, nor cold, nor place, nor destiny can alter or diminish."

It is important to realize that this ideal retained its vigor well into the seventeenth century. Citing the example of Damon and Pythias, Sir Thomas Browne in his *Religio Medici* (c. 1635) exalted the love of a friend above that of parents, wives, and children, and called it inferior only to the love of God and the Holy Trinity. By it men learn "how God loves man." Thus the love of a friend becomes "a mystical union, one soul in two bodies." Familiarity with this ample literature celebrating the glory of male friendship would have justified Shakespeare in calling his affection for Pembroke "dear religious love."

Moreover, the poet could find in real life a parallel to his friendship for Pembroke in the diplomat Herbert Languet's relationship with Sir Philip Sidney, Pembroke's uncle.† In his eighteenth year, just after being graduated from Oxford, Sidney embarked on the grand tour of the Continent, then considered an essential post-graduate education for all scions of the Eng-lish nobility. In Germany he met the fifty-four-year-old Herbert Languet. Both ardent Protestants, they found themselves hold-ing similar opinions on politics and religion, but the corre-spondence shows that the older man admired more than Sid-ney's opinions on these subjects. Languet was obviously greatly taken with the youth's physical beauty, social charm, and the chivalry that made him a model for all English noblemen. Languet filled his letters with philosophical discussion, but he veered easily from affairs of state to private and intimate badinage. Most often he turned to expression of intense and exalted love: "I love all who are dear to you." When Sidney left for Italy, Languet was so overcome with grief that he "shed tears that hardly suffered you to say farewell."

Sidney later became embarrassed by the love expressed in his friend's letters, and protested that if he accepted as truth Languet's extravagant compliments, it would offend against modesty. Languet himself had second thoughts about his fervid

† *Correspondence of Sir Philip Sidney and Herbert Languet.* Edited by William Aspenwold Bradley. Boston, 1912.

language and begged Philip "not to show anyone the foolish letters I send to you. . . . It is enough for me if I succeed in making you believe you are very dear to me." He spoke of his strict observance of the conditions of their friendship as though it had been a sacred, sworn pact and continued to write as to a beloved: "Farewell, love me, from one who loves you better than himself."

Although Shakespeare may well have had some knowledge of the French diplomat's "love" for Sidney, I do not suggest that he modeled his verse letters to Pembroke on Languet's impassioned prose. Yet Languet's role as lover and mentor was much like that which the poet assumed toward his Friend. That the emotion of both was tinged with homosexual feeling is unlikely. Both older men were only proving themselves adept in that dear religious love that animated the widespread cult of male friendship. The sense of realism that permeates every aspect of the sonnet story makes Shakespeare's use of the language of passion to his youthful lord seem like love in the more usual sense of the word.

5. "THE RIVAL POET"

In the sequence, Shakespeare refers to one or more rivals for Lord Herbert's favor. Earlier critics assumed that there was only one rival, and tried to discover who he was. More recently, commentators have generally agreed that there was certainly more than one poet Shakespeare thought to be his rival. The first references to him are vague. In sonnet 23, the poet pleads with his Friend to read his love in his eyes more than in ". . . that tongue that more hath more expressed." The line clearly describes an unidentified individual who has more fully expressed love's ardor for the noble youth than he.

In number 32, written in deep dejection, Shakespeare, speaking directly to his Friend, says in effect, If you should survive me, you will surely hear praise of yourself by better poets than I. When this happens, read their work if you must for its style, but continue to read mine for the deep love it expresses:

> But since he died, and poets better prove,
> Theirs for their style I'll read, his for his love.

This is rather an expression of the modesty traditionally expected of a poet than fear of any rival.

In 38 the poet's reference to rivals is more specific and more hostile. He boasts that his theme is beyond the capacities of the low creatures who in addressing Herbert challenge his right to be the only poet seeking the youth's favor. Shakespeare's answer is that he will continue to play variations on the theme of Herbert's beauty and virtue as long as those qualities can serve as the inspiration of his verse. This is the poet's first intimation that his anxiety over the efforts of commonplace poetasters to supersede him is real.

In sonnet 75, usually described as the first of the Rival Poet series, the author explores his fear that "the filching age" will steal his Friend, now for the first time described as a locked-up "treasure." The thievish culprits are probably the crowd of dissolute companions against whom the poet warns the youth in sonnets 67 to 74.

In the next sonnet, 76, the poet asks his Friend a rhetorical question: If my poetry is so lacking in distinction, why do I not adopt some of the "new-found methods" and "compounds strange" of my avant-garde contemporaries? These phrases serve admirably as a loose description of the distinguishing characteristics of the style of John Donne's early metaphysical poetry. Remembering the wildness of Donne's young days, we feel reasonably justified in assigning him a place among the rakes, who, the poet believes, are leading his Friend astray. Moreover, we know that Donne was once an intimate of the equally profligate Lord William Herbert. According to Ben Jonson, Donne wrote his best pieces before the age of twenty-five, that is, before 1597. In that year Herbert celebrated his eighteenth birthday. The two men were therefore close enough in age to become companions. Later, in 1601, Shakespeare tried his hand at the metaphysical poetry he here depreciates. In this mode he wrote his haunting poem *The Phoenix and the Turtle*. Perhaps he took this way of showing Herbert and his fellow aesthetes that he could, if he chose, write as brilliantly in the metaphysical manner as Donne himself. Why Shakespeare singled Donne out from the crowd of bohemian youths to which Herbert belonged we can only guess. He may have regarded him as the most formidable of his rivals in the group striving for his Friend's favor.

In sonnet 78, the poet complains that his repeated invocation of his Friend as his Muse has provoked the imitation of a crowd of inferior writers. The learned poets in their midst have most obviously benefited from addressing Herbert in laudatory verses. His beauty has taught "heavy ignorance aloft to fly,"—has added feathers to the learned's wing. The representative of these learned poets cannot be the same man as the

creator of "new-found methods." One may guess that he was
Ben Jonson. It is not unlikely that he too was trying to catch
the eye and ear of the rich and reputedly bountiful Lord
William Herbert.

Then, in sonnet 79, the poet laments that, when he alone
called upon his Friend's aid, his verse was worthy of the youth's
"gentle grace," but now his Muse has sickened and yields its
place to a more deserving pen. In sonnet 80, he confesses his
realization that a better spirit, a greater genius, who is dedicating all his powers to praise Herbert, has silenced him. He
believes that his Friend's worth, being as boundless as the
ocean, can, if he chooses, keep afloat the poet's saucy (trim)
bark. Critics have guessed that this greater genius is Marlowe
or Spenser. But there is no evidence, either internal or external, to substantiate these assumptions.

Sonnet 86 contains more valid evidence for identifying a
rival poet than any other in the sequence. And all of it points
to George Chapman.

> Was it the proud full sail of his great verse,
> Bound for the prize of all too precious you,
> That did my ripe thoughts in my brain inhearse,
> Making their tomb the womb wherein they grew?
> Was it his spirit, by spirits taught to write
> Above a mortal pitch, that struck me dead?
> No, neither he, nor his compeers by night
> Giving him aid, my verse astonishèd.
> He, nor that affable familiar ghost
> Which nightly gulls him with intelligence,
> As victors, of my silence cannot boast;
> I was not sick of any fear from thence:
>   But when your countenance filled up his line,
>   Then lacked I matter; that enfeebled mine.

The phrase "the proud full sail of his great verse" is an imaginative description of Chapman's style in his translation of *The
Iliad,* the first seven books of which were first published in
1598. The 14-syllable rhyming verse gives the effect of grandeur
so effectively described in Shakespeare's lines.

The sonnet contains a clearer reference to Chapman in the
phrase "his compeers by night." These were his associates in a
group, probably organized by Sir Walter Raleigh primarily for
the study of navigation, in which the knowledge of astronomy
was fundamental. Shakespeare, in *Love's Labour's Lost,* calls

it the school of night: "Black is the badge of hell, the hue of dungeons, and the school of night."

Thomas Harriot, 1560–1621, a mathematician and astronomer with a wide reputation, was the intellectual leader of the school. Other members were the poets Marlowe and Chapman. Raleigh, Marlowe, and Harriot held religious views so unorthodox that the Jesuit Father Parsons dubbed the group The School of Atheism.

Chapman laid a different emphasis on his studies from that adopted by his colleagues. A mystic, he became interested in what we now call "psychic phenomena" or spiritualism. No one knows what the affable familiar ghost was that nightly gulled Chapman with intelligence. A good guess is that the ghost was a spirit from the other world that was made to materialize as in a modern spiritualistic séance. In attacking this queer mysticism, Shakespeare shows that he is most offended by Chapman's wooing of Lord William.

Shakespeare's assertion that Chapman's ideas were so transcendental that they forced him in shame to bury his own simple thoughts deep in his brain is palpably ironic.

This cursory examination of Shakespeare's direct and oblique references to rival poets in the sonnets shows that he did not constantly fear any single suitor for the Friend's favor, be he Donne, Ben Jonson, or Chapman, or any other contemporary poets suggested by scholars who have written on the sonnets. Shakespeare's anxiety is diffused. His jealousy of those seeking to loosen the bonds of his sacred friendship, and his suspicion of their motives, was much like the jealousy of a lover. Although we have rejected any homosexual taint in the poet's feeling for his Friend, we recognize that the Renaissance cult of male friendship, at least in Shakespeare's case, generated as ardent and complex emotions as a passionate love affair.

6. THE DARK LADY

Critics who decide, as I do, that Lord William Herbert, later the Third Earl of Pembroke, is the Friend to whom Shakespeare addressed most of the sonnets, usually seek to prove that Mary Fitton was the Dark Lady. Although I find it difficult to accept the identification, I will present the evidence that has led to its adoption.

The Dark Lady was almost certainly a lady of high social position. George Lyman Kittredge's conviction that she was somehow connected with Rosaline, the heroine of Shakespeare's

Love's Labour's Lost, is convincing, and recent editors have taken this connection to be a certainty. In the Arden edition of the play (1951), Richard David writes, "Rosaline is clearly a portrait of his (Shakespeare's) own Dark Lady, but from her and her fellows in the Princess' retinue stem a whole race of heroines." Rosaline resembles the Dark Lady in a number of important details. She is a brunette, seductive and easy to seduce. Allusions to her easy virtue recur throughout the comedy.

The Dark Lady's resemblances to Rosaline are so striking that it is natural to infer that she too was one of Queen Elizabeth's maids of honor and that she served as a model for Rosaline. For the Dark Lady is unique. No character like her appears in any other sonnet sequence written during the Renaissance in Italian, French, or English. It is, therefore, tempting to assume that she—and Rosaline—was really Mary Fitton, largely because of Mary Fitton's liaison with Pembroke.

In 1595, when she was seventeen years old, Mary Fitton came down from Cheshire to the Court in London. Her father, Sir Edward Fitton, was in the Irish Administration. The father of Philip and Mary Sidney, the latter Pembroke's mother, used his influence to have Sir Edward knighted. When Mary arrived in London, it was in all the books of hospitality that Lady Pembroke make her welcome at the residence at Wilton. She came to like and admire Mary, and her son developed a passion for the girl. The Queen too found her charming and in 1596 made her one of her maids of honor.

This appointment she owed to Sir William Knollys, then Comptroller of the Queen's Household and an old friend of Mary's father. He seems to have had advance notice of her charm. At least, he wrote to Anne, Mary's sister, effusively promising to play the Good Shepherd and to "defend the innocent lamb against the woeful cruelty and fox-like subtlety" of the young courtiers. At the same time, he wrote to Sir Edward assuring him that "I will with my counsel advise your fair daughter with my true affection, love her and with my sword defend her if need be and I will be careful of her well-doing as if I were her true father." These protestations of fatherly affection came to naught, for almost immediately he fell passionately and hopelessly in love with the irresistible Mary. In a series of letters to her sister Anne, he expatiates on his wretched state, for he was many years older than the girl and already married to an ailing old woman. Besides, Mary increasingly neglects him. The sum of his grief is that, although he is tortured by toothache, Mary no longer comes to bid him good night. When his wife died in 1604 and he was at last free to marry again, Mary had traveled far out of his sphere. So, at the age of sixty-one, he married a nineteen-year-old girl, doubtless an unsatisfactory substitute for the fascinating Mary.

The lines Shakespeare gave "black" Rosaline to speak in *Love's Labour's Lost:*

> The blood of youth burns not with such excess
> As gravity's revolt to wantonness.

neatly describe Sir William's ardor and may have been intended to remind the audience at the Court play of his antics. If Rosaline really was a portrait of the Dark Lady who all the courtiers realized was Mary Fitton, no one in the special audience in the know would miss the topical reference.

Mary broke completely with her suitor the moment she discovered that she could gain the attention of any of the young dandies at Court she chose to beguile. Armed with this assurance, she decided to go in for a gay life. Her companions, the maids of honor, were a wild lot. We are indebted to Sir Nicholas L'Estrange for a vivid picture of Knollys' relationship to the honorable maids.

Perhaps in pursuance of his office of Comptroller of the Queen's Household, Sir William Knollys occupied lodgings adjacent to those of the maids of honor and next door to a room in which the girls "used to frisk and hay about . . . to his extreme disquiet a nights" (the "antic hay" was a brisk and riotous dance). So Sir William "contrived to have their own back door unbolted, strips off [to] his shirt, and so with a pair of spectacles on his nose and Aretino in his hand comes marching in at a postern door of his own chamber, reading very gravely, full upon the faces of them . . . and often traversing the room in this posture above an hour." Presumably his purpose was to quiet and punish the girls. Any other suggestion would, of course, be actionable by the censors. But the significance of his ostentatious reading of one of Pietro Aretino's licentious books, (conceivably the *Dialogue Between Nanna and Antonia on the Life of Courtesans*), would not be lost on the errant maids.

From the first, Mary's mother was worried about the influence of these wild girls on her daughter. On July 3, 1598, she writes to Anne: "If you hear anything of your sister, pray let me know for I never heard from her since." (Since becoming a maid?)

Mary also clearly had some sort of contact with Shakespeare's Company. Conceivably, Herbert had introduced his mistress to some of his friends of the Bankside. At any rate, William Kemp dedicated his *Nine Days Wonder* to Mistress Anne [sic] Fitton, Mayde of Honor to most sacred Mayde Royal, Queen Elizabeth. (He must have meant Mary, because she was a maid of honor and Anne was not.)

In his dedication, Kemp writes: "To shew my duty to your honourable self whose favours among other bountiful friends make me (despite this sad world) judge my heart corke and my heels feathers—But in a word, your poor servant offers the truth of his progress and profit to your honourable view; receive it I beseech you such as it is, rude and plain; for I know your pure judgment looks as soon to see beauty in a Blackamoor, or hear smooth speech from a stammerer, as to find anything but blunt mirth in a Morris dancer, especially such a one as Will Kemp, that hath spent his life in mad jigs and merry jests."

Mary's goings on with Pembroke soon became a public scandal. Sir Rowald Whyte in a letter dispatched to Sir Robert Sidney, shortly after June, 1600, writes as follows: "Old Mrs. Martin, who dwelt at Chopping Court near Ludgate, told me in that time that Mistress Fitton was in great favor, and one of her Majesty's Maids of Honor, and during the time that the Earl of Pembroke favored her, she would put her tire head on and tuck up her clothes and take a long black cloak and march as though she had been a man to meet the said Earl out of Court."

Early in the year 1601, his affair with Mary Fitton and its result was bruited about the Court. On February 5, 1601, Sir Robert Cecil wrote to Sir George Carew as follows: "We have no news but that there is a misfortune befallen Mistress Fitton, for she is proved with child and the Earl of Pembroke, being examined, confesseth a fact, but utterly renounceth marriage. I fear they will both dwell in the Tower, for the Queen hath vowed to send them thither."

Some time in March of this year, 1601, Mary gave birth to a stillborn boy. A letter from Tobie Matthew to Dudley Casteton gives him the news of her delivery. "The Earl of Pembroke is committed to the Fleet; his cause is Mistress Fitton is delivered of a boy who is dead." The Queen punished Mary less severely. She placed her in the care of Lady Hawkins, second wife of Sir John Edgerton. Pembroke's imprisonment was of short duration. Later in the year, the Queen released him and gave him permission to travel. Where he went we do not know.

Pembroke's curt refusal to marry the mother of his illegitimate child, despite the pressure put upon him to do so even by the Queen, was quite in character for the proud self-centered lordling. Sir Edward Fitton, Mary's father, writes on May 16, 1601, a letter to Sir Robert Cecil full of scorn for Herbert's complete indifference to Mary's plight: "I can say nothing of the Earl but my daughter is confident in her chance before God and wisheth that she might but meet before in different scenes [at the altar]. But for myself, I expect no good from him that in all this time hath not showed any kindness. I count my daughter as good a gentlewoman as my Lord is though the dignity of honor [*i.e.*, title] be greater only in him, which hath beguiled her. I fear except my Lord's honesty be the greater virtues" [i.e. unless my lord's honesty be greater than my daughter's virtue, or unless it be the greatest of his virtues and endowments].

After Mary's disgrace at Court, two other much younger men played a leading part in her life, and they too eke out the otherwise deficient background of the sonnet story. Both were sea captains in Elizabeth's Royal Navy, Sir Richard Leveson and William Polewhele. Omerod, in his *History of Cheshire,* believes Mary had two more illegitimate children, by Leveson, but there is some doubt about whether one of those was not the son of Captain Polewhele. Both men lived in Staffordshire where Polewhele was a tenant on Leveson's estate, so that their lives were closely intertwined. When Leveson died in 1606, Polewhele married Mary.

Leveson was a cousin of the Fittons and unquestionably a man of a frank and generous nature. His letters to Anne rival Knollys' in number and intimacy, and are affectionate and amiable. He frequently sends Anne presents and even offers her financial aid. His references to Mary give us a glimpse of her life after 1601. He speaks of her as being with Anne in Cheshire and of her having a "Mistress" in London. Like Knollys, he could not marry Mary for he had a wife, the daughter of Lord Howard of Effingham, who was then confined in a lunatic asylum.

Mary's mother thought that her relations with Leveson were highly improper. She writes Anne in 1606: "I take no joy to hear of your sister, nor of that boy. If it had pleased God when I did bear her, that she and I had been buried, it had saved me from a great deal of sorrow and grief and too from shame and such shame as never had Cheshire woman now than ever. Write no more of her to me."

The boy to whom Lady Fitton refers was probably a son of William Polewhele, born before Mary's marriage to him. At this juncture in Mary's affairs, Lady Frances Stanley, daughter of Ferdinando, Earl of Derby, calls Mary "the vilest woman under the sun," and Polewhele "a very knave who taketh the disgrace of his wife and all her friends to make the world think him worthy of her and she deserved no better." The manor in Staffordshire where Polewhele and his wife Mary lived was the property of Sir Richard Leveson. The lease of this house to Polewhele may have been Sir Richard's way of paying his obvious debt to Mary. Her last marriage was to a Captain Lougher. We know little of him except that he died in 1636, leaving her comfortably provided for, as Captain Polewhele had also done. She lived until 1647 and then faded obscurely, leaving behind, in the manner of another Cheshire creature, a grin.

Mary's career presents us with no specific evidence that she and the Dark Lady were one and the same person. However, a woman of her abandoned nature could easily have become involved in the same situations as those in which the Dark Lady of the sonnet story found herself. Mary's easy virtue would make it simple for her to carry on affairs with two men at the same time. Her later intrigues and marriages with commoners suggest that she would not be too proud to become the mistress of an attractive man of the theater, an intimate friend of her official lover, and an ornament of the stage, of which Pembroke was a generous patron. Mary being the passionate and promiscuous creature that her love life indelibly stamps her to have been, Shakespeare, after his first delight in her favors, would soon realize that his love for her was merely lust and come to despise it and her, as his sonnet against lust amply proves.

After all the facts have been duly considered, perhaps the soundest judgment one can pass on the problem of the identity of the Dark Lady is to say: If she were not Mary Fitton, she must have been another Elizabethan charmer with exactly the same nature.†

† This account of Mary Fitton is based largely on documents printed in two works:

(1.) *Gossip from a Muniment Room, being passages in the lives of Anne and Mary Fitton.* Lady Newdigate-Newdegate. London, 1907.

(2.) *Mary Sidney, Countess of Pembroke.* Frances Berkely Young. London, 1912.

7. OUTLINE OF THE SONNET STORY

The following is an outline of the sonnet story as the editor
believes the individual and grouped poems tell it.

Sonnets 1–17

These sonnets form the first group of poems that the poet
addressed to the youthful Lord William Herbert, who later became the Earl of Pembroke, a youth he had probably not yet
met. They are usually called the "procreation sonnets." In
poem after poem in this group Shakespeare urges the boy to
marry and beget children who will preserve his beauty and his
distinction for the delight of ages yet to come.

Sonnets 18–26

Shakespeare begins to appeal to the youth for his friendship.
Here, as throughout the sequence, he uses "love" in the sense
of friendship. To add a new intensity to his expressions of
devotion, he employs the vocabulary of sexual love to describe
his feelings for the youthful lord. He also states his "eternizing"
theme by asserting that his verse will forever preserve his beloved's beauty and his fame. This second group the poet evidently sent to Pembroke along with the procreation sonnets as
a packet he called a "written ambassage."

Sonnets 127–132

To follow the proper time sequence of the series, we must
now turn to 127–132, the first poems that the poet addressed
to the Dark Lady. He approaches her in a half-teasing manner
suitable to a drawing room. With a touch of irony he praises
her unfashionable black beauty and expresses amorous delight
in her lute playing. It is impossible to determine the exact
moment at which the poet began to compose these poems. It
must have been before he was aware of the lady's intimacy with
Herbert. His wooing was apparently followed by a surprisingly
easy seduction of the girl. Filled with remorse for the lust that
this adventure had stimulated, he writes an excoriation of lust
intended no less for his conscience than for the lady's. Having
thus cleared his mind of the result of their guilty passion, he
returns to his praise of the girl's black beauty in order to
regain her acquiescence to their intimacy, in jeopardy because
of a flash of her momentary disdain, real or affected.

Sonnets 27–47

Returning to the poet's letters to the youth, we find that the poet has been traveling (27–32). Perhaps while he is away he discovers that the young lord has seduced the lady or been seduced by her (33–47). Shakespeare, by confronting him with his breach of their contract of "love," reduces him to repentant tears (34). This display of contrition wins the poet's forgiveness and, in spite of the "trespass," enables him still to find comfort in the youth's beauty, birth, wealth, and wit. However, by the time of the composition of 40, the Friend has again established a sexual relationship with the lady. This is his "second trespass." The poet again excuses the "offence," blaming the lady's irresistible temptation. In 42, the poet is so firmly in control of his emotions that he is able to perform a feat of triumphant rationalization. He informs the lady that, since he and his Friend are one soul in bodies twain, in loving the youth she is really loving only him.

Sonnets 133–142

After the Friend's second seduction of the lady, Shakespeare analyzes the new situation in which he finds her principally at fault. He scolds her for giving her love at the same time both to him and to Pembroke and in 135–137, the so-called Will sonnets, he becomes positively insulting, accusing her of becoming a "bay where all men ride," for she apparently desires more lovers than William Herbert and William Shakespeare. In spite of his clear view of the lady's corrupt nature, he admits that his passion for her dominates his entire being. Yet he confesses that his sin in loving her afflicts him with well-deserved suffering. This admission is a sign of his spiritual recovery.

Sonnets 48–66

This group is marked by the poet's anxiety and deep despair. Disloyalty of friends and mortality are the principal themes.

Sonnets 67–108

After the self-analysis and confession of the previous group, the poet resumes writing letters to his Friend. Sonnets 67–70 urge Pembroke to leave his dissolute companions. But sonnets 75–99 record continuing difficulties. This mood changes sharply in sonnet 100. The poet announces his plan to revamp the

record in a way to cause Pembroke to appear forever as spot-
lessly "fair, kind, and true." To discover for what end, we turn
to sonnets 143–152.

Sonnets 143–152

The first poem in the group addressed to the lady describes
the careful housewife in pursuit of her chickens. By way of this
homely figure, Shakespeare begs the lady to show him again
mere simple kindness in return for which she may still have her
"will." The rest of the poems in this group, except for three
meditations, are confessions of his abject slavery and frantic
passion for a woman whom he realizes he should abhor. The
growing power of this realization mounts in 152 to an assertion
of self-mastery that enables him to dismiss the lady from his
mind and his heart for good and all.

Sonnets 109–126

In these sonnets written last Shakespeare turns to Pembroke
to explain how their love, well-nigh ruined by their rivalry for
the Dark Lady, can be renewed in ways that an analysis of individual sonnets will make clear. The sequence thus closes with
a re-establishment of the friendship that apparently remained
firm to the end of the poet's life.

8. GLOSSES AND NOTES

Glosses are signaled by an asterisk next to the word that re-
quires clarification. An equivalent is then given on the same
line in the right-hand margin, so that the eye, particularly as
it becomes accustomed to the arrangement, can absorb the
meaning at a glance.

It will be noticed that there is sometimes a slight break in
the line in which an asterisk occurs. This signifies that the gloss
covers more than one word and applies jointly to the two or
more words from the break to the asterisk.

Occasionally, two asterisks will be found on one line. When
this occurs, the two glosses are separated by a diagonal stroke.

Notes, signaled by a dagger, appear at the foot of the page.

The Procreation Sonnets / 1–17

Critics have agreed to call the first seventeen sonnets of Shakespeare's sequence "The Procreation Sonnets." They are all addressed to the same handsome young aristocrat, all urging upon him the same duty—that of marrying and begetting children, who will perpetuate his beauty and his name. Each sonnet is a variation on the same theme, and, like musical variations on a stated theme, each displays a different form of artistic ingenuity. In Shakespeare's case the verbal ingenuity often becomes forced and strained, that is, "conceited."

Verbal connections between the individual poems show that Shakespeare designed the entire seventeen sonnets to be read as a group and in the order in which they appear in Thorpe's Quarto. He could hardly have designed the seventeen to serve as an introduction to a piece of fiction. But as reiterated, skillfully varied appeals to a youth, they would seem both natural and artistic.

John Corbin once stigmatized the method Shakespeare adopted in composing these seventeen sonnets as "damnable iteration." No Elizabethan with a grammar-school education would have so regarded it. To anyone thus trained, the poet's method would be evidence of his mastery of "invention," one of the four principal parts of the rhetoric systematically taught in all the grammar schools. "Invention" was the term used to describe an author's systematic search for something to say and for original ways of saying it. By presenting seventeen fresh ways of urging the youth to marry and procreate, the poet showed himself to be a master rhetorician, inviting the admiration of the Earl of Pembroke and even more eagerly that of his famous Countess. He doubtless also hoped to win the approval of their liberally trained fifteen-year-old son.

The problem of a suitable marriage for his eldest son seems to have occupied the Earl during the year 1595. He and his Countess were then trying to arrange a marriage for young Pembroke with Elizabeth Carey, the daughter of Sir George Carey, and the granddaughter of the Lord Chamberlain, the current patron of Shakespeare's Company. The negotiations were broken off because of Herbert's "not liking" the lady. By this time, the poet had probably established a close enough relationship with the Earl and the Countess to be taken into their confidence about the problem of their son's aversion to this marriage. Aware of his refined taste in literature, they clearly hoped that persuasions to marriage written by the author of the enormously popular *Venus and Adonis* might induce the reluctant youth to agree to a union that they believed would redound to the family's political and social advantage. They, therefore, asked Shakespeare to come to their aid.

Shakespeare's response to their proposal was successful in a way they could not have anticipated. He not only wrote seventeen ornate sonnets on the subject they had asked him to develop, but, in the process, he also became a close friend of the young man and his kindly mentor. This family situation forms so natural a reason for the poet's turning from dramatic composition to the writing of sonnets that it seems likely that Shakespeare did not begin his sonnet story until the year 1595; and that it was not the popularity of the vogue that induced him to write his own sort of sugared sonnets, but his response to the request of a great Lord and Lady whose "servant" he had been and whose livery he had worn.

I

In the first of the procreation sonnets, the poet shows his approval of the philosophy of plenitude, of the goodness of God's bounty. Shakespeare instructs the youthful Lord Herbert to show his acceptance of this almost sacred belief by producing children. No one in Shakespeare's day would have considered this theme trivial. Associated with it is the poet's near anguish at the briefness of beauty, whose early death is one of the conquests of devouring time that most distressed Shakespeare at this stage of his life.

From fairest creatures we desire increase,
That thereby beauty's rose might never die,
But as the riper should by time decease,
His tender* heir might bear* his memory: immature / harbor
But thou, contracted* to thine own bright eyes,   betrothed
Feed'st thy light's flame with self-substantial* fuel, *i.e.,* of its own
Making a famine where abundance lies,   substance
Thyself thy foe, to thy sweet self too cruel.
Thou that art now the world's fresh ornament
And only* herald to the gaudy spring,   *i.e.,* chief
Within thine own bud buriest thy content*   *i.e.,* potential child
And, tender churl, makest waste in niggarding.
    Pity the world, or else this glutton be,
    To eat the world's due, by the grave and thee.†

Pity the world, or else this glutton be,
To eat the world's due, by the grave and thee.
To consume what you owe the world, *i.e.,* children,
through death or your refusal to beget offspring.

2

In this sonnet Shakespeare, repeating the commonplaces about old age, encourages the youth to realize that when he has reached the age of forty he will find compensation for the infirmities of old age in the discovery that he has been "new made" by having a child.

When forty winters shall besiege thy brow
And dig deep trenches in thy beauty's field,
Thy youth's proud livery, so gazed on now,
Will be a tattered weed,* of small worth held: garment
Then being asked where all thy beauty lies,
Where all the treasure of thy lusty days,
To say, within thine own deep-sunken eyes,
Were an all-eating shame, and thriftless* praise.   profitless
How much more praise deserved thy beauty's use,*   investment
If thou couldst answer "This fair child of mine
Shall sum my count and make my old excuse,"†
Proving his beauty by succession thine!
    This were to be new made when thou art old,
    And see thy blood warm when thou feel'st it cold.

Shall sum my count and make my old excuse.
Shall close my account with Nature and make an
excuse for my old age.

3

The principal interest in the third sonnet is the poet's reference in lines 9 and 10 to Herbert's mother, the beautiful and talented Countess of Pembroke whom Herbert was said to resemble.

Look in thy glass, and tell the face thou viewest
Now is the time that face should form another;
Whose fresh repair* if now thou not renewest,   state of health
Thou dost beguile the world, unbless some mother.
For where is she so fair whose uneared* womb   untilled
Disdains the tillage of thy husbandry?
Or who is he so fond* will be the tomb   foolish
Of his self-love, to stop posterity?
Thou art thy mother's glass, and she in thee
Calls back the lovely April of her prime:*   spring
So thou through windows of thine age shalt see,
Despite of wrinkles, this thy golden time.
   But if thou live, remembered not to be,*   only to be forgotten
   Die single, and thine image dies with thee.

4

In the fourth sonnet the poet adjures the Friend to realize his beauty is not a legacy but a loan from Nature, which he must someday repay.

Unthrifty loveliness, why dost thou spend
Upon thyself thy beauty's legacy?*   inherited beauty
Nature's bequest gives nothing, but doth lend,
And being frank,* she lends to those are free.*   liberal / generous
Then, beauteous niggard, why dost thou abuse
The bounteous largess* given thee to give?   generosity
Profitless usurer, why dost thou use*   put out for interest
So great a sum of sums, yet canst not live?*   survive
For having traffic with thyself alone,†
Thou of thyself thy sweet self dost deceive.
Then how, when nature calls thee to be gone,
What acceptable audit* canst thou leave?   account
    Thy unused* beauty must be tombed with thee,   uninvested
    Which, used, lives th' executor to be.

For having traffic with thyself alone.
Because you have traffic only with yourself, *i.e.,* with no woman.

5

In the next sonnet the poet employs the figure of the swift progress of the seasons from summer to winter. Then the perfume distilled from summer's flowers is the only valid memorial of summer that remains in the youth's possession.

Those hours that with gentle work did frame*   shape
The lovely gaze* where every eye doth dwell,   *i.e.,* object
Will play the tyrants to the very same   gazed at
And that unfair which fairly doth excel:
For never-resting time leads summer on
To hideous winter and confounds* him there;   destroys
Sap checked with frost and lusty leaves quite gone,
Beauty o'ersnowed and bareness every where:
Then, were not summer's distillation* left,   *i.e.,* perfume
A liquid prisoner pent in walls of glass,
Beauty's effect with beauty were bereft,†
Nor it, nor no remembrance what it was:
    But flowers distilled, though they with winter meet,
      Leese* but their show;* their substance still   lose / appearance
      lives sweet.

Beauty's effect with beauty were bereft.
We should be bereft of the perfume along with the rose, *i.e.,*
of the beauty of your unborn child along with your own.

6

This sixth sonnet develops the metaphor of 4, interest paid on a loan, and of 5, that of the distillation of perfume.

Then let not winter's ragged* hand deface   rough
In thee thy summer, ere thou be distilled:
Make sweet some vial;† treasure* thou some place   enrich
With beauty's treasure, ere it be self-killed.
That use* is not forbidden usury,   interest
Which happies* those that pay the willing loan;   makes happy
That 's for thyself to breed another thee,
Or ten times happier, be it ten for one;†
Ten times thyself were happier than thou art,
If ten of thine ten times refigured* thee: reproduced
Then what could death do, if thou shouldst depart,
Leaving thee living in posterity?
   Be not self-willed, for thou art much too fair
    To be death's conquest and make worms thine heir.

Make sweet some vial. Distill the essence of your beauty, *i.e.,* the perfume, into some vial.

Be it ten for one. That is, ten percent interest, the highest rate permitted by a statute of Henry VIII, revived by Queen Elizabeth.

7

Here the poet employs the image of the eyes following the course of the sun until it sinks, then turning away. In like fashion, the youth is told, when you pass your zenith, you will be looked upon as dead unless you have begotten a son.

Lo, in the orient when the gracious light
Lifts up his burning head, each under eye*   *eye below*
Doth homage to his new-appearing sight,
Serving with looks his sacred majesty;
And having climbed the steep-up heavenly hill,
Resembling strong youth in his middle age,
Yet mortal looks adore his beauty still,
Attending on his golden pilgrimage;
But when from highmost pitch,* with weary car,   *i.e.,* noon
Like feeble age, he reeleth from the day,
The eyes, 'fore duteous, now converted are
From his low tract and look another way:
   So thou, thyself out-going in thy noon,†
    Unlooked on diest, unless thou get* a son.   **beget**

So thou, thyself out-going in thy noon.
So passing beyond your zenith.

8

The figure developed in this sonnet is drawn from lute-playing. To understand it properly, one must remember that the strings on a lute, except for the highest, which was a single string, were tuned in pairs.

Music to hear, why hear'st thou music sadly?†
Sweets with sweets war not, joy delights in joy.
Why lovest thou that which thou receivest not gladly,
Or else receivest with pleasure thine annoy?
If the true concord of well tunèd sounds,
By unions married, do offend thine ear,
They do but sweetly chide thee, who confounds*   wastes
In singleness the parts that thou shouldst bear.*   sing
Mark how one string, sweet husband to another,
Strikes each in each by mutual ordering;*   sympathetic
                                                              vibration
Resembling sire and child and happy mother,
Who, all in one, one pleasing note do sing:
      Whose speechless song, being many, seeming one,
      Sings this to thee: "Thou single wilt prove none."†

Music to hear, why hear'st thou music sadly?
Why are you, whose voice is like music, sad when you hear music?
Whose speechless song, being many, seeming one,
Sings this to thee: "Thou single wilt prove none."
The meaning of this labored conceit is this: As the strings being many,
seem to combine to make one tone, so you who remain single will be
none at all. Perhaps this is an allusion to the proverbial expression,
"One is no number."

9

Can it be, the poet asks the young lord, that you refuse to marry from fear of leaving a widow, when the whole world will be your widow and weep that you have left it no child? Your beauty, if wasted by refusing to breed, becomes extinct.

Is it for fear to wet a widow's eye
That thou consumest thyself in single life?
Ah! if thou issueless shalt hap to die,
The world will wail thee, like a makeless* wife;   mateless
The world will be thy widow, and still* weep   ever
That thou no form of thee hast left behind,
When every private* widow well may keep   particular
By children's eyes her husband's shape in mind.
Look, what an unthrift* in the world doth spend   prodigal
Shifts but his place,† for still the world enjoys it;
But beauty's waste* hath in the world an end,   if wasted
And kept unused, the user so destroys it.
    No love toward others in that bosom sits
      That on himself such murderous shame*   shameful murder
      commits.

Shifts but his place. Is not lost, but passes
into the pockets of other men.

10

Here Shakespeare makes a personal appeal to the youth. Although it is obvious, he says, that you love no one, reserving all your emotion for hatred of yourself, "Make thee another self, for love of me."

For shame! deny that thou bear'st love to any,
Who for thyself art so unprovident.
Grant,* if thou wilt, thou art beloved of many,   <small>let it be granted</small>
But that thou none lovest is most evident;
For thou art so possessed with murderous hate
That 'gainst thyself thou stick'st* not to conspire,   <small>do not scruple</small>
Seeking that beauteous roof* to ruinate   <small>*i.e.,* family</small>
Which to repair should be thy chief desire.
O, change thy thought, that I may change my mind!
Shall hate be fairer lodged than gentle love?
Be, as thy presence is, gracious and kind,
Or to thyself at least kind-hearted prove:
    Make thee another self, for love of me,
    That beauty still may live in thine or thee.

II

As fast as thou shalt wane, so fast thou grow'st
In one of thine, from that* which thou departest;   *i.e.,* beauty
And that fresh blood which youngly* thou bestow'st   in youth
Thou mayst call thine when thou from youth
        convertest.*   changes (to age)
Herein lives wisdom, beauty and increase;
Without this, folly, age and cold decay:
If all were minded so, the times* should cease   generations
And threescore year would make the world away.†
Let those whom Nature hath not made for store,*   source of supply
Harsh, featureless and rude, barrenly perish:
Look, whom she best endowed she gave the more;
Which bounteous gift thou shouldst in bounty*   by being prolific
        cherish:
    She carved thee for her seal, and meant thereby
    Thou shouldst print more, not let that copy die.

And threescore year would make the world away.
If all men died without issue, the human race would end in sixty years.

12

   Contemplating the melancholy changes wrought by Time
the destroyer, the poet warns the youth that his beauty will
suffer the same ruin as all other objects suffer from Time's
relentless warfare, a fate he can avoid only by breeding children. This is one of the most popular and one of the best of
all the sonnets.

When I do count* the clock that tells the time,   take account of
And see the brave* day sunk in hideous night;   splendid
When I behold the violet past prime,
And sable curls all silvered o'er with white;
When lofty trees I see barren of leaves,
Which erst* from heat did canopy the herd,   formerly
And summer's green all girded up* in sheaves,   firmly tied
Borne on the bier with white and bristly beard,
Then of thy beauty do I question make,*   entertain a doubt
That thou among the wastes of time must go,
Since sweets and beauties do themselves forsake
And die as fast as they see others grow;
   And nothing 'gainst Time's scythe can make defence
   Save breed,* to brave* him when he takes   *i.e.*, children / defy
      thee hence.

13

O, that you were yourself!* but, love, you are   forever yourself
No longer yours than you yourself here live:*†   are alive
Against this coming end you should prepare,
And your sweet semblance to some other give.
So should that beauty which you hold in lease
Find no determination;* then you were   have no end
Yourself again, after yourself's decease,
When your sweet issue your sweet form should bear.
Who lets so fair a house fall to decay,
Which husbandry in honour might uphold
Against the stormy gusts of winter's day
And barren rage of death's eternal cold?
    O, none but unthrifts:* dear my love, you know   spendthrifts
    You had a father; let your son say so.

                ... love, you are
No longer yours than you yourself here live.
You can preserve your identity only
while you are alive.

14

Shakespeare here tells the determined youth that he does not derive his power of prognostication where others find it—in the stars—but from the knowledge he obtains from Herbert's eyes.

Not from the stars do I my judgment pluck;*	derive
And yet methinks I have astronomy,*	know astrology
But not to tell of good or evil luck,	
Of plagues, of dearths, or season's quality;	
Nor can I fortune to brief minutes tell,	
Pointing* to each his thunder, rain and wind,	appointing
Or say with princes if it shall go well,	
By oft predict* that I in heaven find:	frequent prognostication
But from thine eyes my knowledge I derive,	
And, constant stars, in them I read such art,	
As truth and beauty shall together thrive,	
If from thyself to store* thou wouldst convert;*	stock (of children) turn
Or else of thee this I prognosticate:	
Thy end is truth's and beauty's doom* and date.*	doomsday end

15

This is a universally admired sonnet. Its subject is one of Shakespeare's favorites: the power of time to consume man and all his works.

When I consider every thing that grows
Holds in perfection but a little moment,
That this huge stage presenteth nought but shows
Whereon the stars in secret influence comment;
When I perceive that men as plants increase,
Cheered and checked* even by the self-same sky,   repressed
Vaunt* in their youthful sap, at height decrease,   exult
And wear their brave state out of memory;
Then the conceit* of this inconstant stay   fanciful idea
Sets you most rich in youth before my sight,
Where wasteful Time debateth with Decay,
To change your day of youth to sullied night;
   And all in war with Time for love of you,
   As he takes from you, I engraft you new.

16

But wherefore do not you a mightier way
Make war upon this bloody tyrant, Time?
And fortify yourself in your decay
With means more blessed than my barren rhyme?
Now stand you on the top of happy hours,
And many maiden gardens, yet unset,*   unplanted
With virtuous wish would bear your living flowers
Much liker than your painted counterfeit:*   portrait
So should the lines of life that life repair,†
Which this, Time's pencil, or my pupil pen,†
Neither in inward worth nor outward fair,
Can make you live yourself in eyes of men.
    To give away yourself keeps yourself still;†
    And you must live, drawn by your own sweet skill.

So should the lines of life that life repair.
So should your lineage repair your life.

Which this, Time's pencil, or my pupil pen.
Pupil pen is an expression of exaggerated modesty that was
conventional with poets of Shakespeare's day.

To give away yourself keeps yourself still.
To produce copies of yourself, *i.e.,* children, will be the best
way to keep memory of you forever alive.

17

Who will believe my verse in time to come,
If it were filled with your most high deserts?
Though yet, heaven knows, it is but as a tomb
Which hides your life and shows not half your parts.* good qualities
If I could write the beauty of your eyes
And in fresh numbers* number all your graces,   lively verses
The age to come would say "This poet lies;
Such heavenly touches* ne'er touched earthly   strokes of the pen
    faces."
So should my papers, yellowed with their age,
Be scorned, like old men of less truth than tongue,
And your true rights* be termed a poet's rage*   *i.e.,* praises /
And stretchèd* metre of an antique song: inspiration
                                                          overwrought
    But were some child of yours alive that time,
    You should live twice, in it and in my rhyme.

Herbert's response to this first group of sonnets was evidently so cordial that the poet assumed he would not be averse to a personal friendship. Shakespeare, therefore, moves the theme of breeding to a new emotional level. He suggests that he knows an ampler way of insuring perpetuation of the youth's line and beauty than that he has been urging in sonnet after sonnet: he can insure eternal life to them both through his verses.

The delight the poet takes in what soon became an intimate relationship stimulates in him a proud self-confidence that sets the tone of all the poems in this group.

18

This famous sonnet is the first Shakespeare wrote on the "eternizing" theme. Critics have accused him of making the youth's charms seem effeminate in this poem.

Shall I compare thee to a summer's day?
Thou art more lovely and more temperate:*   mild
Rough winds do shake the darling buds of May,†
And summer's lease hath all too short a date:*   duration
Sometime too hot the eye of heaven shines,
And often is his gold complexion dimmed;
And every fair* from fair* sometime declines,   fair one / beauty
By chance or nature's changing course untrimmed;*   without ornament
But thy eternal summer shall not fade,
Nor lose possession of that fair thou owest;*   ownest
Nor shall Death brag thou wander'st in his shade,
When in eternal lines to time thou growest:
    So long as men can breathe, or eyes can see,
    So long lives this, and this gives life to thee.

Rough winds do shake the darling buds of May.
May was in Shakespeare's time a summer month.
It continued through a few days of our mid-June.

19

Devouring Time, blunt thou the lion's paws,
And make the earth devour her own sweet brood;
Pluck the keen teeth from the fierce tiger's jaws,
And burn the long-lived phœnix in her blood;†
Make glad and sorry seasons as thou fleet'st,
And do whate'er thou wilt, swift-footed Time,
To the wide world and all her fading sweets;
But I forbid thee one most heinous crime:
O, carve not with thy hours my love's fair brow,
Nor draw no lines there with thine antique* pen;   old-making
Him in thy course untainted* do allow   unharmed
For beauty's pattern to succeeding men.
    Yet do thy worst, old Time: despite thy wrong,
    My love shall in my verse ever live young.

And burn the long-lived phœnix in her blood.
According to the legend, this fabulous Arabian bird lived
500 years. Then it laid an egg and set fire to its nest.
From the ashes a new phoenix was born.

20

The frankness of this sonnet has disturbed many modern readers, but it would not have embarrassed any Elizabethan gentleman, least of all the errant lord to whom it was addressed. In spite of the feminine delicacy of the youth's beauty, and the gentleness of his heart, the poet knows well enough that the object of his devotion is a male and averse to homosexual advances. The only sonnet in the series with double (two-syllable) rhymes throughout—the poem has a joyful, almost rollicking tempo.

A woman's face with Nature's own hand* painted   *i.e.,* not Art's
Hast thou, the master-mistress* of my passion;   both master and mistress
A woman's gentle heart, but not acquainted
With shifting change, as is false women's fashion;
An eye more bright than theirs, less false in rolling,
Gilding the object whereupon it gazeth;
A man in hue,* all "hues" in his controlling,†   *i.e.,* form
Which* steals men's eyes and women's souls amazeth.   *i.e.,* hues
And for a woman wert thou first created;
Till Nature, as she wrought thee, fell a-doting,
And by addition me of thee defeated,*   deprived
By adding one thing* to my purpose nothing.   *i.e.,* a phallus
    But since she pricked thee out* for women's pleasure, chose you
    Mine be thy love, and thy love's use their treasure.

A man in hue, all "hues" in his controlling.
A man in appearance, dominating all other forms of external show by the charm of his own appearance.

21

Shakespeare probably is not attacking the euphuistic extravagances of any one poet here, but the overingenious conceits of a whole school of contemporary sonneteers whose contrived art he repudiates.

So is it not with me as with that Muse
Stirred by* a painted* beauty to his verse,   *inspired / artificial*
Who heaven itself for ornament doth use
And every fair with his fair doth rehearse,*   *mention*
Making a couplement* of proud compare,*   *combination / comparison*
With sun and moon, with earth and sea's rich gems,
With April's first-born flowers, and all things rare
That heaven's air in this huge rondure* hems.   *i.e., of the globe*
O, let me, true in love, but truly write,
And then believe me, my love is as fair
As any mother's child, though not so bright
As those gold candles fixed in heaven's air:
    Let them say more that like of hearsay well.†
    I will not praise that purpose not to sell.†

Let them say more that like of hearsay well.
Let them say more that fall in love
with mere reports of beauty.
I will not praise that purpose not to sell.
Since I am not trying to sell my Friend and his beauty,
I will not overpraise him in the manner of vendors.

22

In this sonnet the poet explodes the convention originating in ancient Greece of a poet's authority depending upon his having reached full maturity, if not actually old age. Shakespeare was actually only in his early thirties when he wrote this poem.

My glass shall not persuade me I am old,
So long as youth and thou are of one date;
But when in thee time's furrows I behold,
Then look I death my days should expiate.*   finish
For all that beauty that doth cover thee
Is but the seemly raiment of my heart,
Which in thy breast doth live, as thine in me:†
How can I then be elder than thou art?
O, therefore, love, be of thyself so wary
As I, not for myself, but for thee will;
Bearing thy heart, which I will keep so chary*   carefully
As tender nurse her babe from faring ill.
    Presume not on* thy heart when mine is slain;   do not claim
    Thou gavest me thine, not to give back again.

Which in thy breast doth live, as thine in me.
This is one of many illustrations of the adage,
"The heart is not where it lives but where it loves."

23

    The poet explains that lack of self-confidence prevents him from fully expressing his love. The figure of a frightened actor stumbling through badly learned lines betrays the frequent irritation of a director or of a fellow actor with which Shakespeare here shows himself painfully familiar.

As an unperfect actor on the stage,
Who with his fear is put besides* his part,   *i.e.,* made to forget
Or some fierce thing replete with too much rage,
Whose strength's abundance weakens his own heart;
So I, for fear of trust,* forget to say   lack of
The perfect ceremony of love's rite,   self-confidence
And in mine own love's strength seem to decay,
O'ercharged with burthen of mine own love's might.
O, let my looks be then the eloquence
And dumb presagers* of my speaking breast;   preliminary
Who plead for love, and look for recompense,   dumb shows
More than that tongue that more hath more expressed.†
    O, learn to read what silent love hath writ:
    To hear with eyes belongs to love's fine wit.

More than that tongue that more hath more expressed.
Let my expression plead for love better than that of a
rival who has more fully expressed more of love's ardor.

24

This elaborately developed conceit of a picture painted by
the poet's eye and its future disposition is a product of forced
ingenuity.

Mine eye hath played the painter and hath stelled*   engraved
Thy beauty's form in table* of my heart;   panel
My body is the frame wherein 'tis held,
And pérspective it is best painter's art.†
For through the painter must you see his skill,
To find where your true image pictured lies;
Which in my bosom's shop is hanging still,*   continues to hang
That hath his windows glazèd with thine eyes.
Now see what good turns eyes for eyes have done:
Mine eyes have drawn thy shape, and thine for me
Are windows to my breast, where-through the sun
Delights to peep, to gaze therein on thee;
    Yet eyes this cunning want* to grace their art,   still lack
    They draw but what they see, know not the heart.

And perspective it is best painter's art.
And the perspective that the frame helps to create
is an artifice of the best painters.

25

Let those who are in favour with their stars
Of public honour and proud titles boast,
Whilst I, whom fortune of such triumph bars,
Unlooked for* joy in that I honour most.   inconspicuously
Great princes' favourites their fair leaves spread
But as the marigold at the sun's eye,
And in themselves their pride lies burièd,
For at a frown they in their glory die.
The painful* warrior famousèd for fight,   hard-working
After a thousand victories once foiled,*   thwarted
Is from the book of honour razèd quite,
And all the rest forgot for which he toiled;
   Then happy I, that love and am beloved
   Where I may not remove nor be removed.†

Where I may not remove nor be removed.
Whom I may not leave and by whom I may not be left.

26

This sonnet is an envoy or covering note sent to the Friend with the written ambassage. After the poet completed and sent the procreation sonnets, he seems to have become acquainted with the young man to whom they were addressed, and at once, fascinated by his beauty, he begins to praise it.

Lord of my love, to whom in vassalage
Thy merit hath my duty* strongly knit,   respect
To thee I send this written ambassage,*   message
To witness duty,* not to show my wit:*   respect / invention
Duty so great, which wit so poor as mine
May make seem bare, in wanting words to show it,
But that I hope some good conceit* of thine   conception
In thy soul's thought, all naked, will bestow it;
Till whatsoever star that guides my moving,*   way of life
Points* on me graciously with fair aspéct,* sheds rays /
               favorable influence
And puts apparel on my tattered loving,
To show me worthy of thy sweet respect:
 Then may I dare to boast how I do love thee;
 Till then not show my head where thou mayst
  prove* me.   test

Thoughts in Absence / 27–32

Readers who wish to follow the stages of this *drame à trois* in supposed chronological order should now turn to the first sonnets Shakespeare addressed to the Dark Lady (127–132). In them he reminds her of his early light-hearted, half-teasing wooing. Poems 127 to 132 were obviously written before Shakespeare suspected the existence of her affair with Herbert.

While he was traveling, probably with his fellow actors in the provinces, Shakespeare sent sonnets 27 and 28 to young Herbert. Both poems lament his separation from his Friend. Sonnets 29 and 30 also record the solace that friendship recollected can afford.

27

"Pilgrim" was equivalent to "lover" in a common Elizabethan metaphor. Jaggard entitled his 1599 anthology, *The Passionate Pilgrim, i.e.,* The Passionate Lover.

Weary with toil,* I haste me to my bed,	*i.e.,* travel
The dear repose for limbs with travel tired;	
But then begins a journey in my head	
To work my mind, when body's work 's expired:	
For then my thoughts, from far where I abide	
Intend* a zealous pilgrimage* to thee,	direct / lover's journey
And keep my drooping eyelids open wide,	
Looking on darkness which the blind do see:	
Save that my soul's imaginary sight*	inward eye
Presents thy shadow* to my sightless view,	apparition
Which, like a jewel hung in ghastly* night,	deathlike
Makes black night beauteous and her old face new.	
Lo, thus, by day my limbs, by night my mind,	
For thee and for myself no quiet find.	

28

How can I then return in happy plight,
That am debarred the benefit of rest?
When day's oppression is not eased by night,
But day by night, and night by day, oppressed?
And each, though enemies to either's* reign,   each other's
Do in consent* shake hands to torture me;   agreement
The one by toil,* the other to complain   travel
How far I toil, still farther off from thee.
I tell the day, to please him thou art bright,
And dost him grace when clouds do blot the heaven:
So flatter I the swart*-complexioned night;   black
When sparkling stars twire* not, thou gild'st the even.   twinkle
   But day doth daily draw my sorrows longer,†
   And night doth nightly make grief's strength
      seem stronger.

But day doth daily draw my sorrows longer.
But each day's journey makes my
grief more intense.

29

The youth's evident acceptance of the poet's friendship delights him and prompts him to celebrate what is soon to become their "dear religious love." One of the most artfully composed and beautifully expressed of all the sonnets, it appears in most anthologies.

When, in disgrace with fortune and men's eyes,
I all alone beweep my outcast state,
And trouble deaf heaven with my bootless* cries,   useless
And look upon myself, and curse my fate,
Wishing me like to one more rich in hope,
Featured like him, like him with friends possessed,
Desiring this man's art and that man's scope,*   range
With what I most enjoy contented least;†
Yet in these thoughts myself almost despising,
Haply I think on thee, and then my state,
Like to the lark at break of day arising
From sullen* earth, sings hymns at heaven's gate;   gloomy
    For thy sweet love remembered such wealth brings
    That then I scorn to change my state with kings.

With what I most enjoy contented least.
I am least contented with the talents
I do possess.

30

Shakespeare now tells the absent youth that the mere thought of him is compensation for all past sorrow. In spite of some artificial wordplay, the sonnet is one of the most admired and most frequently quoted.

When to the sessions of sweet silent thought
I summon up remembrance of things past,
I sigh the lack of many a thing I sought,
And with old woes' new wail my dear time's waste:†
Then can I drown an eye, unused to flow,
For precious friends hid in death's dateless* night,   endless
And weep afresh love's long since canceled* woe,   paid in full
And moan the expense* of many a vanished sight: loss
Then can I grieve at grievances foregone,*   passed
And heavily from woe to woe tell* o'er   count
The sad account of fore-bemoanèd moan,
Which I new pay as if not paid before.
    But if the while I think on thee, dear friend,
    All losses are restored and sorrows end.

And with old woes' new wail my dear time's waste.
And waste my precious time bewailing anew old woes.

31

The poet's thought in this sonnet is so subtle that he has difficulty in expressing it clearly. He tells the youth that he enshrines all of the older man's past loves, even those that he had supposed altogether dead. Yet in them, Shakespeare continues, he sees the image of those he has once loved and lost. This is the last sonnet of the group expressing joy at Herbert's favorable response to the "written ambassage."

Thy bosom is endearèd with all hearts,
Which I by lacking have supposèd dead;
And there reigns love, and all love's loving parts,
And all those friends which I thought burièd.
How many a holy and obsequious* tear   funereal
Hath dear religious love stol'n from mine eye,†
As interest* of the dead, which now appear   claims
But things removed* that hidden in thee lie!   absent
Thou art the grave where buried love doth live,
Hung with the trophies* of my lovers* gone,   memorials / friends
Who all their parts of me* to thee did give: shares in me
That due of many now is thine alone:
    Their images I loved I view in thee,
    And thou, all they, hast all the all of me.†

Hath dear religious love stol'n from mine eye.
This phrase, "dear religious love," expresses the exalted opinion that men of Shakespeare's day held of male friendship.

And thou, all they, hast all the all of me.
"All they," *i.e.,* who express in yourself all that they were.

32

In 32 comes one of those sudden shifts of mood which is such a striking feature of the sequence. The joy in the sonnets immediately preceding gives way to deep dejection. In this mood, the poet counsels that should the youth read his poor lines after he is dead, when better poets are writing about his friend, then the youth must ignore his inferior style and its shortcomings and concentrate on the love the poems express.

If thou survive my well-contented day,*   *i.e.*, day of his burial
When that churl Death my bones with dust
    shall cover,
And shalt by fortune once more re-survey
These poor rude lines of thy deceasèd lover,
Compare them with the bettering* of the time,   improvement
And though they be outstripped by every pen,
Reserve* them for my love, not for their rhyme,   preserve
Exceeded by the height* of happier men.*   *i.e.*, excellence / better writers
O, then vouchsafe me but this loving thought:
"Had my friend's Muse grown with this growing age,
A dearer birth than this his love had brought,
To march in ranks of better equipage:
   But since he died, and poets better prove,
   Theirs for their style I'll read, his for his love."

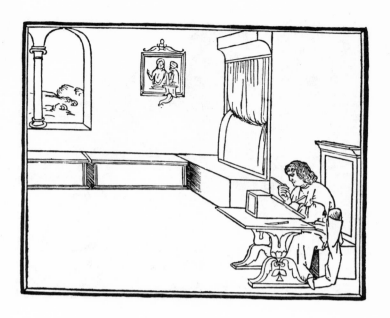

Reactions to His Friend's Disloyalty / 33–47

When convinced of Herbert's intimacy with the lady, the poet sends him this group of sonnets lamenting this disloyalty to their friendship. After the Friend's repentance (34), there is an apparent reconciliation; but sonnets 40 and 41 make it clear that the friendship between Shakespeare and Pembroke is still in danger.

33

Full many a glorious morning have I seen
Flatter the mountain-tops with sovereign eye,
Kissing with golden face the meadows green,
Gilding pale streams with heavenly alchemy;
Anon permit the basest* clouds to ride   darkest
With ugly rack* on his celestial face,   vapor
And from the fórlorn world his visage hide,
Stealing unseen to west with this disgrace:
Even so my sun one early morn did shine
With all-triumphant splendour on my brow;
But, out, alack! he was but one hour mine,
The region* cloud hath masked him from me now.   *i.e.,* of the
    Yet him for this my love no whit disdaineth;   upper air
    Suns of the world may stain* when heaven's   grow dim
      sun staineth.

34

Why didst thou promise such a beauteous day,
And make me travel forth without my cloak,
To let base clouds o'ertake me in my way,
Hiding thy bravery* in their rotten smoke?*   finery / unwhole-
                                                            some vapor
Tis not enough that through the cloud thou break,
To dry the rain on my storm-beaten face,
For no man well of such a salve can speak
That heals the wound and cures not the disgrace:*   scar, *i.e.*,
                                                            humiliation
Nor can thy shame give physic to my grief;
Though thou repent, yet I have still the loss:
The offender's sorrow lends but weak relief
To him that bears the strong offense's cross.
    Ah, but those tears are pearl which thy love sheds,
    And they are rich and ransom all ill deeds.

35

In the first quatrain of 35 Shakespeare extends once more his sentimentally provoked forgiveness, but in terms deliberately ugly. By "salving thy amiss," he tells the youth, you are corrupting yourself and so becoming accessary to the lady's theft.

No more be grieved at that which thou hast done:	
Roses have thorns, and silver fountains mud;	
Clouds and eclipses stain* both moon and sun,	darken
And loathsome canker* lives in sweetest bud.	canker-worm
All men make faults, and even I in this,	
Authòrizing* thy trespass with compare,*	justifying / similes
Myself corrupting, salving thy amiss,	
Excusing thy sins more than thy sins are;†	
For to thy sensual fault I bring in sense—*	reason
Thy adverse party* is thy advocate—	i.e., the lady
And 'gainst myself a lawful plea commence:	
Such civil war is in my love and hate,	
That I an accessary needs must be	
To that sweet thief* which sourly* robs from me.	i.e., the lady / in bitterness

Excusing thy sins more than thy sins are.
Making more excuses for your sins than their actual number.

36

Applying his reason to the youth's sensual fault has resulted in the poet's decision to break with him, perhaps even to refuse to recognize him in public. The disgrace of two men sharing the same mistress has apparently become common knowledge. Strict fidelity to the Renaissance code of male friendship would have demanded that, instead of acquiescing in their rivalry, the poet surrender all his rights and hand the temptress over to Herbert, as Valentine in *The Two Gentlemen of Verona* surrenders Silvia to his rival Proteus, explaining, "All that was mine in Silvia I give thee."

Let me confess that we two must be twain,*	parted
Although our undivided loves are one:	
So shall those blots that do with me remain,	
Without thy help, by me be borne alone.	
In our two loves there is but one respect,*	consideration
Though in our lives a separable* spite,	separating
Which though it alter not love's sole* effect,	unique
Yet doth it steal sweet hours from love's delight.	
I may not evermore acknowledge* thee,	recognize
Lest my bewailèd guilt* should do thee shame,	*i.e.,* with the lady
Nor thou with public kindness* honour me,	politeness
Unless thou take that honour* from thy name:	*i.e.,* which you give me
But do not so; I love thee in such sort,	
As thou being mine, mine is thy good report.†	

Mine is thy good report.
Your reputation is in my keeping.
(This couplet also concludes sonnet 96.)

37

In this and the three following sonnets Shakespeare seeks ways of assuaging the grief caused by separation from his Friend. Incredible though it may seem, some critics take the lameness of line 3 literally; it is, of course, a metaphor which expresses the poet's inability to join in the activities of the young aristocrat.

As a decrepit father takes delight
To see his active child do deeds of youth,
So I, made lame by fortune's dearest* spite,   most grievous
Take all my comfort of thy worth and truth;
For whether beauty, birth, or wealth, or wit,
Or any of these all, or all, or more,
Entitled in thy parts* do crownèd sit,   talents
I make my love engrafted to this store:
So then I am not lame, poor, nor despised,
Whilst that this shadow* doth such substance give†   *i.e.*, picture
That I in thy abundance am sufficed
And by a part of all thy glory live.
    Look, what is best, that best I wish in thee:
    This wish I have; then ten times happy me!

Whilst that this shadow doth such substance give.
While this picture of your qualities that exists in my imagination enables me to share in their reality to such an extent that I am satisfied by their abundance.

38

Shakespeare assures the young nobleman that, as long as the youth's merits continue to inspire his Muse, he will be able to write verse effectively celebrating them. So certain is the poet that his artistic powers will flourish as long as Herbert is their inspiration that, in a burst of enthusiasm and flattery, he addresses Herbert as the "tenth Muse."

How can my Muse want subject to invent,
While thou dost breathe, that pour'st into my verse
Thine own sweet argument,* too excellent   theme
For every vulgar paper* to rehearse?†   *i.e.,* poem
O, give thyself the thanks, if aught in me
Worthy perusal stand against thy sight;*   written for your eye
For who 's so dumb that cannot write to thee
When thou thyself dost give invention light?
Be thou the tenth Muse, ten times more in worth
Than those old nine which rhymers invocate;
And he that calls on thee, let him bring forth
Eternal numbers* to outlive long date.   verses
  If my slight Muse do please these curious* days   critical
  The pain be mine, but thine shall be the praise.

For every vulgar paper to rehearse.
This is the first expression of the poet's jealousy of other poets who are seeking to gain the young Lord's attention and bounty.

39

O, how thy worth with manners* may I sing,   *i.e.*, decently
When thou art all the better part of me?*   *i.e.*, my soul
What can mine own praise to mine own self bring
And what is 't but mine own when I praise thee?
Even for this let us divided live,
And our dear love lose name* of single one,   name only
That by this separation I may give
That due to thee which thou deservest alone.
O absence, what a torment wouldst thou prove,
Were it not thy sour leisure gave sweet leave
To entertain* the time with thoughts of love,   keep occupied
Which time and thoughts so sweetly doth deceive,
    And that thou teachest how to make one twain,†
    By praising him here who doth hence remain!

And that thou teachest how to make one twain.
Absence teaches me how to create two presences
of my absent Friend: he who is actually present
and he whose image my imagination creates.

40

In this slur on the renunciation demanded of an ideal male friendship, the poet, in exaggerated fashion, promises to give up not only the lady they both want, but also all his loves of whatever sort. In a spirit of bitterness, not of generosity, Shakespeare closes the poem with a sneer at the lascivious grace that lends beauty to all Herbert's evil courses.

Take all my loves,* my love, yea, take them all; *those I love
What hast thou then more than thou hadst before?
No love, my love, that thou mayst true love call;
All mine was thine before thou hadst this more.
Then, if for my love* thou my love* receivest, *love of me / one I love / *i.e.*, sexually
I cannot blame thee for my love thou usest;*
But yet be blamed, if thou thyself deceivest *enjoyment / really despises
By willful taste* of what thyself refusest.*
I do forgive thy robbery, gentle thief,
Although thou steal thee all my poverty:* *poor possession
And yet, love knows, it is a greater grief
To bear love's wrong than hate's known* injury. *i.e.*, publicly
    Lascivious grace, in whom all ill well shows,
    Kill me with spites; yet we must not be foes.

41

Although Shakespeare condones the youth's involvement with the Dark Lady by saying that, drawn by his beauty, she has been the erotic aggressor, he gives the poem an undertone of reproof. Yet, he continues, you might have forborn taking my place in her mind and body, for that has resulted in a twofold deception of me: first, by tempting the lady through your beauty; and, then, by employing that same beauty to be false to me. Even to Shakespeare, the future Earl of Pembroke is beginning to appear utterly selfish and self-willed.

Those pretty wrongs that liberty* commits,   lust
When I am sometime absent from thy heart,
Thy beauty and thy years full well befits,
For still temptation follows where thou art.
Gentle thou art, and therefore to be won,
Beauteous thou art, therefore to be assailed;*   tempted
And when a woman woos, what woman's son
Will sourly leave her till she have prevailed?
Aye me! but yet thou mightst my seat* forbear,   place
And chide thy beauty and thy straying youth,
Who* lead thee in their riot* even there   which /
Where thou art forced to break a twofold truth,   debauchery
   Hers, by thy beauty tempting her to thee,
   Thine, by thy beauty being false to me.

42

By a tortuous process of rationalization, the poet tells Herbert that, in loving him, the lady really loves his "other self," *i.e.,* Shakespeare. Hence, there is no deception by either errant lover, and no sin anywhere. In *Troilus and Cressida* Shakespeare calls this type of reasoning "madness of discourse." Here, it is a clear indication that Shakespeare's inventiveness on the subject of divided loving is nearly exhausted. It is, therefore, not surprising that the rest of the sonnets in this group exhibit the very essence of quibbling and logic chopping.

That thou hast her, it is not all my grief,
And yet it may be said I loved her dearly;
That she hath thee, is of my wailing chief,
A loss in love that touches me more nearly.
Loving offenders, thus I will excuse ye:
Thou dost love her, because thou know'st I love her;
And for my sake even so doth she abuse* me, deceive
Suffering my friend for my sake to approve* her. make trial of
If I lose thee, my loss is my love's* gain,   mistress's
And losing her, my friend hath found that loss;
Both find each other, and I lose both twain,
And both for my sake lay on me this cross:
 But here 's the joy: my friend and I are one;
 Sweet flattery! then she loves but me alone.

43

Sonnets 43-47 are the most involved and affected in expression, and more burdened with complicated figures of speech (conceits) than any others in the sequence. By the time Shakespeare reaches sonnet 43, he has exhausted his authentic impulse toward expressing his forgiveness of Herbert's sensual fault; thereafter, following the imitators of Petrarch, he forces his imagination into perverse courses of invention.

The meaning of sonnet 43 remains obscure because of the persistent play on the various meanings of the word "shadow." The apparent meaning of lines 11–14 is the following: In the darkness of my dream, my eyes are drawn to you by the brightness of your apparition.

When most I wink,* then do mine eyes best see,   shut my eyes
For all the day they view things unrespected;*   unnoticed
But when I sleep, in dreams they look on thee,
And, darkly bright, are bright* in dark* directed.   clear / darkness
Then thou, whose shadow* shadows doth make bright,   image
How would thy shadow's form form happy show
To the clear day with thy much clearer light,
When to unseeing eyes thy shade* shines so!   apparition
How would, I say, mine eyes be blessèd made
By looking on thee in the living day,
When in dead night thy fair imperfect shade
Through heavy sleep on sightless eyes doth stay!
   All days are nights to see till I see thee,
    And nights bright days when dreams do show
     thee me.*   i.e., you to me

44

Here, Shakespeare uses the ancient conception of the composition of the human body (see note on line 11) in illuminating the situation between the two men.

If the dull substance of my flesh were thought,
Injurious distance should not stop my way;
For then, despite of space, I would be brought,
From limits* far remote, where* thou dost stay.   districts /
                                                          to where
No matter then although my foot did stand
Upon the farthest earth removed from thee;
For nimble thought can jump both sea and land,
As soon as think the place where he* would be.   *i.e.*, thought
But, ah, thought kills me, that I am not thought,
To leap large lengths of miles when thou art gone,
But that, so much of earth and water wrought,†
I must attend time's leisure* with my moan;   *i.e.*, to reunite us
    Receiving nought by elements so slow*   *i.e.*, earth and water
    But heavy tears, badges of either's woe.†

But that, so much of earth and water wrought.
This is a reference to the ancient conception that man's being,
like all nature's, is composed of four elements: (the flesh)
of earth and water; (thought) of fire and air.
But heavy tears, badges of either's woe.
A badge of woe of both earth and water, because
earth is sluggish, producing melancholy, and water
the substance of tears.

45

The other two, slight* air and purging fire,   unsubstantial
Are both with thee, wherever I abide;
The first my thought, the other my desire,
These present-absent with swift motion slide.
For when these quicker elements are gone
In tender embassy of love to thee,
My life, being made of four,* with two alone   *i.e.,* four elements
Sinks down to death, oppressed with melancholy;
Until life's composition be recured*   restored to
By those swift messengers returned from thee,   proper balance
Who even but now come back again, assured
Of thy fair health, recounting it to me:
  This told, I joy; but then no longer glad,
  I send them* back again, and straight grow sad.   *i.e.,* thought
                                                                     and desire

46

One of the most extended of the poet's many references to
the law, this sonnet depicts a legal action instituted jointly by
the eye and the heart to determine the proper division of
their rights to the youth's portrait. This war between eye and
heart was a favorite subject of the imitators of Petrarch, and
also of Shakespeare.

Mine eye and heart are at a mortal* war,   deadly
How to divide the conquest of thy sight;†
Mine eye my heart thy picture's sight would bar,
My heart mine eye the freedom of that right.
My heart doth plead that thou in him dost lie,
A closet never pierced with crystal eyes,
But the defendant* doth that plea deny,   *i.e.,* the eye
And says in him thy fair appearance lies.
To 'cide* this title is impanelèd   decide
A quest* of thoughts, all tenants to the heart;   jury
And by their verdict is determinèd
The clear eye's moiety* and the dear heart's part: portion
  As thus; mine eye's due is thy outward part,
  And my heart's right thy inward love of heart.

How to divide the conquest of thy sight.
How to determine which of us is to be granted the
exclusive right of gazing at your portrait.

47

The poet thanks his Friend for the gift of his portrait because it has been instrumental in bringing about a settlement of the suit satisfactory to both litigants. Shakespeare's accurate knowledge of the law, as shown in this group of sonnets, has induced some commentators to assume that during his "lost years" he was probably a lawyer's clerk. The use of legal terminology, however, was a widely adopted convention of the sonneteers.

Betwixt mine eye and heart a league is took,*   established
And each doth good turns now unto the other:
When that mine eye is famished for a look,
Or heart in love with sighs himself doth smother,
With my love's picture then my eye doth feast
And to the painted banquet* bids my heart;   i.e., the portrait
Another time mine eye is my heart's guest
And in his thoughts of love doth share a part:
So, either by thy picture or my love,
Thyself away art present still* with me;   always
For thou not farther than my thoughts canst move,
And I am still with them and they with thee;
   Or, if they sleep, thy picture in my sight
   Awakes my heart to heart's and eye's delight.

Anxiety and Depression / 48–66

These eighteen sonnets are a closely integrated sequence which record the painful thoughts and feelings the poet has after discovering the Friend's seduction of the Dark Lady. Though traveling, Shakespeare seems to have had news of Herbert's other involvements. This infidelity fills him with a continuing anxiety and depression which he describes in this group of poems.

48

How careful was I, when I took my way,*	*i.e.,* left home
Each trifle under truest* bars to thrust,	most trustworthy
That to my use it might unusèd stay	
From hands of falsehood,* in sure wards of trust!	*i.e.,* thieves
But thou, to whom my jewels trifles* are,	*i.e.,* compared to you
Most worthy comfort,* now my greatest grief,	enjoyment
Thou, best of dearest and mine only care,	
Art left the prey of every vulgar* thief.	common
Thee have I not locked up in any chest,	
Save where thou art not, though I feel thou art,	
Within the gentle closure of my breast,	
From whence at pleasure thou mayst come and part;*	leave
And even thence thou wilt be stol'n, I fear.	
For truth* proves thievish for a prize so dear.	honesty

49

Against* that time, if ever that time come, *in anticipation of*
When I shall see thee frown on my defects,
When as thy love hath cast* his utmost* sum, *reckoned / total*
Called to that audit by advised respects;* *careful considerations*
Against that time when thou shalt strangely* pass, *as a stranger*
And scarcely greet me with that sun, thine eye,
When love, converted* from the thing it was, *changed*
Shall reasons find of settled* gravity; *i.e., weighty*
Against that time do I ensconce* me here *shelter*
Within the knowledge of mine own desert,
And this my hand against myself uprear,†
To guard the lawful reasons on thy part:
   To leave poor me thou hast the strength of laws,
   Since why to love I can allege no cause.

And this my hand against myself uprear.
I.e., as a witness being sworn.

50

In this sonnet the poet confesses to his Friend that he is exhausted and depressed by the thought that every one of his jade's steps carries him further from his locked-up treasure. The horse seems instinctively to realize that his rider does not wish for speed, in spite of his angry spurring.

How heavy* do I journey on the way,   *sadly*
When what I seek, my weary travel's end,
Doth teach that ease and that repose to say,
"Thus far the miles are measured from thy friend!"
The beast that bears me, tired with my woe,
Plods dully on, to bear that weight in me,
As if by some instinct the wretch did know
His rider loved not speed, being made from* thee: *directed away from*
The bloody spur cannot provoke him on
That sometimes anger thrusts into his hide;
Which heavily he answers with a groan,
More sharp to me than spurring to his side;
   For that same groan doth put this in my mind;
   My grief lies onward, and my joy behind.

51

Developing the whimsical idea that his horse shares his feelings, Shakespeare declares that when he turns his mount toward his Friend, his own eagerness is so great that neither this horse nor any other can keep pace with it.

Thus can my love excuse the slow offense*   offense of slowness
Of my dull bearer when from thee I speed:
From where thou art why should I haste me thence?
Till I return, of posting* is no need.   hurrying
O, what excuse will my poor beast then find,
When swift extremity* can seem but slow?   extreme speed
Then should I spur, though mounted on the wind,
In wingèd speed no motion shall I know:†
Then can no horse with my desire keep pace;
Therefore desire, of perfect'st love being made,
Shall neigh—no dull flesh—in his fiery race;†
But love, for love, thus shall excuse my jade;†
　　Since from thee going he went willful-slow,
　　Towards thee I'll run and give him leave to go.*   walk

In wingèd speed no motion shall I know.
Even though I should fly I should be aware of no
movement toward you.
Shall neigh—no dull flesh—in his fiery race.
Lee's explanation of this puzzling line strikes me as the best:
"Desire which is all spent, and no dull flesh, shall neigh
in the excitement of its impassioned flight."
But love, for love, thus shall excuse my jade.
Because of the horse's love for me, which he shows
by going slow when moving away from you,
my Friend, I will excuse him.

52

So am I as the rich, whose blessèd key
Can bring him to his sweet up-lockèd treasure,
The which he will not every hour survey,
For* blunting the fine point of seldom pleasure.   for fear of
Therefore are feasts so solemn and so rare,
Since, seldom coming, in the long year set,
Like stones of worth they thinly placèd are,
Or captain* jewels in the carcanet.*   chief / gold necklace
So is the time that keeps you as my chest,
Or as the wardrobe which the robe doth hide,
To make some special instant special blest,
By new unfolding his imprisoned pride.
    Blessèd are you, whose worthiness gives scope,
    Being had, to triumph, being lacked, to hope.†

Being had, to triumph, being lacked, to hope.
Blessed are you whose charm is so great that your
presence is a triumph and your absence a hope
of seeing you again.

53

Many critics believe that sonnets 53 and 54 introduce a quite different person from the youth whose sensual fault the poet has previously been lamenting. He seems to be a noble creature who would reject the blandishments of vulgar thieves. Commentators often suggest that in this part of the sequence at least two friends are hodge-podged together. One need not, however, adopt this assumption. The perfunctory sonnets Shakespeare wrote while away were designed as a holding operation to keep his Friend's loyalty. When he returned to find his poems had produced the desired effect, he expressed his gratitude and delight in extravagant praise. The virtues he celebrates, therefore, need not be the result of sober judgment. Moreover, William Herbert was a complicated youth in whom aristocratic virtues and vices mingled, as they did in many of his noble contemporaries.

What is your substance, whereof are you made,
That millions of strange shadows* on you tend?*   images / attend
Since every one hath, every one, one shade,
And you, but one, can every shadow lend.
Describe Adonis, and the counterfeit*   portrait
Is poorly imitated after you;†
On Helen's cheek all art of beauty set,
And you in Grecian tires* are painted new:†   i.e., robes
Speak of the spring and foison* of the year,   i.e., autumn
The one doth shadow of your beauty show,
The other as your bounty doth appear;
And you in every blessèd shape we know.
　In all external grace you have some part,
　But you like none, none you,* for constant heart. i.e., like you

Describe Adonis and the counterfeit / Is poorly imitated after you.
A description of the beautiful Greek youth Adonis, loved by Venus would prove to be an unflattering portrait of you.
And you in Grecian tires are painted new.
You give a new beauty to Helen attired in her Greek robes.

54

O, how much more doth beauty beauteous seem
By that sweet ornament which truth* doth give!   constancy
The rose looks fair, but fairer we it deem
For that sweet odour which doth in it live.
The canker-blooms* have full as deep a dye   wild dog roses
As the perfumèd tincture* of the roses,   color
Hang on such thorns, and play as wantonly*   merrily
When summer's breath their maskèd buds discloses:
But, for* their virtue only is their show,   because
They live unwooed and unrespected* fade;   neglected
Die to themselves. Sweet roses do not so;
Of their sweet deaths are sweetest odours made:
  And so of you, beauteous and lovely youth,
  When that* shall fade, my verse distills your truth.   *i.e.*, youth

55

The litany of praise in the preceding sonnets mounts in 55 to one of the poet's most confident expressions of the triumph of his verse over the universal destruction of "sluttish time." In this way Shakespeare carries his glorification of his Friend into the public domain of the future. Thus the "poor me" of sonnet 49, who could find no reason for being loved, raises himself to a position in the House of Fame as honorable as that of the youth he is extolling.

Not marble, nor the gilded monuments
Of princes, shall outlive this powerful rhyme;
But you shall shine more bright in these contents
Than unswept stone,* besmeared with   *memorial in floor of a church
    sluttish* time.   *dirty
When wasteful war shall statues overturn,
And broils root out the work of masonry,
Nor Mars his sword nor war's quick fire shall burn
The living record of your memory.
'Gainst death and all-oblivious* enmity   *bringing total oblivion
Shall you pace forth;* your praise shall still   *i.e., endure
    find room
Even in the eyes of all posterity
That wear this world out to the ending doom.*†   *judgment day
    So, till the judgment that yourself arise,
    You live in this, and dwell in lovers' eyes.

That wear this world out to the ending doom.
That outlast this world even to the final judgment day.

56

The poet now begs the lovely boy to regard the recent break
in their intimacy as the experience of an engaged pair separated by a broad expanse of water. Nevertheless they come
every day to the water's edge to gaze at each other. In this
situation what they see will be more blessed, their love more
dear. Or, he says, let us consider our separation a kind of
winter that makes the summer the more wished for.

Sweet love,* renew thy force; be it not said   *i.e.*, spirit of love
Thy edge should blunter be than appetite,†
Which but to-day by feeding is allayed,
To-morrow sharpened in his former might:
So, love, be thou; although to-day thou fill
Thy hungry eyes even till they wink* with fullness,   close
To-morrow see again, and do not kill
The spirit of love with a perpetual dullness.
Let this sad interim like the ocean be
Which parts the shore, where two
     contracted new*   newly betrothed
Come daily to the banks, that, when they see
Return of love, more blest may be the view;
   Or call it winter, which, being full of care,
     Makes summer's welcome thrice more wished,
        more rare.

Thy edge should blunter be than appetite.
Interrupted love should be as capable of renewal as appetite,
which every day must be newly satisfied.

57

This sonnet, like 58, expresses a near-servile attitude. In both poems the poet describes himself as the lad's slave.

Being your slave, what should I do but tend*   wait
Upon the hours and times of your desire?
I have no precious time at all to spend,
Nor services to do, till you require.
Nor dare I chide the world-without-end* hour   everlasting
Whilst I, my sovereign, watch the clock for you,   *i.e.*, tedious
Nor think the bitterness of absence sour
When you have bid your servant once adieu;
Nor dare I question with my jealous thought
Where you may be, or your affairs suppose,*   imagine
But, like a sad slave, stay and think of nought
Save, where you are how happy you make those.
   So true a fool is love that in your will,
   Though you do any thing, he thinks no ill.†

So true a fool is love that in your will,
Though you do any thing, he thinks no ill.
Love is such a fool that it disapproves of nothing that your perverse desire brings to birth. In the quarto line 13 reads "Will," *i.e.*, Will Shakespeare. The line then would mean, Love in the person of Will Shakespeare can think no ill of anything that you do.

58

That god forbid that made me first your slave,
I should in thought control your times of pleasure,
Or at your hand the account* of hours to crave,   accounting
Being your vassal, bound to stay your leisure!
O, let me suffer, being at your beck,
The imprisoned absence of your liberty;†
And patience, tame to sufferance,* bide each   to the point of
   check,*   endurance
                                                                      rebuke
Without accusing you of injury.
Be where you list, your charter* is so strong   privilege
That you yourself may privilege* your time   license
To what you will; to you it doth belong
Yourself to pardon of self-doing* crime.   done by yourself
   I am to wait, though waiting so be hell,
   Not blame your pleasure, be it ill or well.

The imprisoned absence of your liberty.
Although during your absence from me you are free to go
wherever you please, nevertheless, the freedom that I gladly grant
you keeps me shut up in solitude. The line is a good example
of Shakespeare's "imagination all compact."

59

The eight sonnets that follow 58 form a unit. In them the poet speaks of the grief over the divided living to which Herbert has forced him to agree. As his mood darkens, he broods again over the wastage wrought by Time, of which their interrupted friendship is a sad example.

If there be nothing new, but that which is	
Hath been before, how are our brains beguiled	
Which, labouring for invention, bear amiss*	improperly
The second burthen of a former child!	
O, that recórd* could with a backward look,	memory
Even of five hundred courses of the sun,	
Show me your image in some antique book,	
Since mind at first in character was done.*	expressed in writing
That I might see what the old world could say	
To this composèd wonder* of your frame;	wonderful composition
Whether we are mended,* or whether better they,	perform better
Or whether revolution be the same.†	
O, sure I am, the wits* of former days	intellectuals
To subjects worse have given admiring praise.	

Or whether revolution be the same.
Or whether change be really no change at all,
i.e., whether history moves in a cyclic course.

60

This is one of the most admired of all the sonnets, both for its form and its eloquence.

Like as the waves make towards the pebbled shore,
So do our minutes hasten to their end;
Each changing place with that which goes before,
In sequent* toil all forwards do contend.   successive
Nativity,† once in the main of light,*   *i.e.,* the firmament
Crawls to maturity, wherewith being crowned,
Crookèd* eclipses 'gainst his glory fight,   malignant
And Time that gave doth now his gift confound.*   destroy
Time doth transfix* the flourish* set on youth   remove / bloom
And delves the parallels in beauty's brow
Feeds on the rarities of nature's truth,
And nothing stands but for his scythe to mow:
   And yet to times in hope* my verse shall stand   *i.e.,* the future
   Praising thy worth despite his cruel hand.

Nativity. This was an astrological term denoting the time of a child's birth in relation to all the starry influences of the moment.

61

In this and the next four sonnets the rhythms of devouring
Time beat incessantly beneath the verbal music.

Is it thy will thy image should keep open
My heavy eyelids to the weary night?
Dost thou desire my slumbers should be broken,
While shadows* like to thee do mock my sight?   images
Is it thy spirit that thou send'st from thee
So far from home into my deeds to pry,
To find out shames and idle* hours in me,†   empty
The scope and tenour* of thy jealousy?*   purport / suspicion
O, no! thy love, though much, is not so great:
It is my love that keeps mine eye awake;
Mine own true love that doth my rest defeat,*   destroy
To play the watchman ever for thy sake:
  For thee watch* I whilst thou dost wake*   keep awake / revel
    elsewhere,
  From me far off, with others all too near.

To find out shames and idle hours in me.
To discover how shamefully I spend my leisure.

62

Sin of self-love possesseth all mine eye
And all my soul and all my every part;
And for this sin there is no remedy,
It is so grounded inward in my heart.
Methinks no face so gracious* is as mine,   attractive
No shape so true, no truth of such account;
And for myself mine own worth do define,†
As I all other in all worths surmount.
But when my glass shows me myself indeed,
Beated and chopped* with tanned antiquity,*   seamed / old age
Mine own self-love quite contrary I read;
Self so self-loving were iniquity.
   'Tis thee, myself,* that for myself I praise   who art myself
   Painting my age with beauty of thy days.

And for myself mine own worth do define.
I place so great value on my own worth that, etc.

63

Against my love shall be,† as I am now,
With Time's injurious hand crushed and o'erworn;*†   worn out
When hours have drained his blood and filled his brow   by Time
With lines and wrinkles; when his youthful morn
Hath traveled on to age's steepy night,
And all those beauties whereof now he's king
Are vanishing or vanished out of sight,
Stealing away the treasure of his spring;
For such a time do I now fortify*   *i.e.*, myself
Against confounding* age's cruel knife,*   destroying / *i.e.*, scythe
That he shall never cut from memory
My sweet love's beauty, though my lover's life:
   His beauty shall in these black lines be seen,
   And they shall live, and he in them still green.

Against my love shall be. In anticipation of the time when, etc.
With Time's injurious hand crushed and o'erworn.
The author's extended reference to his old age is an
expression of the modesty conventionally expected
of a poet and is not to be taken literally.

64

When I have seen by Time's fell hand defaced
The rich-proud cost* of outworn buried age;   *expenditure*
When sometime lofty towers I see down-razed,
And brass* eternal slave to mortal* rage;   *i.e., on tombs /*
                                             i.e., death's
When I have seen the hungry ocean gain
Advantage on the kingdom of the shore,
And the firm soil win of the watery main,
Increasing store* with loss and loss with store;   *abundance*
When I have seen such interchange of state,*   *condition*
Or state* itself confounded* to decay;   *pomp / wasted*
Ruin hath taught me thus to ruminate,
That Time will come and take my love away.
    This thought is as a death, which* cannot choose   *i.e., thought*
    But weep to have* that which it fears to lose. *because of having*

65

This sonnet restates the theme of 63 though in a less effective manner.

Since brass, nor stone, nor earth, nor boundless sea,	
But sad mortality o'er-sways* their power,	surpasses
How with this rage shall beauty hold a plea	
Whose action* is no stronger than a flower?	vigor
O, how shall summer's honey breath hold out	
Against the wreckful* siege of battering days,	destructive
When rocks impregnable are not so stout,	
Nor gates of steel so strong, but* Time decays?	but that
O fearful meditation! where, alack,	
Shall Time's best jewel from Time's chest lie hid?	
Or what strong hand can hold his swift foot back?	
Or who his spoil* of beauty can forbid?	plunder
O, none, unless this miracle have might,	
That in black ink my love* may still shine bright.	*i.e.,* loved one

66

The poet's pondering over death in the four preceding sonnets inevitably culminates in reflecting on his own demise and
the evils of life from which it would release him. A somewhat
more comprehensive summary of mortal ills than Hamlet gives
in his "To be or not to be" soliloquy, both passages are always
taken to be expressions of Shakespeare's own feeling.

Tired with all these,* for restful death I cry,   *i.e., following evils*
As, to behold desert a beggar born,
And needy nothing trimmed in jollity,†
And purest faith unhappily* forsworn,   *evilly*
And gilded honour shamefully misplaced,*   *i.e., above its deserts*
And maiden virtue rudely strumpeted,*   *debauched*
And right perfection wrongfully disgraced,
And strength by limping sway* disablèd,   *being misdirected*
And art* made tongue-tied by authority,   *learning*
And folly, doctor*-like, controlling skill,   *pedantic*
And simple truth miscalled simplicity,*   *stupidity*
And captive good attending captain ill:†
    Tired with all these, from these would I be gone,
    Save that, to die, I leave my love alone.

And needy nothing trimmed in jollity.
Undeserving persons of no account magnificently adorned.
And captive good attending captain ill.
Virtue helplessly following evil.

Corruption and Death / 67–74

The first of these two closely knit groups of four sonnets, presents the poet's efforts to persuade the youth to break with a crowd of dissolute companions. The second group is concerned with age and death.

67

In an elaborate conceit developing the superiority of Nature to artifice, the author accuses the wayward youth of covering his natural beauty with "false painting," *i.e.*, cosmetics. His meaning is that the youth is hiding his natural sound morality by indulgence in the corrupt manners of the rakes who surround him. Moreover, by prostituting his beauty to their immorality he gives such conduct an adventitious attraction. Some literal-minded commentators have assumed that the target of the poet's attack is the young dandy's actual use of paint and powder, but the language is obviously figurative.

Ah, wherefore with infection* should he live	*i.e.*, of immorality
And with his presence grace impiety,	
That sin by him advantage should achieve	
And lace* itself with his society?	adorn
Why should false painting* imitate his cheek,	*i.e.*, cosmetics
And steal dead seeing of his living hue?	
Why should poor beauty indirectly* seek	at second hand
Roses of shadow,* since his rose is true?	painted roses
Why should he live, now Nature bankrupt is,	
Beggared of blood to blush through lively veins?	
For she hath no exchequer now but his,†	
And, proud of many, lives upon his gains.†	
O, him she stores,* to show what wealth she had	preserves
In days long since, before these last so bad.	

For she hath no exchequer now but his.
She has no treasure of beauty but his.
And, proud of many, lives upon his gains.
Nature, proud of her many beautiful forms, now derives her income exclusively from his natural beauty.

68

Shakespeare uses another homely figure to emphasize his conviction that his Friend's beauty partakes of that simple un-
adorned charm that prevailed before artificial aids to beauty
had become fashionable—like the repulsive Elizabethan custom of wearing wigs made of hair shorn from the heads of
dead men.

Thus is his cheek the map* of days outworn,*	image / past
When beauty lived and died as flowers do now,†	
Before these bastard signs of fair* were born,	painted beauty
Or durst inhabit on a living brow;	
Before the golden tresses of the dead,	
The right of sepulchers, were shorn away,	
To live a second life on second head;	
Ere beauty's dead fleece made another gay:	
In him those holy antique hours are seen,	
Without all* ornament, itself and true,	any
Making no summer of another's green,*	verdure
Robbing no old to dress his beauty new;	
And him as for a map doth Nature store,	
To show false Art what beauty was of yore.	

When beauty lived and died as flowers do now.
When beautiful men lived and died in the
colors that Nature had given them.

69

The poet turns from persuading to scolding the youth. He begins by admitting that everyone pays tribute to Herbert's good looks; but on further examination the discerning are grieved to discover that the fair flower of his beauty begins to throw off the rank smell of weeds. Perceptive acquaintances realize that in spite of his beauty, his conduct has made him "common." The word in the context of these rebukes means not only vulgar, but also easy of approach by every sort of person, good or bad.

Those parts of thee that the world's eye doth view
Want nothing that the thought of hearts can mend;
All tongues, the voice of souls,* give thee that due,   *i.e.,* candor
Uttering bare truth, even so as foes commend.*   *i.e.,* sparingly
Thy outward* thus with outward praise is crowned;   appearance
But those same tongues, that give thee so thine own,
In other accents* do this praise confound*   words / destroy
By seeing farther than the eye hath shown.
They look into the beauty of thy mind,
And that, in guess,* they measure by thy deeds;   by guesswork
Then, churls, their thoughts, although their eyes
    were kind,
To thy fair flower add the rank smell of weeds:
    But why thy odour* matcheth not thy show,   appearance
    The soil* is this, that thou dost common grow.   blemish

70

In sonnet 70 the poet tries to salve the wound made by his accusation in 69, admitting that the combination of beauty and virtue like Herbert's is always the target of the envious. Many critics believe that the man described in this poem is not the same person as the "sweet boy" of most of the other sonnets. They are apparently led astray by taking "prime" in line 8 in its modern meaning of the time of the full development of one's powers not yet impaired by age. But the word here has its usual Elizabethan meaning of early spring or early morning. It is true that the poet compliments his Friend on having passed the "ambush of young days," meaning that he has escaped from the snares of sexual temptation. Shakespeare believes, or perhaps only pretends to believe, that Herbert's yielding to the seductions of the Dark Lady was a mere lapse of youth, and that he has escaped from this sort of temptation for good and all. At the age of nineteen Shakespeare had extricated himself without dishonor from the same sort of trap. The couplet expresses the gist of all four poems, *i.e.,* if some *suspicion* of evil did not cling to the youth, he would win everyone's admiration.

That thou art blamed shall not be thy defect,
For slander's mark was ever yet the fair;
The ornament of beauty is suspect,
A crow that flies in heaven's sweetest air.
So thou be good, slander doth but approve
Thy worth the greater, being wooed of time;†
For canker vice the sweetest buds doth love,
And thou present'st a pure unstainèd prime.†
Thou hast passed by the ambush of young days,
Either not assailed, or victor being charged;*   attacked
Yet this thy praise cannot be so thy praise,
To tie up envy evermore enlarged:*   set at liberty
  If some suspect of ill masked* not thy show,   concealed
  Then thou alone kingdoms of hearts shouldst owe.*   possess

Being wooed of time. **Being wooed by the temptations of the age.**
And thou present'st a pure unstainèd prime.
And you exhibit a pure unsmirched springtime.

This second group of four sonnets reveals Shakespeare in a mood of profound discouragement because the youth has apparently ignored the appeal to break with his dissolute companions. The poet turns to thoughts of age and death.

71

In 71, Shakespeare's fear that the lordling will take his warning as an ultimatum makes him melancholy. Into his anxiety there intrudes the thought of his own death and the usual obsequies. He implores Herbert to react to his loss as he fears he will, urging him to mourn only briefly and then to forget the poet forever.

No longer mourn for me when I am dead
Than you shall hear the surly sullen bell†
Give warning to the world that I am fled
From this vile world, with vilest worms to dwell:
Nay, if you read this line, remember not
The hand that writ it; for I love you so,
That I in your sweet thoughts would be forgot,
If thinking on me then should make you woe.
O, if, I say, you look upon this verse
When I perhaps compounded* am with clay,   blended
Do not so much as my poor name rehearse,
But let your love even with my life decay;
   Lest the wise world should look into your moan,
   And mock you with me after I am gone.

Than you shall hear the surly sullen bell.
This was a bell tolled during the funeral service of a man recently dead, and while the funeral procession moved to the cemetery.

72

When the poet dies and the world calls on Herbert to write a laudatory obituary, Shakespeare advises him not to do so. If he did, he would have to lie, and lest Herbert's love tempt him to fabricate such falsehoods, it is better for the young lord to bury Shakespeare's name with his body.

O, lest the world should task you to recite*   tell
What merit lived in me, that you should love
After my death, dear love, forget me quite,
For you in me can nothing worthy prove;*   find
Unless you would devise some virtuous lie,
To do more for me than mine own desert,
And hang more praise upon deceasèd I
Than niggard truth would willingly impart:
O, lest your true love may seem false in this,
That you for love speak well of me untrue,*   untruly
My name be buried where my body is,
And live no more to shame nor me nor you.
    For I am shamed by that which I bring forth,*   *i.e.,* these sonnets
    And so should you,* to love things nothing   *i.e.,* be ashamed
        worth.*   of no value

73

One of the most famous and most artfully composed of all the sonnets in the sequence, this poem forms a quiet interlude in the poet's self-pitying appeal to the youth to forget him. In each quatrain Shakespeare employs a different, elaborately developed figure to express how his approach to old age must seem to his youthful Friend. In the couplet he finds comfort in the assurance that Herbert's love will grow stronger through the fear that he has only a little longer to live.

That time of year thou mayst in me behold
When yellow leaves, or none, or few, do hang
Upon those boughs which shake against the cold,
Bare ruined choirs, where late the sweet birds sang.†
In me thou see'st the twilight of such day
As after sunset fadeth in the west;
Which by and by* black night doth take away,   at once
Death's second self, that seals* up all in rest.   shuts
In me thou see'st the glowing of such fire,
That on the ashes of his youth doth lie,
As the death-bed whereon it must expire,
Consumed* with that* which it was nourished by.   choked /
                                                         i.e., the ashes
  This thou perceivest, which makes thy love more
     strong,
  To love that well which thou must leave ere long.

Bare ruined choirs, where late the sweet birds sang.
The poet compares the leafless boughs of winter to the
Gothic tracery of the ruined towers of destroyed abbeys.

74

The transition from the poet's assurance expressed in the last line of 73 to his inevitable death is artificial. Shakespeare exhorts Herbert to let happen what he fears will happen, assuring the young lord that his spirit will survive and will be incorporated into that of his bereaved Friend.

But be contented: when that fell arrest*   *i.e.,* by Death's officer
Without all bail shall carry me away,
My life hath in this line some interest,*   share
Which for memorial still with thee shall stay.
When thou reviewest this, thou dost review
The very part was consecrate to thee:
The earth can have but earth, which is his due;
My spirit is thine, the better part of me:
So then thou hast but lost the dregs of life,*   *i.e.,* the body
The prey of worms, my body being dead;
The coward conquest of a wretch's knife,†
Too base of thee to be rememberèd.
    The worth of that is that which it contains,*   *i.e.,* the spirit
    And that is this, and this with thee remains.

The coward conquest of a wretch's knife.
In this compact line most critics detect a threat of suicide.

Perils to the Friendship / 75–99

The profligate either ignored Shakespeare's appeal in the previous sonnets or scorned it. This attitude wounded the poet so deeply that he realized their friendship's very existence was at stake. He must now seek to rehabilitate it in every way possible and simultaneously thwart rival poets' efforts to supersede him in the youth's heart and mind.

75

The first sign of Shakespeare's anxiety appears in vacillation between his eagerness to delight in the young man's charms exclusively and his pride-driven impulse to allow the world to share this precious experience with him.

So are you to my thoughts as food to life,
Or as sweet-seasoned* showers are to the ground;   *i.e.,* April's
And for the peace of you* I hold such strife   contentment in you
As 'twixt a miser and his wealth is found;
Now proud as an enjoyer, and anon
Doubting* the filching age will steal his treasure;†   suspecting
Now counting best to be with you alone,
Then bettered* that the world may see my pleasure: made happier
Sometime all full with feasting on your sight,
And by and by* clean starvèd for a look;   at once
Possessing or pursuing no delight,
Save what is had or must from you be took.
   Thus do I pine and surfeit day by day,
   Or gluttoning on all, or all away.†

Doubting the filching age will steal his treasure.
Suspecting that some creature of the filching age, etc.
Thus do I pine and surfeit day by day,
Or gluttoning on all, or all away.
Thus is my eye surfeited with your beauty, while my appetite remains unsatisfied. I either fill myself with your charms when you are present, or have nothing to satisfy my hunger in your absence.

76

Shakespeare assures his Friend that he does not need to experiment with the rhetoric of the metaphysical poets. He is content to clothe his reiterated love in dress familiar to them both which he believes will make his love seem more and more personal: "That every word doth almost tell my name." The phrases "new-found methods" and "compounds strange" probably served to characterize the early poetry of John Donne.

Why is my verse so barren of new pride,*   *i.e.,* novelty
So far from variation or quick* change?   lively
Why with the time* do I not glance aside   following the fashion
To new-found methods and to compounds
     strange?*   *i.e.,* compounded epithets
Why write I still all one, ever the same,*   *i.e.,* the same purpose
And keep invention in a noted weed,*   familiar dress
That every word doth almost tell my name,
Showing their birth and where* they did proceed?   whence
O, know, sweet love, I always write of you,
And you and love are still my argument;*   theme
So all my best is dressing old words new,
Spending again what is already spent:
     For as the sun is daily new and old,
     So is my love still telling what is told.

77

The poet sent number 77 to Herbert commending him to the looking glass, the sun dial, and the commonplace book, or diary, to learn his lesson. The sonnet belongs to the group in which Shakespeare seeks to wean the youth from his wild companions. Exasperated by Herbert's failure to heed the warning against the decay of his morals and the fading of his beauty, the poet recommends that the young lord glance in the mirror and pay attention to the dial both of which will show him the effect "Time's thievish progress to eternity"—a striking phrase—will have on his beauty. The melancholy and desperate thoughts awakened will lead him to regret the carelessness with which he has treated the poet's loving admonitions.

Thy glass* will show thee how thy beauties wear,   mirror
Thy dial* how thy precious minutes waste;   sun dial
The vacant leaves* thy mind's imprint will bear,   *i.e.*, of the diary
And of this book this learning mayst thou taste.
The wrinkles which thy glass will truly show
Of mouthèd graves will give thee memory;
Thou by thy dial's shady stealth* mayst know   slow movement
Time's thievish progress to eternity.
Look, what thy memory cannot contain
Commit to these waste blanks, and thou shalt find
Those children nursed, delivered from thy brain
To take a new acquaintance of thy mind.
  These offices,* so oft as thou wilt look,   functions
  Shall profit thee and much enrich thy book.

78

Everyone's pen has taken the young lord as the subject of
verse, the poet complains. Learned writers, above all, when
addressing him, endow their verse with unaccustomed grace
and lightness. But however much their learning shames Shakespeare's ignorance, they are influenced by Herbert only in their
style, while his verse shows that his Friend is his sole inspiration.

The representative of these learned poets is not likely the
same man as the discoverer of "new-found methods." His virtues are much more like those of rare Ben Jonson, who might
very well have been trying to establish a productive relationship with Lord William Herbert.

So oft have I invoked thee for my Muse
And found such fair assistance in my verse
As* every alien pen hath got my use*   that / habit
And under thee* their poesy disperse.   *i.e.*, thy patronage
Thine eyes, that taught the dumb on high*   in an exalted fashion
          to sing
And heavy ignorance aloft to fly,
Have added feathers to the learnèd's wing†
And given grace a double majesty.
Yet be most proud of that which I compile,
Whose influence* is thine and born of thee: inspiration
In others' works thou dost but mend the style,
And arts* with thy sweet graces gracèd be.   learning
    But thou art all my art, and dost advance*   raise up
    As high as learning my rude ignorance.

Have added feathers to the learnèd's wing.
This is a figure from falconry: missing or
broken feathers were replaced by sound ones.

79

The next three sonnets are among the poorest in the entire sequence. In them the poet languidly repeats ideas that he has just effectively presented. As often before, notably in the first seventeen poems, he writes a number of sonnets on the same subject, as if testing his powers of "invention."

Whilst I alone did call upon thy aid,
My verse alone had all thy gentle grace;
But now my gracious numbers* are decayed,   pleasing verses
And my sick Muse doth give another place.†
I grant, sweet love, thy lovely argument*   subject of your beauty
Deserves the travail of a worthier pen;
Yet what of thee thy poet doth invent
He robs thee of, and pays it thee again.
He lends thee virtue, and he stole that word
For thy behaviour; beauty doth he give,
And found it in thy cheek: he can afford
No praise to thee but what in thee doth live.
    Then thank him not for that which he doth say,
    Since what he owes thee* thou thyself dost pay.   *i.e.,* as his patron

And my sick Muse doth give another place.
This line suggests that in his eagerness to win the contest with a rival poet he has come to realize that he has forced a reluctant Muse.

80

In an awkwardly developed figure of a race between two sailboats, the poet confesses his consciousness that the Rival Poet's superior achievements have made him tongue-tied whenever he tries to celebrate his Friend's fame.

O, how I faint when I of you do write,
Knowing a better spirit* doth use your name,   greater genius
And in the praise thereof spends all his might,
To make me tongue-tied, speaking* of your fame!   trying to speak
But since your worth, wide as the ocean is,
The humble* as the proudest sail doth bear,   *i.e.,* humblest
My saucy bark, inferior far to his,
On your broad main doth wilfully* appear.   daringly
Your shallowest help will hold me up afloat,
Whilst he upon your soundless* deep doth ride;   unfathomed
Or, being wrecked, I am a worthless boat,
He of tall building and of goodly pride:
    Then if he thrive and I be cast away,
    The worst* was this ; my love was my decay.*   *i.e.,* that could be said / cause of ruin

81

Or* I shall live your epitaph to make,   either
Or you survive when I in earth am rotten;
From hence your memory death cannot take,
Although in me each part* will be forgotten.   characteristic
Your name from hence immortal life shall have,
Though I, once gone, to* all the world must die: for
The earth can yield me but a common* grave,   lowly
When you entombèd in men's eyes shall lie.
Your monument shall be my gentle verse,
Which eyes not yet created shall o'er-read;
And tongues to be your being shall rehearse,
When all the breathers of this world are dead;
  You still shall live—such virtue hath my pen—
  Where breath most breathes, even in the mouths of
  men.

82

If Herbert doubts that it is only Shakespeare's Muse that can bring him immortal fame, then he must not be taken in by the exaggerations and strained rhetoric of the poet's rivals. The simple truth about him, simply expressed, is the most fitting praise to Herbert's fair nature.

I grant thou wert not married to my Muse,
And therefore mayst without attaint* o'erlook*   disgrace / peruse
The dedicated* words which writers use   used in dedications
Of their fair subject, blessing every book.†
Thou art as fair in knowledge as in hue,*   complexion
Finding thy worth a limit past* my praise;   reach beyond
And therefore art enforced to seek anew
Some fresher stamp of the time-bettering days,
And do so, love; yet when they have devised
What strainèd* touches rhetoric can lend,   exaggerated
Thou truly fair wert truly sympathized*   expressed
                                                        sympathetically
In true plain words by thy true-telling friend;
   And their gross painting might be better used
   Where cheeks need blood; in thee it is abused.*   misused

Blessing every book. The patron blesses by accepting the works dedicated to him and rewarding their authors.

83

I never saw that you did painting* need,   *i.e.*, rhetoric
And therefore to your fair* no painting set;   beauty
I found, or thought I found, you did exceed
The barren tender of a poet's debt:†
And therefore have I slept in your report,†
That you yourself, being extant, well might show
How far a modern quill doth come too short,
Speaking of worth, what worth in you doth grow.
This silence for my sin you did impute,
Which shall be most my glory, being dumb;
For I impair not beauty being mute,
When others would give life and bring a tomb.
    There lives more life in one of your fair eyes
    Than both your poets* can in praise devise.   Shakespeare
                                                                 and his rival

The barren tender of a poet's debt.
The poet's worthless proffer of repayment of an obligation.
And therefore have I slept in your report.
Out of idleness I have stopped praising you.

84

Who is it that says most? which can say more
Than this rich praise, that you alone are you?
In whose confine immurèd is the store
Which should example where your equal grew.
Lean penury within that pen doth dwell
That to his subject lends not some small glory;
But he that writes of you, if he can tell
That you are you, so dignifies his story.
Let him but copy what in you is writ,
Not making worse what nature made so clear,
And such a counterpart shall fame* his wit,   make famous
Making his style admirèd every where.
    You to your beauteous blessings add a curse,
    Being fond on* praise, which makes your praises   doting on
      worse.*   *i.e.*, debases you

85

My tongue-tied Muse in manners* holds her still,*   fittingly /
                                                           keeps silent
While comments of your praise, richly compiled,*   composed
Reserve their character* with golden* quill,   handwriting /
                                                          everlasting
And precious* phrase by all the Muses filed.   polished
I think good thoughts, whilst other write good words,
And, like unlettered* clerk, still cry "Amen"   illiterate cleric,
                                                        i.e., the rival
To every hymn that able spirit affords,
In polished form of well refinèd pen.
Hearing you praised, I say " 'Tis so, 'tis true,"
And to the most of praise add something more;
But that is in my thought, whose love to you,
Though words come hindmost,† holds his rank before.
   Then others for the breath of words respect,
   Me for my dumb thoughts, speaking in effect.

Though words come hindmost. Though my words are less effective
than those of my rivals.

86

Having shown better manners by giving up flattery, Shakespeare breaks out against another rival poet whom most critics
have identified as George Chapman. The striking image, in
the first two lines, of piracy on the high seas and particularly
of "the proud full sail of his great verse" describe Chapman's
style. The sonnet contains other more specific allusions to
Chapman, which are fully set forth in the essay on the Rival
Poet (pp. 16–19).

Was it the proud full sail of his great verse,
Bound for the prize of all too precious you,
That did my ripe thoughts in my brain inhearse,*   entomb
Making their tomb the womb wherein they grew?
Was it his spirit, by spirits taught to write
Above a mortal pitch, that struck me dead?
No, neither he, nor his compeers by night
Giving him aid, my verse astonishèd.*   stunned
He, nor that affable familiar ghost
Which nightly gulls* him with intelligence,*   cheats / messages
As victors, of my silence cannot boast;
I was not sick of any fear from thence:
    But when your countenance* filled up his line,   patronage
    Then lacked I matter; that enfeebled mine.

87

Farewell! thou art too dear for my possessing,
And like enough thou know'st thy estimate:*   value
The charter* of thy worth gives thee releasing;   privilege granted
My bonds in thee are all determinate.*   ended
For how do I hold thee but by thy granting?
And for that riches where is my deserving?
The cause of this fair gift in me is wanting,
And so my patent* back again is swerving.   grant
Thyself thou gavest, thy own worth then not knowing,
Or me, to whom thou gavest it, else mistaking;
So thy great gift, upon misprision growing,
Comes home again, on better judgment making.†
　　Thus have I had thee, as a dream doth flatter,
　　In sleep a king, but waking no such matter.

So thy great gift, upon misprision growing,
Comes home again, on better judgment making.
So your love, founded on a mistaken estimate of me, returns to you,
now that you have appraised me (and my work) truly.

88

In the next three sonnets the poet continues to lament his Friend's inconstancy and the loss of his love. The extreme statements of sacrificial devotion in these poems seems fulsome, but the lack of restraint is Elizabethan. Sonnet 88 is filled with the mortified spirit of the confessional, but stated with a simplicity and directness that give it restrained eloquence.

When thou shalt be disposed to set me light,*   value me little
And place my merit in the eye of scorn,
Upon thy side against myself I'll fight,
And prove thee virtuous, though thou art forsworn.*   perjured
With mine own weakness being best acquainted,
Upon thy part* I can set down a story   behalf
Of faults concealed,* wherein I am attainted;   i.e., from the world
That thou in losing* me shalt win much glory: forgetting
And I by this will be a gainer too;
For bending all my loving thoughts on thee,
The injuries that to myself I do,
Doing thee vantage,* double-vantage me.   good
    Such is my love, to thee I so belong,
    That for thy right* myself will bear all wrong.   advantage

89

Say that thou didst forsake me for some fault,
And I will comment* upon that offense: discourse
Speak of my lameness, and I straight will halt,*†   limp
Against thy reasons* making no defense.   remarks
Thou canst not, love, disgrace me half so ill,
To set a form upon desirèd change,*   make look respectable
As I'll myself disgrace; knowing thy will,
I will acquaintance* strangle and look strange;*   familiarity /
Be absent from thy walks; and in my tongue   like a stranger
Thy sweet belovèd name no more shall dwell,
Lest I, too much profane, should do it wrong,
And haply of our old acquaintance tell.
    For thee, against myself I'll vow debate,*   quarrel
    For I must ne'er love him whom thou dost hate.

I straight will halt. See sonnet 37.

90

This lyric expression of injured love, though hackneyed in theme, has been greatly admired by most critics for its restrained eloquence.

Then hate me when thou wilt; if ever, now;
Now, while the world is bent my deeds to cross,*   thwart
Join with the spite of fortune, make me bow,
And do not drop in for an after-loss:*   future grief
Ah, do not, when my heart hath 'scaped this sorrow,
Come in the rearward of a conquered woe;†
Give not a windy night a rainy morrow,
To linger out* a purposed overthrow.   protract
If thou wilt leave me, do not leave me last,
When other petty griefs have done their spite,
But in the onset* come: so shall I taste   beginning
At first the very worst of fortune's might;
   And other strains* of woe, which now seem woe,   feelings
   Compared with loss of thee will not seem so.

Come in the rearward of a conquered woe.
Afflict me after I have conquered the woe of one misfortune.

91

Sonnets 91–93 are linked verbally and emotionally, and rise to a climax in 93. They are utterances of despair. The Friend seems to have made no reassuring response to the poet's self-abasement in the previous poems. These are the last of the widely scattered sonnets concerning the rival poet or poets. In 91 Shakespeare enumerates his Friend's aristocratic diversions only to assert that his love is a better interest than any of them.

Some glory in their birth, some in their skill,
Some in their wealth, some in their body's force;
Some in their garments, though new-fangled ill;*   fashionably ugly
Some in their hawks and hounds, some in their horse;
And every humour* hath his adjunct pleasure,   temperament
Wherein it finds a joy above the rest:
But these particulars are not my measure;*   *i.e.,* of happiness
All these I better in one general best.
Thy love is better than high birth to me,
Richer than wealth, prouder than garments' cost,
Of more delight than hawks or horses be;
And having thee, of all men's pride I boast:†
  Wretched in this alone, that thou mayst take
  All this away and me most wretched make.

And having thee, of all men's pride I boast.
I boast of having in your love the equivalent of
all the sources of pride of which aristocrats boast.

92

In 92 the poet expresses a kind of lyrical optimism. Should his Friend die, he would enjoy the double happiness of knowing that he will live no longer than Pembroke's love endures, and will be able to escape grief at losing his love by death.

But do thy worst to steal thyself away,
For term of life thou art assurèd mine;
And life no longer than thy love will stay,
For it depends upon that love of thine.
Then need I not to fear the worst of wrongs,
When in the least of them my life hath end.†
I see a better state to me belongs
Than that which on thy humour* doth depend: whim
Thou canst not vex me with inconstant mind,
Since that my life on thy revolt doth lie.*   *i.e., your desertion
O, what a happy title do I find,   would kill me
Happy to have thy love, happy to die!†
    But what's so blessed-fair that fears no blot?
    Thou mayst be false, and yet I know it not.

*Then need I not to fear the worst of wrongs,
When in the least of them my life hath end.*
Then I need not fear the entire loss of your love when the first intimation of its loss would kill me.
Happy to have thy love, happy to die.
Happy to die because by dying I will escape the experience of losing your love.

93

In 93 Shakespeare takes comfort in the fact that the youth's countenance and demeanor display only love, whatever his deep feelings may be; so the poet is forced to assume a resolute cheerfulness like that of a husband who knows his wife is betraying him.

So shall I live, supposing thou art true,
Like a deceivèd husband; so love's face
May still seem love to me, though altered new;*   *i.e.,* new
Thy looks with me, thy heart in other place: mannered
For there can live no hatred in thine eye,
Therefore in that I cannot know thy change.
In many's looks* the false heart's history   casts of countenance
Is writ in moods and frowns and wrinkles strange,
But heaven in thy creation did decree
That in thy face sweet love should ever dwell;
Whate'er thy thoughts or thy heart's workings be,
Thy looks should nothing thence but sweetness tell.
 How like Eve's apple doth thy beauty grow,†
 If thy sweet virtue answer not* thy show.   corresponds
                 not with

How like Eve's apple doth thy beauty grow.
Eve's apple was good to behold but disastrous to taste. The line means:
Like the apple, your beauty is wonderful to admire, but
dangerous if regarded as a revelation of your real nature.

94

In a bitterly ironic tone, the poet accuses his Friend of awakening love that he is too cold to return. Such creatures as Herbert, Shakespeare sarcastically continues, are the proper recipients of heaven's graces because they do not wantonly waste them. This is a picture of a selfish, haughty lordling, who hoards barren emotion. His deeds become more offensive because of their deceptive appearance of rectitude.

They that have power to hurt and will do* none,   *i.e.,* return
That do not do the thing they most do show,†
Who, moving others, are themselves as stone,
Unmovèd, cold and to temptation slow;
They rightly do inherit* heaven's graces   use correctly
And husband* nature's riches from expense;*   hoard / waste
They are the lords and owners of their faces,
Others but stewards of their excellence.
The summer's flower is to the summer sweet,
Though to itself it only live and die,
But if that flower with base infection meet,
The basest weed outbraves* his dignity: surpasses
    For sweetest things turn sourest by their deeds;
    Lilies that fester smell far worse than weeds.

That do not do the thing they most do show.
That do not return the love they awaken.

95

How sweet and lovely dost thou make the shame
Which, like a canker* in the fragrant rose,   canker-worm
Doth spot the beauty of thy budding name!
O, in what sweets dost thou thy sins inclose!
That tongue that tells the story of thy days,
Making lascivious comments on thy sport,*   sensual pleasures
Cannot dispraise but in a kind of praise;
Naming thy name blesses an ill report.†
O, what a mansion have those vices got
Which for their habitation chose out thee,
Where beauty's veil doth cover every blot
And all things turn to fair that eyes can see!
　　Take heed, dear heart, of this large privilege;
　　The hardest knife ill used doth lose his edge.

Naming thy name blesses an ill report.
The mere uttering of your name, like a priest's sign of the cross,
takes all the curse from the evil that is reported of you.

96

The subject of 96 is identical with that of 95, except that the poet is more explicit about the nature of Pembroke's immorality. Yet he is able to transmute the youth's faults into graces.

Some say thy fault is youth, some wantonness;
Some say, thy grace is youth and gentle sport;*   amorous dalliance
Both grace and faults are loved of more and less:*   aristocrats and common men
Thou makest faults graces that to thee resort.
As on the finger of a thronèd queen
The basest jewel will be well esteemed,
So are those errors* that in thee are seen   vices
To truths translated* and for true things deemed.   transformed
How many lambs might the stern* wolf betray,   ferocious
If like a lamb he could his looks translate!*   change his looks to a lamb's
How many gazers mightst thou lead away,
If thou wouldst use the strength of all thy state!*   high rank
    But do not so; I love thee in such sort,
    As thou being mine, mine is thy good report.†

But do not so; I love thee in such sort,
As thou being mine, mine is thy good report.
This couplet is exactly like the final couplet of 36. Some critics think Shakespeare repeats the lines to carry the Earl's mind back to the happier
days of their relationship; other critics believe it to be a typesetter's mistake.

97

In this and the two following sonnets Shakespeare changes tactics in his efforts to lure Pembroke away from his evil companions and back to his own company. Instead of deploring the Earl's vices, the poet laments his continued separation from his Friend with a grace and controlled emotion that render this sonnet and 98 two of the most beautiful poems in the entire sequence.

How like a winter hath my absence been
From thee, the pleasure of the fleeting year:
What freezings have I felt, what dark days seen!
What old December's bareness every where!
And yet this time removed* was summer's time; of absence
The teeming autumn, big with rich increase,
Bearing the wanton burthen of the prime,* spring
Like widowed wombs after their lord's decease:
Yet this abundant issue seemed to me
But hope of orphans and unfathered fruit;†
For summer and his pleasures wait on thee,
And, thou away, the very birds are mute;
  Or, if they sing, 'tis with so dull a cheer* cheerfulness
  That leaves look pale, dreading the winter's near.

But hope of orphans and unfathered fruit.
But expectation of children whose father is dead.

98

From you have I been absent in the spring,
When proud-pied* April, dressed in all his trim,*   coat of many
                                                     colors / finery
Hath put a spirit of youth in every thing,
That heavy* Saturn† laughed and leaped with him.*   sorrowful /
                                                      i.e., April
Yet nor the lays of birds, nor the sweet smell
Of different flowers in odour and in hue,
Could make me any summer's story tell,
Or from their proud lap pluck them where they grew:
Nor did I wonder at the lily's white,
Nor praise the deep vermilion in the rose;
They were but sweet, but figures* of delight,   symbols
Drawn after you, you pattern of all those.
    Yet seemed it winter still, and, you away,
    As with your shadow* I with these did play.   portrait

That heavy Saturn laughed and leaped with him.
Because of its remoteness and slow motion, Saturn was supposed to cause
sluggishness. Men under its influence were afflicted with a double melancholy.

99

This poem is not a true sonnet; it is fifteen lines long. Joseph Quincy Adams plausibly suggests that the poet realized that it betrayed so obvious a failure of inspiration that he never took the trouble to make it over into sonnet form.

The forward* violet thus did I chide: early
Sweet thief, whence didst thou steal thy sweet
    that smells.
If not from my love's breath? The purple pride
Which on thy soft cheek for complexion dwells
In my love's veins thou hast too grossly dyed.
The lily I condemnèd for thy hand,†
And buds of marjoram* had stolen thy hair;   i.e., reddish brown
The roses fearfully* on thorns did stand,   uneasily
One blushing shame, another white despair;
A third, nor red nor white, had stol'n of both,
And to his robbery had annexed thy breath;
But, for his theft, in pride of all his growth
A vengeful canker* eat him up to death.   canker-worm
    More flowers I noted, yet I none could see
    But sweet or colour it had stol'n from thee.

The lily I condemnèd for thy hand.
For trying to imitate the whiteness of thy hand.

When the long breach in the friendship between the two men ended, Shakespeare's spirits grew buoyant and he reiterates his earlier expressions of delight in the youth's charms. Although the poet designed these nine poems to form a group, their organization differs from that of other groups in the sequence because these poems are all different expressions of a state of well-being. Not until we reach sonnet 107 do we discover the reasons for the poet's euphoria.

In sonnet 100 he appropriately begins with chiding his truant Muse for her long failure to celebrate his Friend's beauty and to commend her resistance to all efforts of Time to smirch it.

100

Where art thou, Muse, that thou forget'st so long
To speak of that which gives thee all thy might?
Spend'st thou thy fury* on some worthless song,   *inspiration*
Darkening thy power to lend base subjects light?
Return, forgetful Muse, and straight redeem
In gentle numbers* time so idly spent;   *noble verses*
Sing to the ear that doth thy lays esteem
And gives thy pen both skill and argument.*   *subject*
Rise, resty* Muse, my love's sweet face survey   *lazy*
If Time have any wrinkle graven there.
If any, be a satire to decay,
And make Time's spoils despisèd every where.
   Give my love fame faster than Time wastes life;
   So thou prevent'st his scythe and crooked knife.*   *i.e., scythe*

101

O truant Muse, what shall be thy amends
For thy neglect of truth in beauty dyed?
Both truth and beauty on my love depends;
So dost thou too, and therein dignified.*   are dignified
Make answer, Muse: wilt thou not haply say,
"Truth needs no colour, with his colour fixed;†
Beauty no pencil, beauty's truth to lay;*   *i.e.,* on canvas
But best is best, if never intermixed"?
Because he needs no praise, wilt thou be dumb?
Excuse not silence so, for 't lies in thee
To make him much outlive a gilded tomb
And to be praised of ages yet to be.
    Then do thy office,* Muse; I teach thee how   perform your
    To make him seem long hence as he shows now.   function

Truth needs no colour, with his colour fixed.
Truth needs no embellishment because its own beauty is unchangeable.

102

In one of the loveliest poems in the entire sequence, Shake-speare appeals to his Muse to revive the spell cast both on him and on Pembroke during the first days of their friendship. Harking back to their springtime rapture, Shakespeare promises that the summer of their friendship will be as beautiful as the nightingale's song.

My love is strengthened, though more weak in seeming;
I love not less, though less the show appear:
That love is merchandized* whose rich esteeming   treated as merchandise
The owner's tongue doth publish every where.
Our love was new, and then but in the spring,
When I was wont to greet it with my lays;
As Philomel* in summer's front† doth sing,   the nightingale
And stops her pipe in growth of riper days:
Not that the summer is less pleasant now
Than when her mournful hymns did hush the night,
But that wild music* burthens every bough,   *i.e.*, songbirds
And sweets grown common lose their dear delight.
    Therefore, like her, I sometime hold my tongue,
    Because I would not dull* you with my song.   bore

As Philomel in summer's front. Front means forehead. The phrase means early summer.

103

Alack, what poverty my Muse brings forth,
That having such a scope* to show her pride,   free play
The argument,* all bare, is of more worth   theme
Than when it hath my added praise beside!
O, blame me not, if I no more can write!
Look in your glass, and there appears a face
That over-goes* my blunt* invention quite,   surpasses /
Dulling my lines and doing me disgrace.   awkward
Were it not sinful then, striving to mend,
To mar the subject that before was well?
For to no other pass my verses tend
Than of your graces and your gifts to tell;
    And more, much more, than in my verse can sit,
    Your own glass shows you when you look in it.

104

Shakespeare continues to ring changes on his Friend's personal charms, reminding him that they are as compelling as they were when the two of them first met three years before. Though this is the only specific time reference in the sequence, we shall see that all nine poems in this group were written at approximately the same time, and, if sonnet 107 is properly interpreted, that date is 1601. With this line of reasoning, Shakespeare must therefore have met Herbert in 1598. Such a late date, however, is fatal to the conjecture that the two first met in 1595, when Pembroke made his initial visit to London. Nevertheless, Shakespeare could well have composed the procreation sonnets, the written ambassage, and many of the other poems before he actually met Pembroke.

To me, fair friend, you never can be old,
For as you were when first your eye I eyed,
Such seems your beauty still. Three winters' cold
Have from the forests shook three summers' pride,
Three beauteous springs to yellow autumn turned
In process* of the seasons have I seen,   course
Three April perfumes in three hot Junes burned,
Since first I saw you fresh, which yet are green.
Ah, yet doth beauty, like a dial-hand,*   shadow on
                                                       the sun dial
Steal from his figure, and no pace perceived;
So your sweet hue, which methinks still doth stand,
Hath motion, and mine eye may be deceived:
    For fear of which, hear this, thou age unbred;
    Ere you were born was beauty's summer dead.

105

Shakespeare now seeks to assure himself that Pembroke, despite his liaison with the poet's mistress, nevertheless always remained faithful to their sacred bond of friendship.

Let not my love be called idolatry,
Nor my belovèd as an idol show,*   appear
Since all alike my songs and praises be
To one, of one, still such, and ever so.
Kind is my love to-day, to-morrow kind,
Still constant in a wondrous excellence;
Therefore my verse to constancy confined,
One thing expressing, leaves out difference.*   *i.e.,* differences
"Fair, kind, and true," is all my argument,
"Fair, kind, and true," varying to other words;
And in this change is my invention spent,
Three themes in one, which wondrous scope affords.
   "Fair, kind, and true," have often lived alone,
   Which three till now never kept seat in one.

106

Although in sonnet 105 Shakespeare exonerates himself of the charge of idolatry, in 106 he comes perilously near pagan worship. For the Muse, whom he begins by chiding as truant, now composes one of the most eloquent of his eulogies to the youth's beauty.

When in the chronicle of wasted time
I see descriptions of the fairest wights,
And beauty making beautiful old rhyme
In praise of ladies dead and lovely knights,
Then, in the blazon* of sweet beauty's best,   display
Of hand, of foot, of lip, of eye, of brow,
I see their antique pen would have expressed
Even such a beauty as you master* now.   possess
So all their praises are but prophecies
Of this our time, all you prefiguring;
And, for* they looked but with divining* eyes,   because /
They had not skill enough your worth to sing: prophetic
   For we, which now behold these present days,
    Have eyes to wonder, but lack tongues to praise.

107

Usually described as the "dated sonnet," this poem has stimulated many differing interpretations. Written in 1601 (see the Introduction for the editor's discussion of the dating), it is significant in the changing relationship between the two men. It also was meaningful because Shakespeare had just escaped from the danger of his Company's involvement with the Essex rebellion and because the Queen, furious with Pembroke for fathering Mary Fitton's child and refusing to marry her, had sent Pembroke to jail and then rusticated him to Wilton. Shakespeare might well have considered that an appropriate moment to express his continuing devotion to Herbert who was now "in disgrace with fortune and men's eyes."

Not mine own fears, nor the prophetic soul
Of the wide world dreaming on things to come,
Can yet the lease* of my true love control,   duration
Supposed as forfeit to a cónfined doom.*   imprisonment
The mortal moon* hath her eclipse endured,   *i.e.,* The Queen
And the sad augurs mock their own presage;
Incertainties now crown themselves assured,
And peace proclaims olives of endless age.
Now with the drops of this most balmy time
My love looks fresh, and Death to me subscribes,*   submits
Since, spite of him, I 'll live in this poor rhyme,
While he insults* o'er dull and speechless tribes: *i.e.,* triumphs
  And thou in this shalt find thy monument,
    When tyrants' crests and tombs of brass are spent.

108

If these nine sonnets were designed as a group, the last poem rounds out the whole. In the first quatrain, Shakespeare confesses he has nothing new to add on the subject of Herbert's charms. And even the most sympathetic reader will agree.

What's in the brain, that ink may character,*   write
Which hath not figured to thee my true spirit?
What's new to speak, what new to register,
That may express my love, or thy dear merit?
Nothing, sweet boy; but yet, like prayers divine,
I must each day say o'er the very same;
Counting no old thing old, thou mine, I thine,
Even as when first I hallowed thy fair name.
So that eternal love in love's fresh case*   covering
Weighs not the dust and injury of age,
Nor gives to necessary wrinkles place,
But makes antiquity* for aye his page;*   old age / servant
   Finding the first conceit* of love there bred,   conception
   Where time and outward form would show it dead.

In Retrospect / 109–126

In these last sonnets, Shakespeare explains how his friendship with Pembroke, almost ruined by the rivalry for the Dark Lady, can be renewed. The sequence closes with the reestablishment of the attachment between the poet and Pembroke which apparently remained secure for the rest of Shakespeare's life.

109

O, never say that I was false of heart,
Though absence seemed my flame to qualify.*   moderate
As easy might I from myself depart
As from my soul, which in thy breast doth lie:
That is my home of love: if I have ranged,*   strayed
Like him that travels, I return again;
Just to the time, not with the time exchanged,†
So that myself bring water for my stain.
Never believe, though in my nature reigned
All frailties that besiege all kinds of blood,*   passion
That it could so preposterously be stained,
To leave* for nothing all thy sum of good;   to desert
 For nothing this wide universe I call,
  Save thou, my rose; in it thou art my all.

Just to the time, not with the time exchanged.
True to this phase of our love, but not changed by the opinions of the world.

IIO

The poet reveals what has been weighing on his mind, the fear that his affair with the Dark Lady has made him unworthy of Pembroke's love.

Many critics believe that the first two lines indicate Shakespeare's shame for his profession as an actor, but the rest of the poem does not confirm this opinion. Rather the poet seems to be saying that by forming new emotional relationships of which Pembroke disapproved, he injured his own self-respect.

Alas, 'tis true I have gone here and there,
And made myself a motley* to the view,   a fool
Gored* mine own thoughts, sold cheap what is   deeply wounded
    most dear,
Made old offenses of affections new;†
Most true it is that I have looked on truth
Askance* and strangely:* but, by all above,   disdainfully /
                                        distantly
These blenches* gave my heart another youth,   disdainful looks
And worse essays* proved thee my best of love.   trials of
                                     worse lovers
Now all* is done, have what* shall have no end: *i.e.*, such trials /
Mine appetite I never more will grind   my love
On newer proof, to try an older friend,†
A god in love, to whom I am confined.
    Then give me welcome, next my heaven the best,
    Even to thy pure and most most loving breast.

Made old offenses of affections new.
Established new loves that offend my old ones.
Mine appetite I never more will grind
On newer proof, to try an older friend.
I will never whet my appetite for your love on new friends in order to discover your love's value.

III

The poet does advance another possible reason for his fear that Pembroke's affection for him is cooling: his career in the theater.

O, for my sake do you with Fortune chide,
The guilty goddess of my harmful deeds,†
That did not better for my life provide
Than   public means* which public* manners   *i.e.*, acting /
    breeds.   common
Thence comes it that my name receives a brand,
And almost thence my nature is subdued*   subjugated
To what it works in, like the dyer's hand:
Pity me then and wish I were renewed;*   restored
Whilst, like a willing patient, I will drink
Potions of eisel* 'gainst my strong infection;   vinegar
No bitterness that I will bitter think,
Nor double penance, to correct correction.†
   Pity me then, dear friend, and I assure ye
   Even that your pity is enough to cure me.

The guilty goddess of my harmful deeds.
The goddess who is responsible for my professional activities that injure my reputation.

No bitterness that I will bitter think,
Nor double penance, to correct correction.
I will consider no remedy too bitter, nor will I shun double penance, provided it corrects my conduct.

112

  Shakespeare thanks Pembroke for the love and pity lavished
upon him, especially at this moment when he is humiliated by
a mysterious "vulgar scandal." So long as his Friend cherishes
him thus, the scorn and neglect of others do not disturb him.

Your love and pity doth the impression fill
Which vulgar* scandal stamped upon my brow;   public
For what care I who calls me well or ill,
So you o'er-green* my bad, my good allow?*   cover as with
You are my all the world, and I must strive   grass / commend
To know my shames and praises from your tongue;
None else to me, nor I to none alive,†
That my steeled sense or changes right or wrong.
In so profound abysm I throw all care
Of others' voices, that my adder's sense
To critic and to flatterer stoppèd are.
Mark how with my neglect I do dispense:†
  You are so strongly in my purpose* bred   will (*i.e.*, plans)
  That all the world besides methinks are dead.

None else to me, nor I to none alive.
There are no others in the world whose opinions influence me, and I take
none into account.
Mark how with my neglect I do dispense.
Mark how little I care for the neglect of others.

113

The next pair of sonnets adopts a familiar rhetorical device that exploits the relation of eye to mind. In this final group of poems addressed to Pembroke, Shakespeare tells the youth that after they have parted, the mental image of the young Earl so dominates his vision that it makes his eye blind to what is actually before it.

Since I left you mine eye is in my mind,†
And that which governs me to go about
Doth part his function and is partly blind,
Seems seeing, but effectually* is out;*   actually / blinded
For it no form delivers to the heart
Of bird, of flower, or shape, which it doth latch:*   lay hold of
Of his quick* objects hath the mind no part,   live
Nor his own vision holds what it doth catch;
For if it see the rudest or gentlest sight,
The most sweet favour* or deformed'st creature,   face
The mountain or the sea, the day or night,
The crow or dove, it shapes them to your feature:†
     Incapable of more, replete with you,
     My most true mind thus makes mine eye.

Since I left you mine eye is in my mind.
Since we parted, my mental image of you is so vivid it keeps me from seeing anything else.
It shapes them to your feature. Everything that the eye sees is instantly changed to your features.

114

Or whether doth my mind, being crowned with you,*   brimful of
Drink up the monarch's plague, this flattery?
Or whether shall I say, mine eye saith true,
And that your love taught it this alchemy,†
To make of monsters and things indigest*   shapeless
Such cherubins as your sweet self resemble,
Creating every bad a perfect best,
As fast as objects to his beams assemble?†
O, 'tis the first; 'tis flattery in my seeing,
And my great mind most kingly drinks it up:
Mine eye well knows what with his gust* is 'greeing,*   taste /
And to his palate doth prepare the cup: agreeable
   If it be poisoned, 'tis the lesser sin
   That mine eye loves it and doth first begin.

And that your love taught it this alchemy.
And that my love of you, like alchemy that changes base metals into gold,
converts everything I see into your golden image.
As fast as objects to his beams assemble.
It was an old idea that the eye actually threw out beams by the light
of which objects became visible.

115

This is one of the many sonnets in which the poet chides Time for its tyranny, for its "millioned" accidents which impair vows of friendship.

Those lines that I before have writ do lie,
Even those that said I could not love you dearer:
Yet then my judgment knew no reason why
My most full flame should afterwards burn clearer.
But reckoning Time, whose millioned* accidents   millionfold
Creep in 'twixt vows, and change decrees of kings,
Tan sacred beauty, blunt the sharp'st intents,*   ambitions
Divert strong minds to the course of altering things;†
Alas, why, fearing of Time's tyranny,
Might I not then say "Now I love you best,"
When I was certain o'er incertainty,
Crowning the present, doubting of the rest?
   Love is a babe; then might I not say so,
    To give full growth to that which still doth grow?

Divert strong minds to the course of altering things.
Turn strong minds from accomplishment of their purpose to the acceptance of mutability.

116

Perhaps the most admired and most quoted of all the sonnets, 116 follows 115 naturally, for here the poet shows his
Friend the way to keep their mutual dear religious love inde-
pendent of the innumerable accidents of Time. Many readers
will be disappointed to learn that it is not a love sonnet addressed to a woman completely different from the Dark Lady.

Let me not to the marriage of true minds
Admit impediments. Love is not love
Which alters when it alteration finds,
Or bends with the remover to remove:†
O, no; it is an ever-fixèd mark,*   sea-mark (beacon)
That looks on tempests and is never shaken;
It is the star* to every wandering bark,   *i.e.,* the North Star
Whose worth 's unknown, although his height
      be taken.†
Love's not Time's fool,* though rosy lips and cheeks   mocks not
                                                              Time
Within his bending* sickle's compass come;   crooked
Love alters not with his brief hours and weeks,
But bears it out* even to the edge of doom.   survives
   If this be error and upon* me proved,   against
   I never writ, nor no man ever loved.

Or bends with the remover to remove.
Changes love's abode because of inconstancy.
Whose worth's unknown, although his height be taken.
Whose occult influence is unknown, even though its altitude
can be calculated for the purposes of navigation.

117

Admitting that he has been false to the ideals of friendship between two married minds, Shakespeare gives Pembroke the lame excuse that his lapses were his way of testing his Friend's constancy and love.

Accuse me thus: that I have scanted* all   slighted
Wherein I should your great deserts repay.
Forgot upon your dearest love to call,
Whereto all bonds* do tie me day by day;   obligations
That I have frequent* been with unknown minds,*   familiar / *i.e.,*
And given to time your own dear-purchased right;   nonentities
That I have hoisted sail to all the winds
Which should transport me farthest from your sight.
Book* both my willfulness and errors down.   register
And on just proof surmise accumulate;†
Bring me within the level* of your frown,   range
But shoot not at me in your wakened hate;
   Since my appeal says I did strive to prove
    The constancy and virtue of your love.

And on just proof surmise accumulate.
Add to what you can reasonably prove all that you suspect.

118

Shakespeare describes his unfaithfulness to his Friend as a purge taken to eliminate the poisons accumulated from his unrelieved feeding on Pembroke's sweetness. This figure of a purge is not to modern taste. J. J. Chapman, in his *A Glance toward Shakespeare,* thought it "disgusting." Perhaps the poet counted on his Friend's finding the figure absurd enough to be amusing.

Like as, to make our appetites more keen,
With eager* compounds we our palate urge;*   bitter / stimulate
As, to prevent our maladies unseen,
We sicken to shun sickness when we purge;
Even so, being full of your ne'er-cloying sweetness,
To bitter sauces did I frame my feeding;
And sick of welfare found a kind of meetness*   fitness
To be diseased, ere that there was true needing.
Thus policy* in love, to anticipate   prudence
The ills that were not, grew to faults assured,*   positive
And brought to medicine a healthful state,
Which, rank of* goodness, would by ill be cured: replete with
   But thence I learn, and find the lesson true,
   Drugs poison him that so fell sick of you.

119

Shakespeare admits that under the spell of the Dark Lady
and her siren's tears he developed a maddening fever. Yet he
discovers that his sexual excitement has benefited his real love
for Pembroke: For love that seems to be a ruin, when repaired,
becomes a fairer, stronger edifice.

What potions have I drunk of Siren* tears,   *i.e.,* the Dark Lady's
Distilled from limbecks* foul as hell within,   stills
Applying* fears to hopes and hopes to fears,   *i.e.,* as poultices
Still losing when I saw myself to win!
What wretched errors hath my heart committed,
Whilst it hath thought itself so blessèd never!
How have mine eyes out of their spheres been fitted,*   convulsed
In the distraction of this madding fever!
O benefit of ill! now I find true
That better is by evil still made better;
And ruined love, when it is built anew,
Grows fairer than at first, more strong, far greater.
  So I return rebuked to my content,
  And gain by ill thrice more than I have spent.

That these five sonnets form an integrated group is proved
by the verbal correspondences, enabling the "strong minds" of
115 to become the "true minds" of 116. The medical jargon of
118 continues in the poultices of 119. And the line "But thence
I learn, and find the lesson true," is echoed in "O benefit of
ill! now I find true" of 119. Here the poet enunciates the truth
of the entire penultimate group. From the paradox of apothe-
cary stuff and grindstone the author rises to the spiritual
mystery of suffering and sin. Weak minds may be corrupted
and destroyed by evil, but strong and true minds survive, and
are purified and strengthened by it—a profound statement of
the mystery of the impact of sin upon a sensitive human being.
Through meeting his ordeal successfully, the poet has achieved
a notable triumph over his sexual degradation, and boldly con-
fronts Pembroke in the light of it. Thus, 119 sums up the
experience of the first part of the sequence and comments on
its significance. A long and rugged path it proves to have been
from the written ambassage and the drawing-room badinage
with the Lady to this expression of deep spiritual insight.

120

From the vantage point of his moral triumph, the poet continues his retrospective view of his relationship with Pembroke. Their estrangement and the suffering it has entailed was Pembroke's second "trespass" with the Dark Lady. Here, for the first time, Shakespeare admits his own transgression against their love.

That you were once unkind befriends me now,
And for that sorrow which I then did feel
Needs must I under my transgression bow,
Unless my nerves were brass or hammered steel.
For if you were by my unkindness shaken,
As I by yours, you've passed a hell of time;
And I, a tyrant, have no leisure taken
To weigh* how once I suffered in your crime.*   consider /
                                                        i.e., offense
O, that our night of woe might have remembered*   reminded me
My deepest sense, how hard true sorrow hits,
And soon to you, as you to me, then tendered
The humble salve which wounded bosoms fits!
    But that your trespass now becomes a fee;*†   compensation
    Mine ransoms yours, and yours must ransom me.

Your trespass now becomes a fee. But that trespass of yours becomes
compensation that I offer as payment for my own trespass,
i.e., transgression.

121

After admitting his own sin, the poet criticizes outsiders who have attacked him for what he lightly dubs his "frailties." Chief among these is his sportive blood, his erotic impulses. In this sonnet Shakespeare addresses his Friend as follows: You and I had much rather be guilty of sensuality than slandered by persons who are themselves guilty of the same sin—unless these critics believe that all men commit adultery. The tone is sarcastic, bursting with scorn and anger.

'Tis better to be vile than vile esteemed,
When not to be receives reproach of being;†
And the just pleasure lost, which is so deemed
Not by our feeling, but by others' seeing:†
For why should others' false adulterate* eyes   licentious
Give salutation to* my sportive blood?   excite
Or on my frailties why are frailer spies,
Which in their wills count bad what I think good?
No, I am that I am, and they that level*   aim
At my abuses reckon up their own:
I may be straight, though they themselves be bevel;*   crooked
By their rank* thoughts my deeds must not be shown;   foul
    Unless this general* evil they maintain,   universal
    All men are bad and in their badness reign.*   exult

When not to be receives reproach of being.
When a person, though not vile, is reproached for being so.
And the just pleasure lost, which is so deemed
Not by our feeling, but by others' seeing.
And the lawful pleasure lost, which is deemed vile not from any sense of shame on our part, but by others who merely look upon us and condemn us.

122

This trivial exchange interrupts the poet's pondering over his own morals and those of Pembroke.

Thy gift, thy tables,* are within my brain   notebooks
Full charactered* with lasting memory,   written
Which shall above that idle rank* remain,   empty leaves
Beyond all date, even to eternity:
Or, at the least, so long as brain and heart
Have faculty by nature to subsist;
Till each to razed* oblivion yield his part   razing
Of thee, thy record never can be missed.
That poor retention* could not so much hold,   *i.e.,* notebooks
Nor need I tallies thy dear love to score;*   keep account of
Therefore to give them from me was I bold,
To trust those tables that receive thee more:†
    To keep an adjunct to remember thee
    Were to import* forgetfulness in me.   imply

Therefore to give them from me was I bold,
To trust those tables that receive thee more.
Therefore I was bold enough to give them away so I might depend
wholly on my memory, which is more fully stored with records
of your love than any notebook.

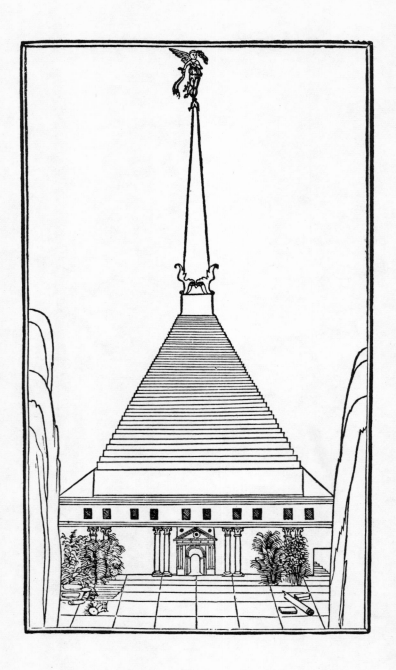

123

The group ends with three valedictory sonnets in which Shakespeare considers the influence of the passage of Time upon the constancy of his affection.

No, Time, thou shalt not boast that I do change:
Thy pyramids built up with newer might†
To me are nothing novel, nothing strange;
They are but dressings* of a former sight.   refurbishings
Our dates* are brief, and therefore we admire   years
What thou dost foist upon us that is old;
And rather make them born to our desire
Than think that we before have heard them told.
Thy registers and thee I both defy,
Not wondering at the present nor the past,
For thy recòrds and what we see doth lie,
Made more or less by thy continual haste.
   This I do vow, and this shall ever be,
   I will be true, despite thy scythe and thee.

Thy pyramids built up with newer might.
The Elizabethans did not distinguish between pyramids and obelisks. The latter were erected as a striking feature of King James' delayed royal entry into London on March 15, 1604. Thomas Dekker described these shafts as sixty feet high and lighted from within. Shakespeare apparently finds these novel constructions nothing but copies of ancient monuments.

124

The poet assures Pembroke that his affection has not changed because of the present unfavorable political and personal circumstances of his Friend's career. "Thrallèd discontent" in line 7 means discontent produced by oppression or more likely by imprisonment. Even a deserved bad reputation is temporary, the poet reminds him, and the culprit may yet die in the odor of sanctity.

If my dear love were but the child of state,
It might for Fortune's bastard be unfathered,†
As subject to Time's love or to Time's hate,
Weeds among weeds, or flowers with flowers gathered.
No, it was builded far from accident;*   chance
It suffers not in smiling pomp, nor falls
Under the blow of thrallèd discontent,*   imprisonment
Whereto the inviting time our fashion calls:†
It fears not policy,* that heretic,   political intrigue
Which works on leases of short-numbered hours.
But all alone stands hugely politic,†
That it nor grows with heat nor drowns with showers.
    To this I witness call the fools* of time,   playthings
    Which die for goodness, who have lived for crime.

If my dear love were but the child of state,
It might for Fortune's bastard be unfathered.
If my loyalty were dependent upon your political prosperity, it might
be regarded as a fatherless child of Fortune.
Whereto the inviting time our fashion calls.
When the passage of the time that favored us puts us out of fashion.
But all alone stands hugely politic.
But love, standing by itself, uninfluenced by political events,
is vastly wise in being loyal forever.

125

The poet confesses defeat for his efforts to re-establish the full vigor of the subsiding friendship. Though both his loves lie in ruins and his repeated assurances that his verses will bring Pembroke immortal fame have come to naught, yet the sonnet contains an assertion of personal victory. Giving up all artificial stimulation to living, such as grindstones and purges, for devotion generated in the heart, the poet will no longer forgo "compound sweet" for "simple savour."

Were 't aught to me I bore the canopy,†
With my extern the outward honouring,
Or laid great bases for eternity,
Which prove more short than waste or ruining?
Have I not seen dwellers on form and favour
Lose all, and more, by paying too much rent,
For compound sweet forgoing simple savour,
Pitiful thrivers, in their gazing spent?
No, let me be obsequious* in thy heart,   devoted
And take thou my oblation,* poor but free,   offering
Which is not mixed with seconds, knows no art
But   mutual render,* only me for thee.   return in kind
    Hence, thou suborned informer! a true soul
    When most impeached stands least in thy control.

Were 't aught to me I bore the canopy.
In ceremonial processions courtiers often held a canopy over the monarch's chair. In this passage the poet says: I do what I can to pay public homage to Pembroke in spite of my defeated efforts to win immortal fame for him.

126

This poem, in rhymed couplets, marks the end of the sonnets written to Pembroke and the last in time of the entire
sequence. The widely accepted idea that the "lovely boy" is
Cupid is untenable. Many critics have pointed out that no
allegorical figure could be less appropriately associated with
an hourglass and sickle than Cupid. As a god, he was immortal
and forever a child. Like the rest of the series, the sonnet is
addressed to the Friend. Although "lovely boy" may seem an
inappropriate way of saluting Pembroke at this, the last recorded stage of their friendship, the poet surely chose the
phrase advisedly. Perhaps he hoped the epithet would carry
the grown man's mind back to the lyrical addresses of their
first days. Mournfully he warns Pembroke that, although still
retaining the beauty and other charms of his youth, he can
only delay Time's triumph. Powerless to make Time stop, he
must finally succumb to the universal foe.

O thou, my lovely boy, who in thy power
Dost hold Time's fickle glass, his sickle, hour;
Who hast by waning grown, and therein show'st
Thy lovers withering as thy sweet self grow'st;
If Nature, sovereign mistress over wrack,*   destruction
As thou goest onwards, still will pluck thee back,
She keeps thee to this purpose, that her skill
May time disgrace and wretched minutes kill.
Yet fear her, O thou minion* of her pleasure!   darling
She may detain, but not still keep, her treasure:
   Her audit, though delayed, answered must be
   And her quietus* is to render* thee.   formal discharge /
                                                  surrender

In closing the sonnets addressed to Pembroke this way,
Shakespeare preserves and accentuates the rueful spirit which
informs the entire valedictory group, and it sounds more
mournfully here than elsewhere in the sequence. A reluctant
farewell to his Friend's youthful charms, the poem develops
the theme of the triumphs of Time the destroyer.

Enter the Dark Lady / 127–132

These sonnets are the first Shakespeare addressed to the Dark Lady. We can only guess at what point in the story he wrote and sent them but probably he began to compose them shortly after he had dispatched his written ambassage to young Lord Herbert.

127

This first sonnet addressed to the Dark Lady contains no intimation of the love for her that was shortly to become a fever in the poet's blood. The tone is humorous and skeptical and he amiably teases the girl about her unfashionable beauty.

In the old age black* was not counted fair,　　　*i.e.,* a brunette
Or if it were, it bore not beauty's name;
But now is black beauty's successive* heir,　　　legitimate
And beauty slandered with a bastard shame:†
For since each hand hath put on nature's power,†
Fairing the foul with art's false borrowed face,
Sweet beauty hath no name, no holy bower,†
But is profaned, if not lives in disgrace.
Therefore my mistress' eyes are raven black,
Her eyes so suited,* and they mourners seem　　　*i.e.,* like the ravens
At such who, not born fair, no beauty lack,
Slandering creation* with a false esteem:　　　nature
　Yet so they mourn, becoming of* their woe,　　　adorning
　That every tongue says beauty should look so.

And beauty slandered with a bastard shame.
Blond beauty is now slandered as the suspected product of cosmetics.
For since each hand hath put on nature's power.
Since each woman has taken over nature's work.
Sweet beauty hath no name, no holy bower.
Natural beauty has no unstained reputation, no sanctuary where it is worshiped as sacred.

128

The poet betrays his growing attraction to the lady. Though
he enjoys her playing of the virginal (a small legless type of
harpsichord) and wishes her fingers to draw music from it, he
wants her lips for himself to kiss.

How oft, when thou, my music, music play'st,
Upon that blessed wood* whose motion sounds   keys of the
                                                      virginal
With thy sweet fingers, when thou gently sway'st
The wiry concord that mine ear confounds,*†   blends
Do I envy those jacks† that nimble leap
To kiss the tender inward of thy hand,
Whilst my poor lips, which should that harvest reap,
At the wood's boldness by thee blushing stand.
To be so tickled, they would change their state
And situation with those dancing chips,
O'er whom thy fingers walk with gentle gait,
Making dead wood more blest than living lips.
   Since saucy jacks so happy are in this,
   Give them thy fingers, me thy lips to kiss.

The wiry concord that mine ear confounds.
The sounds of the individual strings that in my ear blend into harmony.
Do I envy those jacks. Shakespeare here, for the only time in all his
work, makes a mistake in his use of musical terminology. The sounds
of the virginal are made by a quill that plucks the strings. His figure,
therefore, is not applicable to the playing of a virginal.

129

This furious diatribe against lust has elicited extravagant praise from most commentators. Bernard Shaw, for example, describes the poem as "the most merciless passage" in English literature, while Theodore Watts Duncan, satisfied only with a superlative, calls it "the greatest sonnet in the world." To be sure, a few dissidents find it a pathological expression of remorse for what Shakespeare feels is a deadly sin. It is difficult to imagine why the poet should follow the two previous lighthearted sonnets with this display of ethical fervor. The most likely explanation is that his flirtation has led to a surprisingly easy seduction of the girl and he feels compelled to share with her his painful meditations on the nature of the lust.

The expense* of spirit* in a waste of shame	loss / vitality
Is lust in action; and till action, lust	
Is perjured, murderous, bloody, full of blame,	
Savage, extreme, rude,* cruel, not to trust;	brutal
Enjoyed no sooner but despisèd straight;	
Past reason hunted; and no sooner had,	
Past reason hated, as a swallowed bait,	
On purpose laid to make the taker mad:	
Mad in pursuit, and in possession so;*	i.e., mad
Had, having, and in quest to have,* extreme;	in pursuit
A bliss in proof, and proved, a very woe;†	
Before, a joy proposed; behind, a dream.†	
All this the world well knows; yet none knows well	
To shun the heaven that leads men to this hell.	

A bliss in proof, and proved, a very woe.
A bliss while being enjoyed; afterwards a veritable woe.
Before a joy proposed; behind, a dream.
Before it has been experienced, a joy looked forward to; afterwards, a vague memory.

130

Taken by itself, this sonnet is a satire on the vacuous arti-
ficiality of Petrarch's Italian and French imitators, specifically
on their far-fetched comparisons. It occupies an interesting
place in the history of the poet's entanglement with the Dark
Lady. In 129 his first sexual encounter with her had produced
remorse that canceled the bliss. Sonnet 130 is a jocose expression of another phase of his disillusionment, this time with
the lady's beauty. He treats the subject with a stark realism
new to the sonnet. Hyder Rollins suggests, obviously with
tongue in cheek, that the wild-spirited girl had adopted the
brand-new fad of smoking, which Shakespeare nowhere
approves.

My mistress' eyes are nothing* like the sun;	not at all
Coral is far more red than her lips' red:	
If snow be white, why then her breasts are dun;	
If hairs be wires, black wires grow on her head.	
I have seen roses damasked,* red and white,	mingled
But no such roses see I in her cheeks;	
And in some perfumes is there more delight	
Than in the breath that from my mistress reeks.*	exhales
I love to hear her speak, yet well I know	
That music hath a far more pleasing sound:	
I grant I never saw a goddess go,*	walk
My mistress, when she walks, treads on the ground:	
And yet, by heaven, I think my love as rare*	worthy of praise
As any she* belied with false compare.	woman

131

A tension has developed between poet and lady. The word "tyrannous" suggests she may momentarily have withdrawn her favors—just the sort of teasing to stimulate the fervent expressions of love that inform this sonnet.

Thou art as tyrannous, so as thou art,†
As those whose beauties proudly make them cruel;†
For well thou know'st to my dear doting heart
Thou art the fairest and most precious jewel.
Yet, in good faith, some say that thee behold,
Thy face hath not the power to make love groan:
To say* they err I dare not be so bold,   *i.e., publicly*
Although I swear it to myself alone.
And to be sure that is not false I swear,
A thousand groans, but thinking on thy face,
One on another's neck,* do witness bear   *in quick succession*
Thy black is fairest in my judgment's place.†
   In nothing art thou black save in thy deeds,
     And thence this slander, as I think, proceeds.

Thou art as tyrannous, so as thou art.
You are as tyrannous as you can be, being black, but not beautiful.
As those whose beauties proudly make them cruel.
Like those who are made cruel through pride in their beauty.
Thy black is fairest in my judgment's place.
Your brunette features seem fairest at my judgment seat.

132

Sonnet 132 declares Shakespeare's delight in all aspects of
natural beauty and feminine charm. What better phrase could
be imagined to express a lady's playing on the spinet than
"[The keys] o'er whom thy fingers walk with gentle gait"? Or
a more imaginative evocation of the day fading into evening
than "that full star that ushers in the even"? The early stages
of Shakespeare's attraction to the Dark Lady were instinct with
tenderness and usually devoid of sensuality.

Thine eyes I love, and they, as pitying me,
Knowing thy heart torments me with disdain,
Have put on black and loving mourners be,
Looking with pretty ruth upon my pain.
And truly not the morning sun of heaven
Better becomes the gray cheeks of the east,
Nor that full star that ushers in the even
Doth half that glory to the sober west,
As those two mourning eyes become thy face:
O, let it then as well beseem thy heart
To mourn for me, since mourning doth thee grace,
And suit thy pity like in every part.†
   Then will I swear beauty herself is black,
   And all they foul* that thy complexion lack.   ugly

And suit thy pity like in every part.
And clothe your pity in black alike for every part of the region
of your eyes, *i.e.,* your brows and lashes.

The Dark Lady / 133–142

Shakespeare now addresses the Dark Lady directly and analyzes her infidelity with Pembroke. Though he recognizes her corrupt nature, his passion for her still rules his entire being and his suffering, therefore, is well-deserved.

133

Shakespeare reappraises the present state of the relationship between the three principal characters of the sonnet story.

Beshrew that heart that makes my heart to groan
For that deep wound it gives my friend and me!
Is 't not enough to torture me alone,
But slave to slavery* my sweet'st friend must be?   to your enslavement
Me from myself thy cruel eye hath taken,
And my next self* thou harder hast engrossed:*   alter ego / monopolized
Of him, myself, and thee, I am forsaken;
A torment thrice threefold thus to be crossed.
Prison my heart in thy steel bosom's ward,*   protection
But then my friend's heart let my poor heart bail;
Whoe'er keeps me, let my heart be his guard;†
Thou canst not then use rigour in my jail.
    And yet thou wilt; for I, being pent in thee,
    Perforce am thine, and all that is in me.

Whoe'er keeps me, let my heart be his guard.
Whoever my jailer is, let my heart keep his from like imprisonment (by suffering in his place).

134

The poet becomes more explicit. He will end his affair with her if she will but restore Pembroke's ideal friendship with him. Yet, in almost the same breath, he admits he knows she is obdurate and will scorn his plea.

So, now I have confessed that he is thine
And I myself am mortgaged to thy will,*   desire
Myself I 'll forfeit, so that other mine*   *i.e.,* the Friend
Thou wilt restore, to be my comfort still:
But thou wilt not,* nor he will not be free,   *i.e.,* restore him
For thou art covetous and he is kind;
He learned but surety-like to write for me,†
Under that bond that him as fast doth bind.
The statute of thy beauty thou wilt take,†
Thou usurer, that put'st forth all to use,*   interest
And sue a friend came* debtor for my sake;   who became
So him I lose through my unkind abuse.†
    Him have I lost; thou hast both him and me:
    He pays the whole, and yet am I not free.†

He learned but surety-like to write for me.
He learned like one who out of friendship endorses a note.
The statute of thy beauty thou wilt take, / Thou usurer.
Your beauty is a security for money loaned that you will demand as
ruthlessly as a usurer.
My unkind abuse. The ill treatment that you inflict on me.
He pays the whole, and yet am I not free.
Although he is liable for the whole debt, yet I am not free from the
obligation.

135

Sonnets 135 and 136 are the so-called Will sonnets, in which the poet scolds the lady for conduct almost as loose as total promiscuity.

In 135 he plays like an adept on the various Elizabethan meanings of "Will": (1) the poet's name, (2) that of William Herbert, (3) volition, (4) desire. The sexual references are brutally frank. He is begging her to choose him as her one lover.

Whoever hath her wish, thou hast thy "Will,"
And "Will" to boot, and "Will" in overplus;
More than enough am I that vex thee still,
To thy sweet will making addition thus.
Wilt thou, whose will is large and spacious,
Not once vouchsafe to hide my will in thine?
Shall will in others seem right gracious,
And in my will no fair acceptance shine?
The sea, all water, yet receives rain still,
And in abundance addeth to his store;
So thou, being rich in "Will," add to thy "Will"
One will of mine, to make thy large "Will" more.
    Let no unkind, no fair beseechers kill;
      Think all but one, and me in that one "Will."

136

The poet tells the lady that she can ease the embarrassment caused by his frank description of her sensuality by admitting that it is enough to grant his admittance into the fellowship of her many lovers.

If thy soul check* thee that I come so near,*   chide /
Swear to thy blind soul that I was thy "Will,"   *i.e.,* the truth
And will, thy soul knows, is admitted there;
Thus far for love, my love-suit, sweet, fulfill.
"Will" will fulfill the treasure of thy love,
Aye, fill it full with wills, and my will one.
In things of great receipt* with ease we prove   large matters
Among a number one is reckoned none:†
Then in the number let me pass untold,*   uncounted
Though in thy store's account I one must be;
For nothing hold me, so it please thee hold
That nothing me, a something sweet to thee:
    Make but my name thy love, and love that still,
    And then thou lovest me, for my name is "Will."

Among a number one is reckoned none.
This is an allusion to the proverb, "One is no number."

137

This sonnet marks a complete change from the pleading of the previous poems to a blistering attack on the lady's corrupt nature. Having had an example of her flagrant deception and having been intolerably flouted, the poet chides himself for having allowed her beauty to blind him to her promiscuity.

Thou blind fool, Love, what dost thou to mine eyes,
That they behold, and see not what they see?
They know what beauty is, see where it lies,
Yet what the best is take the worst to be.
If eyes, corrupt by over-partial looks,
Be anchored in the bay where all men ride,
Why of eyes' falsehood hast thou forgèd hooks
Whereto the judgment of my heart is tied?
Why should my heart think that* a several* plot   *i.e.*, that woman / enclosed
Which my heart knows the wide world's
     common place?*   a common (park)
Or mine eyes seeing this, say this is not
To put fair truth upon so foul a face?
   In things right true my heart and eyes have erred,
   And to this false plague are they now transferred.

138

This sonnet first appeared in the collection of poems called *The Passionate Pilgrim* in a version based on a corrupt text, and apparently representing an attempted reconstruction of the poem from someone's unreliable memory. It continues to express the bitterness of 137, but in a lighter key. There is no reason for suspecting that it was not intended for the eyes of the lady. It is the poet's most effective protest against his reluctant infatuation.

When my love swears that she is made of truth,
I do believe her, though I know she lies,
That she might think me some untutored* youth,   naïve
Unlearnèd in the world's false subtleties.
Thus vainly thinking that she thinks me young,
Although she knows my days are past the best,
Simply I credit* her false-speaking tongue: believe
On both sides thus is simple truth suppressed.
But wherefore says she not she is unjust?*   faithless
And wherefore say not I that I am old?
O, love's best habit* is in seeming trust,   deportment
And age in love loves not to have years told:
    Therefore I lie with her and she with me,
    And in our faults by lies we flattered be.†

And in our faults by lies we flattered be.
In our respective faults we are both flattered by the pretense of belief in compliments that we know are lies.

139

O call not me to justify the wrong
That thy unkindness lays upon my heart;
Wound me not with thine eye, but with thy tongue;
Use power with power, and slay me not by art.*   magic
Tell me thou lovest elsewhere; but in my sight,
Dear heart, forbear to glance thine eye aside:
What need'st thou wound with cunning, when
     thy might
Is more than my o'er-pressed* defense can bide?*   too hard pressed /
Let me excuse thee: ah, my love well knows   endure
Her pretty looks have been mine enemies;
And therefore from my face she turns my foes,*   *i.e.,* her looks
That they elsewhere might dart their injuries:
  Yet do not so; but since I am near slain,
    Kill me outright with looks, and rid* my pain.   dispatch

140

Be wise as thou art cruel; do not press
My tongue-tied patience with too much disdain;
Lest sorrow lend me words, and words express
The manner of my pity-wanting* pain.   unpitied
If I might teach thee wit, better it were,
Though not to love, yet, love, to tell me so;
As testy* sick men, when their deaths be near,   fretful
No news but health from their physicians know;
For, if I should despair, I should grow mad,
And in my madness might speak ill of thee:
Now this ill-wresting world is grown so bad,
Mad slanderers by mad ears believèd be.†
    That I may not be so, nor thou belied,
    Bear thine eyes straight, though thy proud heart go
      wide.†

Now this ill-wresting world is grown so bad.
Mad slanderers by mad ears believèd be.
This world that puts the worst possible interpretation on everything.
Bear thine eyes straight, though thy proud heart go wide.
Aim straight even though the arrow goes wide of the mark—a
metaphor from the sport of archery.

141

The poet realistically appraises the situation in which he and the lady are involved. At last he confesses that he does not love her with his eyes, yet neither eyes nor mind can dissuade his heart from being her slave. In a flash of spiritual insight he confesses that his sinning has been a boon to him because it serves as purgatorial punishment.

In faith, I do not love thee with mine eyes,
For they in thee a thousand errors note;
But 'tis my heart that loves what they despise,
Who, in despite of view,* is pleased to dote;   what he sees
Nor are mine ears with thy tongue's tune delighted;
Nor tender feeling, to base touches prone,
Nor taste, nor smell, desire to be invited
To any sensual feast with thee alone:
But my five wits† nor my five senses can
Dissuade one foolish heart from serving thee,
Who leaves unswayed the likeness of a man,†
Thy proud heart's slave and vassal wretch to be:
   Only my plague thus far I count my gain,
   That she that makes me sin awards me pain.

Five wits. Imagination, fantasy, judgment, wit, memory.
Who leaves unswayed the likeness of a man.
Which leaves me governed only by my heart, and so no better than a sham likeness of a man.

142

In this last sonnet of the first group addressed to the Dark Lady, the poet admits she must hate the sinful love she has aroused in him, for her own promiscuous loving knows the hatred of such passion. Since they are both in the same immoral situation, they should pity each other.

Love is my sin, and thy dear* virtue hate,   cherished
Hate of my sin, grounded on sinful loving:
O, but with mine compare thou thine own state,
And thou shalt find it merits not reproving;
Or, if it do, not from those lips of thine,
That have profaned their scarlet ornaments
And sealed false bonds of love as oft as mine,
Robbed others' beds' revénues of their rents.†
Be it lawful I love thee, as thou lovest those
Whom thine eyes woo as mine importune thee:
Root pity in thy heart, that, when it grows,
Thy pity may deserve to pitied be.
    If thou dost seek to have what* thou dost hide,   *i.e.,* pity
    By self-example mayst thou be denied!

Robbed others' beds' revénues of their rents.
This line has been taken as proof that the lady was married, but the plurals of "other" and "bed" make the inference impossible. The lady has broken vows of fidelity in the beds of many lovers.

Exit the Dark Lady / 143–152

This last group of sonnets to the Dark Lady was apparently written after an indeterminate period of time. It begins with a playful appeal for her mere kindness and concludes by vowing final separation.

143

The barnyard figure is unique in the sonnets. Shakespeare takes this homely way of telling the lady that he is aware of her resolute pursuit of his Friend. Some critics, missing the jocose temper of the figure, believe Shakespeare loses all his dignity by making what they conceive to be a servilely pathetic appeal for the attention she now lavishes on his rival.

Lo, as a careful* housewife runs to catch	provident
One of her feathered creatures broke away,	
Sets down her babe, and makes all swift dispatch	
In pursuit of the thing she would have stay;	
Whilst her neglected child holds her in chase,	
Cries to catch her whose busy care is bent	
To follow that which flies before her face,	
Not prizing* her poor infant's discontent:	regarding
So runn'st thou after that which flies from thee,	
Whilst I thy babe chase thee afar behind;	
But if thou catch thy hope,* turn back to me,	*i.e.,* Herbert
And play the mother's part, kiss me, be kind:	

   So will I pray that thou mayst have thy "Will,"
   If thou turn back and my loud crying still.

144

This so-called key sonnet would fit logically into almost any spot in the tense little tragicomedy. It makes no important contribution to the part of the story with which this group of sonnets is concerned. Nor does it bear any close relationship to the poem which precedes it. However, the lady's pursuit of Pembroke, described in 143, would be likely to have shocked Shakespeare into a fresh appraisal of the embarrassing part he is playing in the *drame à trois*.

Two loves I have of comfort and despair,
Which like two spirits do suggest me still:†
The better angel is a man right fair,
The worser spirit a woman coloured ill.*   *i.e.,* a brunette
To win me soon to hell, my female evil
Tempteth my better angel from my side,
And would corrupt my saint to be a devil,
Wooing his purity with her foul pride.*   lust
And whether that my angel be turned fiend
Suspect I may, yet not directly tell;
But being both from* me, both to each friend,*   far from /
I guess one angel in another's hell:†   mutually friendly
  Yet this shall I ne'er know, but live in doubt,
  Till my bad angel fire my good one out.

Suggest me still. Continue to prompt me to comfort or despair.
I guess one angel in another's hell.
This is a reference to a tale in Boccaccio's *Decameron*.

145

This poem is written in eight-syllable lines, rhyming *a b a b* and ending with a couplet. Its relation to the rest of the group is not clear. It may be the poet's plaintive acceptance of the lady's pity for which he has been pleading. Perhaps he felt that a poem in this form expressed better than a sonnet the flippancy of his attitude, for its emotional superficiality is calculated.

Those lips that Love's own hand did make
Breathed forth the sound that said "I hate,"
To me that languished for her sake:
But when she saw my woeful state,
Straight in her heart did mercy come,
Chiding that tongue that ever sweet
Was used in giving gentle doom;*   polite censure
And taught it thus anew to greet;
"I hate" she altered with an end,
That followed it as gentle day
Doth follow night, who, like a fiend,
From heaven to hell is flown away;
   "I hate" from hate away she threw,
   And saved my life, saying "not you."†

"I hate" from hate away she threw,
And saved my life, saying "not you."
She removed the words "I hate" some distance from hatred and changed the purport of the line by adding "not you."

146

One of Shakespeare's most personal expressions of religious conviction, this meditation expresses with somber eloquence a central tenet of orthodox Christianity, Catholic as well as Protestant. The poet would think it wise to show this petition to his soul to the lady before he sends her four sonnets which inveigh against her irresistible temptation to sexual indulgence. He warns her too that his deep religious feeling has increased his determination to escape from her evil bondage.

Poor soul, the centre of my sinful earth,
Thrall to these rebel powers* that thee array,*   *i.e.*, the body / afflict
Why dost thou pine within and suffer dearth,
Painting thy outward walls so costly gay?
Why so large cost, having so short a lease,
Dost thou upon thy fading mansion spend?
Shall worms, inheritors of this excess,*   expenditure
Eat up thy charge? is this thy body's end?
Then, soul, live thou upon thy servant's loss,
And let that pine to aggravate* thy store;   increase
Buy terms divine* in selling hours of dross;   *i.e.*, eternity
Within be fed, without be rich no more:
   So shalt thou feed on Death, that feeds on men,
   And Death once dead, there's no more dying then.

147

One of the most moving expressions in literature of the agony and the disgust of a man who has become the slave of sexual desire, this poem reveals the ill-starred result of Shakespeare's determination to escape the lady's evil fascination. He has apparently yielded to her temptation again, probably for the last time, but the experience disgusts him even while he is enjoying her.

My love is as a fever, longing still
For that which longer nurseth the disease;
Feeding on that which doth preserve the ill,
The uncertain sickly appetite to please.
My reason, the physician to my love,
Angry that his prescriptions are not kept,*   followed
Hath left me, and I desperate now approve*   find by experience
Desire is death, which physic did except.*   refuse
Past cure I am, now reason is past care,
And frantic-mad with evermore unrest;
My thoughts and my discourse as madmen's are,
At random from the truth vainly* expressed;   foolishly
   For I have sworn thee fair, and thought thee bright,
   Who art as black as hell, as dark as night.

148

O me, what eyes hath Love put in my head,
Which have no correspondence with true sight!
Or, if they have, where is my judgment fled,
That censures* falsely what they see aright?   judges
If that be fair whereon my false eyes dote,
What means the world to say it is not so?
If it be not, then love doth well denote*   indicate
Love's eye is not so true as all men's: no,†
How can it? O, how can Love's eye be true,
That is so vexed with watching* and with tears?   lying awake
No marvel then, though I mistake my view,*   what I see
The sun itself sees not till heaven clears.
   O cunning Love! with tears thou keep'st me blind,
   Lest eyes well-seeing thy foul faults should find.

Love's eye is not so true as all men's.
A lover's eyes are more inaccurate than those of any other man.

149

The poet replies with almost painful seriousness to the lady's coquettish accusation that he no longer loves her.

Canst thou, O cruel! say I love thee not,
When I against myself with thee partake?*   take sides
Do I not think on thee, when I forgot
Am of myself, all* tyrant, for thy sake?   a complete
Who hateth thee that I do call my friend?
On whom frown'st thou that I do fawn upon?
Nay, if thou lour'st on me, do I not spend
Revenge upon myself with present moan?
What merit do I in myself respect,*   regard
That is so proud thy service to despise,
When all my best doth worship thy defect,
Commanded by the motion of thine eyes?
   But, love, hate on, for now I know thy mind;
   Those that can see thou lovest, and I am blind.

150

In 150 Shakespeare repeats the theme of 148, admitting that
he loves those qualities in the lady which everyone else abhors.

O, from what power hast thou this powerful might
With insufficiency* my heart to sway?   *i.e., defects*
To make me give the lie to my true sight,
And swear that brightness doth not grace the day?
Whence hast thou this becoming* of things ill,   grace
That in the very refuse of thy deeds
There is such strength and warrantise* of skill,   guarantee
That, in my mind, thy worst all best exceeds?
Who taught thee how to make me love thee more,
The more I hear and see just cause of hate?
O, though I love what others do abhor,
With others thou shouldst not abhor my state:
   If thy unworthiness raised love in me,
   More worthy I to be beloved of thee.

151

Shakespeare devotes this and sonnet 152 to the same situation, probably the lady's most recent betrayal with a new lover, painful confirmation of her promiscuity. The tone of this sexually frank letter is jocular.

Love* is too young to know what conscience is;   *i.e.,* Cupid
Yet who knows not conscience† is born of love?
Then, gentle cheater,* urge not my amiss,*   swindler / offenses
Lest guilty of my faults thy sweet self prove:
For, thou betraying me, I do betray
My nobler part to my gross body's treason;
My soul* doth tell my body that he may   vitality
Triumph in love; flesh stays no farther reason,*   excuse
But rising at thy name doth point out thee
As his triumphant prize. Proud of this pride,*   passion
He is contented thy poor drudge to be,
To stand in thy affairs, fall by thy side.
   No want of conscience hold it that I call
   Her "love" for whose dear love I rise and fall.

Conscience. (1) Mental awareness; (2) Knowledge.

152

In loving thee thou know'st I am forsworn,*   broke my oath
But thou art twice forsworn, to me love swearing;
In act thy bed-vow broke, and new faith torn,
In vowing new hate after new love bearing.
But why of two oaths' breach do I accuse thee,
When I break twenty? I am perjured most;
For all my vows are oaths but to misuse* thee,   deceive
And all my honest faith in thee is lost:
For I have sworn deep oaths of thy deep kindness,*   affection
Oaths of thy love, thy truth, thy constancy;
And, to enlighten* thee, gave eyes to blindness,   shed light upon
Or made them swear against the thing they see;
   For I have sworn thee fair; more perjured I,
   To swear against the truth so foul a lie!

153–154

These two sonnets have no discernible relationship to the sonnet story. Intruders into Thorpe's manuscript, each is a translation of an epigram in *The Greek Anthology,* a collection of about 4500 short Greek poems written between the Hellenistic Alexandrian age and the early Middle Ages. Shakespeare found the epigram translated in Giles Fletcher's "Licia" (1593).

153

Cupid laid by his brand and fell asleep:
A maid of Dian's this advantage found,
And his love-kindling fire did quickly steep
In a cold valley-fountain of that ground;
Which borrowed from this holy fire of Love
A dateless* lively heat, still to endure,   eternal
And grew a seething* bath, which yet men prove   boiling
Against strange maladies a sovereign* cure.   efficacious
But at my mistress' eye Love's brand new-fired,
The boy for trial needs would touch my breast;
I, sick withal, the help of bath desired,
And thither hied, a sad distempered* guest,   diseased
   But found no cure: the bath for my help lies
    Where Cupid got new fire, my mistress' eyes.

154

The little Love-god lying once asleep
Laid by his side his heart-inflaming brand,
Whilst many nymphs that vowed chaste life to keep
Came tripping by; but in her maiden hand
The fairest votary took up that fire
Which many legions of true hearts had warmed;
And so the general* of hot desire   chief master
Was sleeping by a virgin hand disarmed.
This brand she quenchèd in a cool well by,
Which from Love's fire took heat perpetual,
Growing a bath and healthful remedy
For men diseased; but I, my mistress' thrall,
   Came there for cure, and this by that I prove.
    Love's fire heats water, water cools not love.

SONGS FROM THE PLAYS

Mark Van Doren describes the songs in Shakespeare's dramas as "shooting like stars across the plays." This charming metaphor is a symbol of their essence only if we remember that these stars do not come from some outer region of the poet's imagination. On the contrary, each one is generated in the atmosphere and action of the scene in which it shines, and bears a close relationship to a significant moment in the growth of the plot.

I shall regard as songs only those lyrics that some character or group of musicians plays and sings. Other short lyrics, however musical their quality, merely recited by a character I shall ignore. Not all the words of the songs included in this essay were written by Shakespeare. Some are Shakespeare's versions of traditional ballads, familiar to nearly every spectator in a typical Elizabethan audience. Some are Shakespeare's complete revisions of the words of popular songs. Some are poems, written by other authors, usually unknown, that the poet thought would be effective in a given context. The songs, as will be presently seen, are of many different sorts and suitable for many different kinds of occasions.

The arrangement of those described below follows the chronological order of the plays from which they have been taken.

Two Gentlemen of Verona (1592)

Who is Silvia? What is she,
That all our swains commend her?
Holy, fair and wise is she,
The heaven such grace did lend her,
That she might admirèd be.

Is she kind as she is fair?
For beauty lives with kindness.
Love doth to her eyes repair
To help him of his blindness,
And being helped, inhabits there.

Then to Silvia, let us sing
That Silvia is excelling,
She excels each mortal thing
Upon the dull earth dwelling.
To her let us garlands bring.

This song, one of the earliest that Shakespeare wrote, is
played and sung by a group of musicians under Silvia's window. It is the result of Proteus' instructions to Thurio, Valentine's silly rival for the girl's hand, to

lay lime to tangle her desires
By wailful sonnets, whose composèd rhymes
Should be full-fraught with serviceable vows.

Thurio eagerly seizes upon the suggestion and, having apparently composed the lines himself, he engages some professional musicians to produce the serenade. In spite of some
pretty phrases, it is a mild caricature of the Elizabethan conventions of poetical compliment. Thurio's praise of Silvia,
particularly in the third stanza, is offensively extravagant. The
flattery is so heavy-footed that Silvia protests:

Think'st thou I am so shallow, so conceitless
To be seducèd by thy flattery?

The song, when properly understood, becomes a striking
exhibition of Thurio's stupidity.

A Midsummer Night's Dream (1594–1595)

You spotted snakes with double tongue,
  Thorny hedgehogs, be not seen;
Newts and blindworms, do no wrong,
  Come not near our Fairy Queen.

  Philomele,* with melody   the nightingale
  Sing in our sweet lullaby;
Lulla, lulla, lullaby, lulla, lulla, lullaby:
  Never harm,
  Nor spell nor charm,
Come our lovely lady nigh.
So, good night, with lullaby.

Weaving spiders, come not here,
  Hence, you long-legged spinners, hence!
Beetles black, approach not near:
  Worm nor snail, do no offence.
  Philomele with melody, &c.

The fairies' song was probably rendered by child actors who had been trained to sing and dance. At the command of Titania, their Queen, the fairies dance around her, lulling her to sleep. This is an effective way of invoking the atmosphere of Fairy Land.

           *   *   *

The ousel* cock so black of hue,   blackbird
  With orange-tawny bill,
The throstle* with his note so true,   thrush
  The wren with little quill,

The finch, the sparrow and the lark,
  The plain-song* cuckoo gray,   simple air
Whose note full many a man doth mark,
  And dares not answer nay.

Bottom sings this song while watching over the sleeping Titania. It is a grotesque equivalent of the song the fairies have just sung.

The Merchant of Venice (1595)

Tell me, where is fancy* bred,   love
Or in the heart, or in the head?
How begot, how nourishèd?
   Reply, reply.
It is engendered in the eyes,
With gazing fed; and fancy dies
In the cradle where it lies.

   Let us all ring fancy's knell:
   I'll begin it,—Ding, dong, bell.

Ding, dong, bell.

This song, the only one in the comedy, is a device for allow-
ing Bassanio time to consider which of the three caskets, gold,
silver, or lead, he should choose. It contains hints that the
leaden casket is the right one. The lines warn him to beware
of what is pleasing only to the eye, for the appeal of super-
ficial beauty is only transient. Bassanio got the point at once.
When the music fades, he wisely remarks:

   So may the outward shows be least themselves.
   The world is still deceived with ornament.

The song also contains a more obvious hint. The end
rhymes of the first three lines, "bred," "head," "nourishèd,"
would suggest to the attentive Bassanio, "lead." The relation
of the song to the dramatic situation is thus vital for the suitor
and for the expectation of the audience.
   The song was sung by musicians attached to Portia's household, for in Elizabethan establishments like hers it was usual
for musicians to be part of the ménage. The refrains were
probably sung in parts by the entire group.

Much Ado About Nothing (1598)

Sigh no more, ladies, sigh no more!
  Men were deceivers ever,
One foot in sea and one on shore,
  To one thing constant never.
Then sigh not so, but let them go,
  And be you blithe and bonny,
Converting all your sounds of woe
  Into Hey nonny, nonny.

Sing no more ditties, sing no moe,
  Of dumps* so dull and heavy!   mournful songs
The fraud of men was ever so,
  Since summer first was leavy:
  Then sigh not so, &c.

Balthasar sings this song for the benefit of Benedick. It is intended to persuade him to abandon his bachelor state. *Much Ado* is the first of Shakespeare's plays in which a character in the play is the vocalist. Balthasar's announcement of the subject of the song connects it with the action: "Because you talk of wooing, I will sing."

*   *   *

Pardon, goddess of the night,
Those that slew thy virgin knight;
For the which, with songs of woe,
Round about her tomb they go.
  Midnight, assist our moan;
  Help us to sigh and groan,
    Heavily, heavily.
  Graves, yawn and yield your dead,
  Till death be uttered,
    Heavily, heavily.

The text does not indicate the singer of this dirge. Claudio, visiting the supposed tomb of Hero, in a church, gives the command: "Now, music, sound, and sing your solemn hymn." To which order the song is an answer.

As You Like It (1600)

Under the greenwood tree
Who loves to lie with me,
And turn his merry note,
Unto the sweet bird's throat,
Come hither, come hither, come hither!
  Here shall he see
  No enemy
But winter and rough weather.

*   *   *

Who doth ambition shun
And loves to live i' the sun,
Seeking the food he eats
And pleased with what he gets,
Come hither, come hither, come hither!
  Here shall he see
  No enemy
But winter and rough weather.

These songs, sung by Amiens, have no relation to the action. They serve only to establish the pastoral atmosphere.

*   *   *

If it do come to pass
  That any man turn ass,
  Leaving his wealth and ease,
  A stubborn will to please,
Ducdame, ducdame, ducdame!†
  Here shall he see
  Gross fools as he,
An if he will come to me.

This parody of Jaques' is most effective if he croaks it in an absurd attempt to imitate Amiens' dulcet voice.

*   *   *

Ducdame is a trisyllable. It is perhaps a corruption of the gypsy's "du Krame" meaning I prophesy.

Blow, blow, thou winter wind,
Thou art not so unkind
   As man's ingratitude.
Thy tooth is not so keen,
Because thou art not seen,
   Although thy breath be rude.
Heigh-ho! sing, heigh-ho! unto the green holly!
Most friendship is feigning, most loving mere folly:
   Then, heigh-ho, the holly!
   This life is most jolly.

Freeze, freeze, thou bitter sky,
That dost not bite so nigh
   As benefits forgot.
Though thou the waters warp,*   *freeze*
Thy sting is not so sharp
   As friend remembered not.
Heigh-ho! sing, &c.

Amiens sings this song in response to the Duke's "Give us some music; and, good cousin, sing." It is a pessimistic variant of "Under the Greenwood Tree."

*   *   *

What shall he have that killed the deer?
His leather skin and horns to wear.
   Then sing him home.
    (The rest shall bear this burden.)†
Take thou no scorn to wear the horn;*   *i.e.,* of a cuckold
It was a crest ere thou wast born:
   Thy father's father wore it,
   And thy father bore it.
The horn, the horn, the lusty horn,
Is not a thing to laugh to scorn.

This song of the huntsman was probably sung by Amiens.

*   *   *

Bear the burden. A play on the double meaning of the phrase (1) carry the deer (2) sing the chorus.

It was a lover and his lass,
   With a hey, and a ho, and a hey nonino,
That o'er the green corn-*field did pass   grain-
   In springtime, the only pretty ring-time,
When birds do sing, hey ding a ding, ding.
Sweet lovers love the spring.

Between the acres of the rye,
   With a hey, and a ho, and a hey nonino,
These pretty country folks would lie,
   In springtime, &c.

This carol they began that hour,
   With a hey, and a ho, and a hey nonino,
How that a life was but a flower
   In springtime, &c.

And therefore take the present time,
   With a hey, and a ho, and a hey nonino;
For love is crownèd with the prime*   *i.e.*, spring
   In springtime, &c.

These lines are sung by two pages. They may have sung antiphonally, but more likely in unison.

Twelfth Night (1601)

O mistress mine, where are you roaming?
O, stay and hear; your true love's coming,
   That can sing both high and low.
Trip no further, pretty sweeting;
Journeys end in lovers meeting,
   Every wise man's son doth know.

What is love? 'Tis not hereafter;
Present mirth hath present laughter;
   What 's to come is still unsure:
In delay there lies no plenty;
Then come kiss me, sweet and twenty!
   Youth's a stuff will not endure.

Feste, Olivia's domestic minstrel, joins the roistering of Sir Toby Belch and his poltroonish companion, Sir Andrew Aguecheek. The two knights ask Feste for a song. He replies, "Would you have a love song or a song of good life?" Sir Toby is all for "A love song, a love song," and Sir Andrew chimes in with "Ay ay! I care not for good life." In answer to this boisterous request Feste sings this magical lyric. "O Mistress Mine" was the title of a piece of music in Thomas Morley's (1557–1604) "Concert Lessons," published in 1599, just about a year before *Twelfth Night* was produced. However, no words were attached to the music in Morley's collection. Shakespeare probably fitted his words to Morley's music. Another possibility is that Shakespeare completely rewrote the words of a popular song.

*   *   *

Come away, come away, death,
  And in sad cypress let me be laid.
Fly away, fly away, breath;
  I am slain by a fair cruel maid.
My shroud of white, stuck all with yew.
  O, prepare it!
My part of death, no one so true
  Did share it.

Not a flower, not a flower sweet,
  On my black coffin let there be strown;
Not a friend, not a friend greet
  My poor corpse, where my bones shall be thrown.
A thousand thousand sighs to save,
  Lay me, O, where
Sad true lover never find my grave,
  To weep there!

This song serves as a prelude to a boisterous evening of singing and carousing by the two knights. It is also sung by Feste to feed the Duke's affected love melancholy and by its funereal tone to laugh at it.

The Duke introduces the song as follows:

O, fellow, come, the song we had last night.
Mark it, Cesario; it is old and plain.
The spinsters and the knitters in the sun,
And the free maids that weave their threads with bones*   bobbins
Do use to chant it.

These lines suggest the folk character of the piece and make it probable that it is Shakespeare's version of a traditional ballad.

*   *   *

I am gone, sir;
  And anon, sir,
I'll be with you again,
  In a trice,
  Like to the old Vice,
Your need to sustain;

Who, with dagger of lath,
In his rage and his wrath,
  Cries, aha! to the devil.
Like a mad lad,
Pare thy nails, dad;
  Adieu, goodman devil.

This song covers Feste's exit at the end of a scene in which he has been tantalizing Malvolio in a dungeon where the absurd fellow has been thrust on the pretense that he had lost his mind. It enables Feste to move slowly off the stage and disappear at the insulting last line.

The Vice in the morality plays was a buffoon, armed with a small wooden dagger, with which he used to beat the Devil. The Fiend sometimes carried him off the stage on his back. Feste talks of the Devil, who, he pretends, is in possession of Malvolio's lost wits.

*   *   *

When that I was and a little tiny boy,
  With hey, ho, the wind and the rain,
A foolish thing was but a toy,
  For the rain it raineth every day.

But when I came to man's estate,
  With hey, ho, &c.
'Gainst knaves and thieves men shut their gate,
  For the rain, &c.

But when I came, alas! to wive,
  With hey, ho, &c.
By swaggering could I never thrive,
  For the rain, &c.

But when I came unto my beds,
  With hey, ho, &c.
With tosspots still had drunken heads,
  For the rain, &c.

A great while ago the world begun,
  With hey, ho, &c.
But that's all one, our play is done,
  And we'll strive to please you every day.

Feste sings the epilogue to the comedy around a refrain in which the audience may have joined. The meaning of this song is: When I was a boy, no one took seriously the things that I did. When I became a man, men shut their gates against me, as though I was a thief and a knave. The only women who would sleep with me were drunken sots.

Many critics have denounced this song as complete nonsense and are sure that it could not have been written by Shakespeare. But the meaning which I have given to the song makes it an appropriate finale of a merry, festive comedy.

Hamlet (1601–1602)

How should I your true-love know
  From another one?
By his cockle hat* and staff,   a pilgrim hat
  And his sandal shoon.

He is dead and gone, lady,
  He is dead and gone;
At his head a grass-green turf,
  At his heels a stone.

*   *   *

To-morrow is Saint Valentine's day,
  All in the morning betime,*   early
And I a maid at your window,
  To be your Valentine.
Then up he rose, and donned his clothes,
  And dupped* the chamber door;   opened
Let in the maid, that out a maid
  Never departed more.

*   *   *

By Gis* and by Saint Charity,   Jesus
   Alack, and fie for shame!
Young men will do 't, if they come to 't;
   By Cock, they are to blame.
Quoth she, "Before you tumbled me,
   You promised me to wed."

"So would I ha' done, by yonder sun,
   An thou hadst not come to my bed."

   The mad Ophelia sings these excerpts from three different
bawdy songs which stay suppressed in her subconscious, until
insanity releases them. They are proof that her malady was
erotic insanity caused by the thwarting of her love for Hamlet
when she thought it on the verge of fruition.

                    *   *   *

In youth, when I did love, did love,
   Methought it was very sweet,
To contract, Oh, the time for, ah, my behove,
Oh, methought, there was nothing meet.

But age, with his stealing steps,
   Hath clawed me in his clutch,
And hath shipped me intil the land,
   As if I had never been such.

A pick-axe, and a spade, a spade,
   For and a shrouding sheet;
O, a pit of clay for to be made
   For such a guest is meet.

   The Gravedigger at work on Ophelia's grave sings these
stanzas from a ballad entitled "The Aged Lover Reminisceth
Love" from Lord Vaux's, *The Image of Death*. His memory
of the lines is confused, so that he corrupts all the stanzas,
making them nonsense. The "Ohs" and "Ah" are grunts,
punctuating the fellow's exertions with his spade.

Troilus and Cressida (1601–1602)

Love, love, nothing but love, still love, still more!
  For, O, love's bow
  Shoots buck and doe;
The shaft confounds
  Not that it wounds,
But tickles still the sore.

These lovers cry, O ho! They die!
  Yet that which seems the wound to kill
Doth turn O ho! to ha! ha! he!
  So dying love lives still.
O ho! awhile, but ha! ha! ha!
O ho! groans out for ha! ha! ha!—hey ho!

Pandarus sings this song in response to Helen's "Let thy song be love. This love will undo us all. O Cupid, Cupid, Cupid!" He is scoffing at the liaison of Troilus and Cressida which he is promoting with lascivious satisfaction.

Othello (1604)

And let me the canakin clink, clink;
And let me the canakin clink.
  A soldier's a man;
  A life's but a span;
Why, then, let a soldier drink.

*   *   *

King Stephen was a worthy peer,
  His breeches cost him but a crown;
He held them sixpence all too dear,
  With that he called the tailor lown.
He was a wight of high renown,
  And thou art but of low degree.
'Tis pride that pulls the country down;
  Then take thine auld cloak about thee.

Iago sings these two songs as part of his method of getting Cassio drunk and quarrelsome. The first is a traditional drinking song; the second was an old song entitled "Bell My Wife" and familiar to everyone in Shakespeare's audience.

*   *   *

The poor soul sat sighing by a sycamore tree,
  Sing all a green willow;*
Her hand on her bosom, her head on her knee,
Sing willow, willow, willow.
The fresh streams ran by her, and murmured
    her moans;
Sing willow, willow, willow;
  Her salt tears fell from her, and softened the stones;
Sing willow, willow, willow.

symbol of
abandoned love

This song is sung by Desdemona as Emilia prepares her for the bed on which Othello is to strangle her. She says it is a song that one of her mother's maids, named Barbara, used to sing after her lover had forsaken her.

Measure for Measure (1604)

Take, O, take those lips away
  That so sweetly were forsworn;
And those eyes, the break of day
  Lights that do mislead the morn;
But my kisses bring again, bring again;
Seals of love, but sealed in vain, sealed in vain.

This is the only song in *Measure for Measure*. It is rendered by a boy, as Mariana appears on the stage for the first time. We have earlier been told her sad story. Angelo had been betrothed to her by a legal ceremony, but when she lost her dowry, he swallowed his vows, pretending that he had heard that her reputation was bad, so he left her in tears. The song is the wail of her broken heart. It serves as her musical theme. The song has attracted many composers.

Antony and Cleopatra (1607–1608)

Come, thou monarch of the vine,
Plumpy Bacchus with pink eyne!
In thy fats our cares be drowned
With thy grapes our hairs be crowned.
Cup us, till the world go round,
Cup us, till the world go round!

This stanza from a hymn is sung by a boy as part of the revels of Pompey, Octavius Caesar, and Antony on Pompey's

galley. While the boy sings, the three join hands as a symbol
of their political unity. A hymn is appropriate to the occasion
because the Romans attached religious significance to the
drinking of wine, God's gift of inspiration to man. Curiously,
the song is modeled on a famous hymn of the medieval church,
Veni Creator.

The Winter's Tale (1611)

When daffodils begin to peer,
  With heigh! the doxy* over the dale,   beggar's whore
Why, then comes in the sweet o' the year;
  For the red blood reigns in the winter's pale.*   pallor *and* domain

The white sheet bleaching on the hedge,
  With heigh! the sweet birds, O, how they sing!
Doth set my pugging tooth* on edge;   taste for thievery
  For a quart of ale is a dish for a king.

The lark, that tirra-lyra chants,
  With heigh! with heigh! the thrush and the jay,
Are summer songs for me and my aunts,*   loose women
  While we lie tumbling in the hay.

All the songs in this play are sung by Autolycus, the thieving
rogue.

*   *   *

I have served Prince Florizel and in my time
wore three-pile;* but now I am out of service;   velvet

But shall I go mourn for that, my dear?
  The pale moon shines by night;
And when I wander here and there,
  I then do most go right.

If tinkers may have leave to live,
  And bear the sow-skin budget,*   wallet
Then my account I well may give,
  And in the stocks avouch it.

This song is a kind of musical soliloquy, in which Autolycus
tells the audience what kind of a gay rogue he is.

*   *   *

Jog on, jog on, the foot-path way,
  And merrily hent* the stile-a.   climbed
A merry heart goes all the day,
  Your sad tires in a mile-a.

    This is Autolycus' first exit song.

*   *   *

Lawn as white as driven snow;
Cyprus black as e'er was crow;
Gloves as sweet as damask roses;
Masks for faces and for noses;
Bugle bracelet, necklace amber,
Perfume for a lady's chamber;
Golden quoifs and stomachers,
For my lads to give their dears;
Pins and poking-sticks of steel,
What maids lack from head to heel.
Come buy of me, come! come buy, come buy!
Buy, lads, or else your lasses cry. Come buy!

    Autolycus has gone to a country fair in the guise of a
peddler and sings this advertisement of his wares.

*   *   *

Get you hence, for I must go
Where it fits not you to know.
Whither? O whither? Whither?
It becomes thy oath full well,
Thou to me thy secrets tell.
Me too, let me go thither.
Or thou goest to the grange* or mill.   remote farm house
If to either, thou dost ill.
Neither. What, neither? Neither.
Thou hast sworn my love to be.
Thou hast sworn it more to me.
Then whither goest? Say, whither?

    Later, two shepherdesses, Mopsa and Dorcas, join in sing-
ing this trio.

*   *   *

Will you buy any tape,
  Or lace for your cape,
My dainty duck, my dear-a?
  Any silk, any thread,
  Any toys* for your head,   trifles
Of the new'st and fin'st, fin'st wear-a?
  Come to the pedlar;
  Money's a medler,*   busybody
That doth utter* all men's ware-a.   circulate

As Autolycus departs in company with the two wenches, for
both of whom he has promised to buy presents, he continues
the advertisement of his wares.

The Tempest (1611)

Come unto these yellow sands,
  And then take hands.
Curtsied when you have and kissed
  The wild waves whist,*   hushed
Foot it featly* here and there;   gracefully
And, sweet sprites, the burthen bear.* refrain sing

        *   *   *

Full fathom five thy father lies;
  Of his bones are coral made;
Those are pearls that were his eyes;
  Nothing of him that doth fade
But doth suffer a sea-change
Into something rich and strange.
Sea-nymphs hourly ring his knell:
             Ding-dong.

Ariel, while invisible, sings this song to console the ship-
wrecked Prince Ferdinand.

        *   *   *

While you here do snoring lie,
Open-eyed conspiracy
  His time doth take,
If of life you keep a care,
Shake off slumber, and beware.
  Awake, awake!

Gonzalo is an honest old counselor of Alonso, King of Naples. Ariel awakens him just in time to thwart a plot hatched by Sebastian, brother of the King of Naples, and Antonio, Prospero's brother, to murder Alonso and establish Sebastian as king in his place.

*   *   *

The master, the swabber, the boatswain and I,
    The gunner and his mate,
Loved Mall, Meg, and Marian, and Margery,
    But none of us cared for Kate;
    For she had a tongue with a tang,
    Would cry to a sailor, Go hang!
She loved not the savour of tar nor of pitch;
Yet a tailor might scratch her where'er she did itch.
    Then to sea, boys, and let her go hang!

This song is boisterously whooped out by Stephano, the drunken butler or steward. It is punctuated by swigs from his bottle. It forms his introduction to the audience appropriately with a landsman's idea of a sailor's chantey.

*   *   *

No more dams I'll make for fish;
    Nor fetch in firing
    At requiring;
Nor scrape trenchering, nor wash dish.
    'Ban, 'Ban, Ca—Caliban
    Has a new master. Get a new man.

This is a song, sung by the drunken Caliban in glee at the hope that Stephano and Trinculo, Alonso's jester, whom he takes for merchant of the moon, will free him from Prospero's control.

*   *   *

Where the bee sucks, there suck I;
In a cowslip's bell I lie;
There I couch when owls do cry.
On the bat's back I do fly
After summer merrily.
Merrily, merrily shall I live now
Under the blossom that hangs on the bough.

Ariel sings this song to himself while he helps Prospero don his magician's robes.

VENUS AND ADONIS

Venus and Adonis and *The Rape of Lucrece* were almost surely written sometime between the summer of 1592 and that of 1594. During these two years, except for brief intervals, a prolonged epidemic of the plague kept all the London theaters closed. Shakespeare's company preserved its organization and its financial health by touring the provinces, but the poet apparently stayed behind to exploit the chance to establish a literary reputation which his plays had not brought him. At that time no one regarded stage plays as works of literature. When Ben Jonson in 1616 published his plays in a folio volume, and called them *Works,* he was widely derided for his presumption.

A few critics believe that Shakespeare wrote the poem much earlier, conceivably even before he left Stratford for London. In any case, he called *Venus and Adonis* "the first heir of my invention." It is a frankly erotic work designed to please the young aristocrat to whom it was dedicated. For, like every Elizabethan poet, Shakespeare needed a patron, and his choice of Henry Wriothesley, the Third Earl of Southampton, was a shrewd one. This volatile and prodigal young lord had just come into a large fortune and was ambitious to be known as a patron of the arts. Thomas Nashe, in dedicating *The Unfortunate Traveller* to him, describes Southampton as "A dear lover, and cherisher . . . as well of the lovers of Poets as of Poets themselves."

Shakespeare's Dedicatory Epistle shows that he had not obtained permission to seek the Earl's patronage—that, in fact, he had never met the noble lord "Right Honourable," he begins, "I know not how I shall offend in dedicating my unpolisht lines to your Lordship, nor how the worlde will censure me for choosing so strong a prop to support so weak a burden." Though this may sound to modern ears a trifle servile, the dedication contains none of the nauseous flattery found in many similar addresses to patrons. The tone is both modest and manly. In calling the poem "the first heir of my invention" Shakespeare meant the first of his works intended for publication as literature.

The poem appeared in 1593 in a slender volume, beautifully printed by Shakespeare's friend, Richard Field, and advertised to be sold for 6d. The text of this work and of *The Rape of Lucrece* are both so good that the inference is unavoidable that Shakespeare himself corrected the proof—the only two of all his works upon which he bestowed any editorial care. In less than a decade seven new editions were published, proof of the poem's immediate and wide popularity. It naturally appealed especially to young men. The author of the Cambridge University play called *The Return from Parnassus* has one of the students—he is, one must admit, a bit of a fool—exclaim, "Let this dunceified world esteem of Spenser and Chaucer; I'll worship sweet Master Shakespeare, and to honour him will lay his *Venus and Adonis* under my pillow."

Fortunately for Shakespeare, Southampton was delighted with the poem and evidently rewarded its author handsomely. This we can infer from the dedication of a second poem, *The Rape of Lucrece,* to Southampton in the following year (1594).

"The love I dedicate to your Lordship," it begins, "is without end. . . . The warrant I have of your Honourable disposition, not the worth of my untutored Lines, makes it assured of acceptance." The tone of this dedication is so warm that we may assume that in the interval between the appearance of the two poems, Shakespeare had won Southampton's friendship and obtained an entree into the gay and cultivated circle of which the young Earl was the center.

Narrative love poems were widely popular in Shakespeare's day. Although the poet must have read most of them, it is difficult to choose which one may have been his model for *Venus and Adonis.* The ultimate source for all of them was Ovid's *Metamorphoses.* It served as a Latin textbook in many Elizabethan grammar schools. Of all these Ovidian poems, Shakespeare's was by far the most popular. It was reprinted fifteen times between 1593 and 1636, more often than any of the plays.

The verse form, *a b a b c c,* was one that had recently become popular for every sort of poem. The most famous work written in this meter was Spenser's elegy on the death of Sir Philip Sidney entitled *Astrophel* (1596). It was also the verse form of Lodge's erotic poem, *Glaucus and Scilla* (1589), which served as one of the closest models for *Venus and Adonis.*

The story is simple. The Goddess of Love tries desperately, but unsuccessfully, to seduce the beautiful Greek youth Adonis. With difficulty he escapes from her torrid wooing to prepare himself for a hunt of a wild boar the next day. In terror Venus hears the sound of the hunt, catches sight of the boar, and soon after comes upon the lifeless body of Adonis, his blood dyeing the flowers among which he lies. The poem ends with a long lament of Venus.

Shakespeare devotes most of his attention to Venus and her techniques of seduction. This was undoubtedly the feature of the poem that gained it immediate popularity. It is not much to modern taste. Henry Simon suggests that, now when every contemporary novel describes love-making with even more candor, the interest in Venus' sensual wiles has greatly diminished.

The influence of Ovid, called throughout the Renaissance "the amorous schoolmaster," can be detected everywhere in *Venus and Adonis*. He could teach one how to arouse passion, and also how to allay it. Some critics have called the poem a mere pageant of gesture. It exhibits the author's mastery of all the approved devices of rhetoric. The tale is hardly more than a string upon which Shakespeare hung his rhetorical jewels: complaints, laments, panegyrics, and diatribes. Venus' diatribe against Death is one of the most skillfully wrought passages in the poem. The style is elaborate: a medley of antitheses, alliterations, and epigrams.

The glory of *Venus and Adonis* lies in its display of a gorgeous youthful imagination as it plays upon the sights and sounds of Nature. Indeed, Nature, both animate and inanimate, achieves the importance of a character in the poem. The passages which have been most admired from the days of Hazlitt and Coleridge to the present are the hunting scenes, reported as if from personal observation, and the description of the flight of the poor Wat, the hunted hare. However, to overstress these decorous features of *Venus and Adonis* is to throw the aesthetic effect of the poem out of focus. Its real achievement is its reflection of the glow and excitement of the sensuous delight of the poet's youth and of the Elizabethan age, and above all, the ardent beauty of its voluptuous situations and descriptions.

VENUS AND ADONIS

Even as the sun with purple-coloured face
Had ta'en his last leave of the weeping* morn,   *dewy*
Rose-cheeked Adonis hied him to the chase;
Hunting he loved, but love he laughed to scorn:
  Sick-thoughted Venus makes amain* unto him,   *hurries*
  And like a bold-faced suitor 'gins to woo him.

'Thrice fairer than myself,' thus she began,
'The field's chief flower, sweet above compare,
Stain* to all nymphs, more lovely than a man,   *injury*
More white and red than doves or roses are;   10
  Nature that made thee, with herself at strife,
  Saith that the world hath ending with thy life.

'Vouchsafe, thou wonder, to alight thy steed,
And rein his proud head to the saddle-bow;
If thou wilt deign this favour, for thy meed*   *reward*
A thousand honey secrets shalt thou know:
  Here come and sit, where never serpent hisses,
  And being set,* I'll smother thee with kisses;   *seated*

'And yet not cloy thy lips with loathed satiety,
But rather famish them amid their plenty,   20
Making them red and pale with fresh variety;
Ten kisses short as one, one long as twenty:
  A summer's day will seem an hour but short,
  Being wasted* in such time-beguiling sport.'   *spent*

With this she seizeth on his sweating palm,
The precedent* of pith* and livelihood,   *evidence / vigor*
And, trembling in her passion, calls it balm,
Earth's sovereign salve to do a goddess good:
  Being so enraged, desire doth lend her force
  Courageously to pluck* him from his horse.   *drag*

Over one arm the lusty courser's rein,
Under her other was the tender boy,
Who blushed and pouted in a dull disdain,
With leaden appetite, unapt to toy;*   *i.e., for dalliance*
  She red and hot as coals of glowing fire,
  He red for shame, but frosty in desire.

The studded bridle on a ragged* bough   rough
Nimbly she fastens—O, how quick is love!—
The steed is stallèd up, and even now
To tie the rider she begins to prove:*   try
    Backward she pushed him, as she would be thrust,
    And governed him in strength, though not in lust.

So soon was she along as he was down,
Each leaning on their elbows and their hips:
Now doth she stroke his cheek, now doth he frown,
And 'gins to chide, but soon she stops his lips;
    And kissing speaks, with lustful language broken,
    'If thou wilt chide, thy lips shall never open.'

He burns with bashful shame; she with her tears
Doth quench the maiden burning of his cheeks;   50
Then with her windy sighs and golden hairs
To fan and blow them dry again she seeks:
    He saith she is immodest, blames her miss;*   misdoing
    What follows more she murders with a kiss.

Even as an empty eagle, sharp by fast,
Tires* with her beak on feathers, flesh and bone,   tears
Shaking her wings, devouring all in haste,
Till either gorge* be stuffed or prey be gone;   crop
    Even so she kissed his brow, his cheek, his chin,
    And where she ends she doth anew begin.   60

Forced to content,* but never to obey,   acquiescence
Panting he lies and breatheth in her face;
She feedeth on the steam as on a prey,
And calls it heavenly moisture, air of grace;
    Wishing her cheeks were gardens full of flowers,
    So they were dewed with such distilling showers.

Look, how a bird lies tangled in a net,
So fastened in her arms Adonis lies;
Pure shame and awed resistance* made him fret,   fear to resist
Which bred more beauty in his angry eyes: 70
    Rain added to a river that is rank*   overfull
    Perforce will force it overflow the bank.

Still she entreats, and prettily entreats,
For to a pretty ear she tunes her tale;
Still is he sullen, still he lours and frets,
'Twixt crimson shame, and anger ashy-pale;
    Being red, she loves him best; and being white,
    Her best is bettered with a more* delight.   greater

Look how he can, she cannot choose but love;
And by her fair immortal hand she swears,   80
From his soft bosom never to remove,
Till he take* truce with her contending tears,   make a
    Which long have rained, making her cheeks all wet;
    And one sweet kiss shall pay this countless debt.

Upon this promise did he raise his chin,
Like a dive-dapper* peering through a wave,   dabchick
                                          (little grebe)
Who, being looked on, ducks as quickly in;
So offers he to give what she did crave;
    But when her lips were ready for his pay,
    He winks,* and turns his lips another way.   shuts his eyes

Never did passenger* in summer's heat   wayfarer
More thirst for drink than she for this good turn.
Her help she sees, but help she cannot get;
She bathes in water, yet her fire must burn:
    'O, pity,' 'gan she cry, 'flint-hearted boy!
    'Tis but a kiss I beg; why art thou coy?

'I have been wooed, as I entreat thee now,
Even by the stern and direful god of war,
Whose sinewy neck in battle ne'er did bow,
Who conquers where he comes in every jar;*   quarrel
    Yet hath he been my captive and my slave,
    And begged for that which thou unasked shalt have.

'Over my altars hath he hung his lance,
His battered shield, his uncontrollèd crest,*   plume
And for my sake hath learned to sport and dance,
To toy, to wanton,* dally, smile and jest;   act lewdly
    Scorning his churlish drum and ensign red,
    Making my arms his field, his tent my bed.

'Thus he that overruled I overswayed,
Leading him prisoner in a red-rose chain: 110
Strong-tempered steel his stronger strength obeyed,
Yet was he servile to my coy disdain.
   O, be not proud, nor brag not of thy might,
   For mastering her that foiled the god of fight!

'Touch but my lips with those fair lips of thine—
Though mine be not so fair, yet are they red—
The kiss shall be thine own as well as mine:
What see'st thou in the ground? hold up thy head:
   Look in mine eyeballs, there thy beauty lies;
   Then why not lips on lips, since eyes in eyes?   120

'Art thou ashamed to kiss? then wink* again,   close your eyes
And I will wink; so shall the day seem night;
Love keeps his revels where there are but twain;
Be bold to play, our sport is not in sight:*   seen
   These blue-veined violets whereon we lean
   Never can blab, nor know not what we mean.

'The tender spring upon thy tempting lip
Shews thee unripe; yet mayst thou well be tasted:
Make use of time, let not advantage slip;
Beauty within itself should not be wasted: 130
   Fair flowers that are not gathered in their prime
   Rot and consume themselves in little time.

'Were I hard-favoured,* foul, or wrinkled-old,   ugly
Ill-nurtured, crooked, churlish, harsh in voice,
O'erworn,* despised, rheúmatic and cold,   worn out
Thick-sighted,* barren, lean, and lacking juice,   dim-eyed
   Then mightst thou pause, for then I were not for
     thee;
   But having no defects, why dost abhor me?

'Thou canst not see one wrinkle in my brow;
Mine eyes are grey and bright and quick in turning;   140
My beauty as the spring doth yearly grow,
My flesh is soft and plump, my marrow burning;
   My smooth moist hand, were it with thy hand felt,
   Would in thy palm dissolve, or seem to melt.

'Bid me discourse, I will enchant thine ear,
Or, like a fairy trip upon the green,
Or, like a nymph with long dishevelled hair,
Dance on the sands, and yet no footing* seen: mark of feet
    Love is a spirit all compact of fire,
    Not gross to sink, but light, and will aspire.*   ascend

'Witness this primrose bank whereon I lie;
These forceless flowers like sturdy trees support me;
Two strengthless doves will draw me through the sky,
From morn till night, even where I list to sport me:
    Is love so light, sweet boy, and may it be
    That thou shouldst think it heavy unto thee?

'Is thine own heart to thine own face affected?
Can thy right hand seize love* upon thy left?   clasp as a lover
Then woo thyself, be of thyself rejected,
Steal thine own freedom, and complain on theft.   160
    Narcissus† so himself himself forsook,
    And died to kiss his shadow in the brook.

'Torches are made to light, jewels to wear,
Dainties to taste, fresh beauty for the use,
Herbs for their smell, and sappy plants to bear;
Things growing to* themselves are growth's abuse: for
    Seeds spring from seeds and beauty breedeth beauty;
    Thou wast begot; to get* it is thy duty.   beget

'Upon the earth's increase why shouldst thou feed,
Unless the earth with thy increase be fed?   170
By law of nature thou art bound to breed,
That thine may live when thou thyself art dead;
    And so, in spite of death, thou dost survive,
    In that thy likeness still is left alive.'

By this, the love-sick queen began to sweat,
For, where they lay, the shadow had forsook them,
And Titan,* tired in the mid-day heat,   the sun
With burning eye did hotly overlook them,
    Wishing Adonis had his team to guide,
    So he were like him and by Venus' side.   180

Narcissus. A Greek youth who refused all offers of love. He fell in love
with his image reflected in a pool and pined away, a victim of
self-love.

And now Adonis, with a lazy spright,*   spirit
And with a heavy, dark, disliking eye,
His louring* brows o'erwhelming his fair sight,   frowning
Like misty vapours when they blot the sky,
    Souring* his cheeks, cries 'Fie, no more of love!   soiling
    The sun doth burn my face; I must remove.'*   depart

'Ay me,' quoth Venus, 'young, and so unkind!
What bare* excuses makest thou to be gone!   inadequate
I'll sigh celestial breath, whose gentle wind
Shall cool the heat of this descending sun: 190
    I'll make a shadow for thee of my hairs;
    If they burn too, I'll quench them with my tears.

'The sun that shines from heaven shines but warm,
And, lo, I lie between that sun and thee:
The heat I have from thence doth little harm,
Thine eye darts forth the fire that burneth me;
    And were I not immortal, life were done
    Between this heavenly and earthly sun.

'Art thou obdúrate, flinty, hard as steel?
Nay, more than flint, for stone at rain relenteth:*   softens
Art thou a woman's son, and canst not feel
What 'tis to love? how want of love tormenteth?
    O, had thy mother borne so hard a mind,
    She had not brought forth thee, but died unkind.*   childless

'What am I, that thou shouldst contemn* me this?   refuse
Or what great danger dwells upon my suit?
What were thy lips the worse for one poor kiss?
Speak, fair;* but speak fair words, or else be mute: civilly
    Give me one kiss, I'll give it thee again,
    And one for interest, if thou wilt have twain.   210

'Fie, lifeless picture, cold and senseless stone,
Well painted idol, image dull and dead,
Statue contenting but the eye alone,
Thing like a man, but of no woman bred!
    Thou art no man, though of a man's complexion,
    For men will kiss even by their own direction.'

This said, impatience chokes her pleading tongue,
And swelling passion doth provoke a pause;
Red cheeks and fiery eyes blaze forth her wrong;
Being* judge in love, she cannot right her   *though she is
   cause: 220
    And now she weeps, and now she fain would speak,
    And now her sobs do her intendments* break.   *intentions

Sometimes she shakes her head, and then his hand,
Now gazeth she on him, now on the ground;
Sometimes her arms infold him like a band:
She would, he will not in her arms be bound;
    And when from thence he struggles to be gone,
    She locks her lily fingers one in one.

'Fondling,'* she saith, 'since I have hemmed thee   *darling
   here
Within the circuit of this ivory pale,*   *enclosure
I'll be a park, and thou shalt be my deer;
Feed where thou wilt, on mountain or in dale:
    Graze on my lips, and if those hills be dry,
    Stray lower, where the pleasant fountains lie.

'Within this limit is relief* enough,   *i.e., food
Sweet bottom-grass* and high delightful plain,   *valley grown
Round rising hillocks, brakes* obscure* and   *thickets / dark
   rough,
To shelter thee from tempest and from rain:
    Then be my deer, since I am such a park;
    No dog shall rouse thee, though a thousand bark.'   240

At this Adonis smiles as in disdain,
That in each cheek appears a pretty dimple:
Love made those hollows, if himself were slain,
He might be buried in a tomb so simple;
    Foreknowing well, if there he came to lie,
    Why, there Love lived, and there he could not die.

These lovely caves, these round enchanting pits,
Opened their mouths to swallow Venus' liking.
Being mad before, how doth she now for wits?
Struck dead at first, what needs a second striking?   250
    Poor queen of love, in thine own law forlorn,
    To love a cheek that smiles at thee in scorn!

Now which way shall she turn? what shall she say?
Her words are done, her woes the more increasing;
The time is spent, her object will away
And from her twining arms doth urge releasing.
   'Pity,' she cries, 'some favour, some remorse!'*   tenderness
   Away he springs, and hasteth to his horse.

But, lo, from forth a copse that neighbours by,
A breeding jennet,* lusty, young and proud,   young mare
Adonis' trampling courser* doth espy,   swift steed
And forth she rushes, snorts and neighs aloud:
   The strong-necked steed, being tied unto a tree,
   Breaketh his rein and to her straight goes he.

Imperiously he leaps, he neighs, he bounds,
And now his woven girths he breaks asunder;
The bearing earth with his hard hoof he wounds,
Whose hollow womb resounds like heaven's thunder;
   The iron bit he crusheth 'tween his teeth,
   Controlling what he was controllèd with.   270

His ears up-pricked; his braided hanging mane
Upon his compassed* crest now stand on end;   arched
His nostrils drink the air, and forth again,
As from a furnace, vapours doth he send:
   His eye, which scornfully glisters* like fire,   glitters
   Shows his hot courage and his high desire.

Sometimes he trots, as if he told* the steps,   counted
With gentle majesty and modest pride;
Anon he rears upright, curvets* and leaps,   prances
As who should say 'Lo, thus my strength is tried;   280
   And this I do to captivate the eye
   Of the fair breeder that is standing by.'

What recketh he his rider's angry stir,*   excitement
His flattering 'Holla' or his 'Stand, I say'?
What cares he now for curb or pricking spur?
For rich caparisons* or trappings gay?   ornamental coverings
   He sees his love, and nothing else he sees,
   For nothing else with his proud sight agrees.

Look, when a painter would surpass the life,
In limning* out a well proportioned steed,   painting
His art with nature's workmanship at strife,
As if the dead the living should exceed;
    So did this horse excel a common one
    In shape, in courage, colour, pace and bone.

Round-hoofed, short-jointed, fetlocks shag* and long,   shaggy
Broad breast, full eye, small head and nostril wide,
High crest, short ears, straight legs and passing strong,
Thin mane, thick tail, broad buttock, tender hide:
    Look, what a horse should have he did not lack,
    Save a proud rider on so proud a back.   300

Sometime he scuds* far off, and there he stares;   moves swiftly
Anon he starts* at stirring of a feather;   jumps
To bid the wind a base he now prepares,†
And whether he run or fly they know not whether;
    For through his mane and tail the high wind sings,
    Fanning the hairs, who wave like feathered wings.

He looks upon his love and neighs unto her;
She answers him, as if she knew his mind:
Being proud, as females are, to see him woo her,
She puts on outward strangeness, seems unkind,   310
    Spurns* at his love and scorns the heat he feels,   kicks
    Beating his kind embracements with her heels.

Then, like a melancholy malcontent,
He vails* his tail, that, like a falling plume,   lowers
Cool shadow to his melting buttock lent:
He stamps, and bites the poor flies in his fume.*   anger
    His love, perceiving how he was enraged,
    Grew kinder, and his fury was assuaged.

His testy master goeth about* to take him;   attempts
When, lo, the unbacked breeder, full of fear,   320
Jealous of catching, swiftly doth forsake him,
With her the horse, and left Adonis there:
    As they were mad, unto the wood they hie them,
    Out-stripping crows that strive to over-fly them.

To bid the wind a base he now prepares.
To challenge the wind in a contest for speed.

All swoln with chafing, down Adonis sits,
Banning* his boisterous and unruly beast: cursing
And now the happy season once more fits,
That love-sick Love by pleading may be blest;
  For lovers say, the heart hath treble wrong
  When it is barred the aidance of the tongue.   330

An oven that is stopped, or river stayed,
Burneth more hotly, swelleth with more rage:
So of concealèd sorrow may be said;
Free vent of words love's fire doth assuage;
  But when the heart's attorney* once is mute,   *i.e.,* the tongue
  The client breaks, as desperate in his suit.

He sees her coming, and begins to glow,
Even as a dying coal revives with wind,
And with his bonnet* hides his angry brow,   cap
Looks on the dull earth with disturbèd mind,   340
  Taking no notice that she is so nigh,
  For all askance he holds her in his eye.†

O, what a sight it was, wistly to view
How she came stealing* to the wayward boy!   furtively
To note the fighting conflict of her hue,
How white and red each other did destroy!
  But now her cheek was pale, and by and by*   at once
  It flashed forth fire, as lightning from the sky.

Now was she just before him as he sat,
And like a lowly lover down she kneels;   350
With one fair hand she heaveth* up his hat,   raises
Her other tender hand his fair cheek feels:
  His tenderer cheek receives her soft hand's print,
  As apt as new-fallen snow takes any dint.

O, what a war of looks was then between them!
Her eyes petitioners to his eyes suing;
His eyes saw her eyes as they had not seen them;
Her eyes wooed still, his eyes disdained the wooing:
  And all this dumb play* had his* acts made   dumb show / its
  plain
  With tears, which chorus-like her eyes did rain.   360

For all askance he holds her in his eye.
For he watches her sidewise, *i.e.,* with mistrust.

Full gently now she takes him by the hand,
A lily prisoned in a gaol of snow,
Or ivory in an alabaster band;
So white a friend engirts* so white a foe: clasps
   This beauteous combat, wilful and unwilling,
   Showed like two silver doves that sit a-billing.

Once more the engine of her thoughts began:
'O fairest mover on this mortal round,
Would thou wert as I am, and I a man,
My heart all whole as thine, thy heart my wound;   370
   For one sweet look thy help* I would assure thee,   cure
   Though nothing but my body's bane* would cure thee.'   death

'Give me my hand,' saith he; 'why dost thou feel it?'
'Give me my heart,' saith she, 'and thou shalt have it;
O, give it me, lest thy hard heart do steel it,
And being steeled, soft sighs can never grave it;*   fix indelibly
   Then love's deep groans I never shall regard,
   Because Adonis' heart hath made mine hard.'

'For shame,' he cries, 'let go, and let me go;
My day's delight is past, my horse is gone,   380
And 'tis your fault I am bereft him* so: of him
I pray you hence, and leave me here alone;
   For all my mind, my thought, my busy care,
   Is how to get my palfrey* from the mare.'   saddle horse

Thus she replies: 'Thy palfrey, as he should,
Welcomes the warm approach of sweet desire:
Affection is a coal that must be cooled;
Else, suffered,* it will set the heart on fire: allowed (to burn)
   The sea hath bounds, but deep desire hath none;
   Therefore no marvel though thy horse be gone.   390

'How like a jade* he stood, tied to the tree,   worn-out horse
Servilely mastered with a leathern rein!
But when he saw his love, his youth's fair fee,*   reward
He held such petty bondage in disdain;
   Throwing the base thong from his bending crest,
   Enfranchising his mouth, his back, his breast.

'Who sees his true-love in her naked bed,
Teaching the sheets a whiter hue than white,
But, when his glutton eye so full hath fed,
His other agents aim at like delight?   400
    Who is so faint, that dares not be so bold
    To touch the fire, the weather being cold?

'Let me excuse thy courser, gentle boy;
And learn of him, I heartily beseech thee,
To take advantage on presented joy;
Though I were dumb, yet his proceedings teach thee:
    O, learn to love; the lesson is but plain,
    And once made perfect, never lost again.'

'I know not love,' quoth he, 'nor will not know it,
Unless it be a boar, and then I chase it;   410
'Tis much to borrow, and I will not owe it;
My love to love is love but to disgrace it;
    For I have heard it is a life in death,
    That laughs, and weeps, and all but with a breath.

'Who wears a garment shapeless and unfinished?
Who plucks the bud before one leaf put forth?
If springing things be any jot diminished,
They wither in their prime,* prove nothing worth: youth
    The colt that's backed and burthened being young
    Loseth his pride, and never waxeth strong.   420

'You hurt my hand with wringing;* let us part,   pressing it
And leave this idle* theme, this bootless chat: foolish
Remove your siege from my unyielding heart;
To love's alarms* it will not ope the gate: attack
    Dismiss your vows, your feignèd tears, your flattery;
    For where a heart is hard they make no battery.'*   enforced
                                                          entrance

'What! canst thou talk?' quoth she, 'hast thou a tongue?
O, would thou hadst not, or I had no hearing!
Thy mermaid's voice hath done me double wrong;
I had my load before, now pressed* with bearing: pressed down
    Melodious discord, heavenly tune harsh-sounding,
    Ear's deep-sweet music, and heart's deep-sore wounding.

'Had I no eyes but ears, my ears would love
That inward beauty and invisible;
Or were I deaf, thy outward parts would move
Each part in me that were but sensible:*   impressionable
　　Though neither eyes nor ears, to hear nor see,
　　Yet should I be in love by touching thee.

'Say, that the sense of feeling were bereft me,
And that I could not see, nor hear, nor touch,   440
And nothing but the very smell were left me,
Yet would my love to thee be still as much;
　　For from the stillitory* of thy face excelling*   still / exquisite
　　Comes breath perfumed, that breedeth love by
　　　smelling.

'But, O, what banquet were thou to the taste,
Being nurse and feeder of the other four!
Would they not wish the feast might ever last,
And bid Suspicion double-lock the door,
　　Lest Jealousy, that sour unwelcome guest,
　　Should by his stealing in disturb the feast?'   450

Once more the ruby-coloured portal opened,
Which to his speech did honey passage yield;
Like a red morn, that ever yet betokened
Wreck to the seaman, tempest to the field,
　　Sorrow to shepherds, woe unto the birds,
　　Gusts and foul flaws* to herdmen and to herds.   winds

This ill presage advisedly* she marketh: deliberately
Even as the wind is hushed before it raineth,
Or as the wolf doth grin before he barketh,
Or as the berry breaks before it staineth,   460
　　Or like the deadly bullet of a gun,
　　His meaning struck her ere his words begun.

And at his look she flatly falleth down,
For looks kill love, and love by looks reviveth:
A smile recures* the wounding of a frown;   heals
But blessed bankrupt, that by love so thriveth!
　　The silly boy, believing she is dead,
　　Claps her pale cheek, till clapping makes it red;

And all amazed brake off his late intent,
For sharply he did think to reprehend her,   470
Which cunning love did wittily prevent:
Fair fall* the wit that can so well defend her!   good luck to
   For on the grass she lies as she were slain,
   Till his breath breatheth life in her again.

He wrings her nose, he strikes her on the cheeks,
He bends her fingers, holds her pulses hard,
He chafes her lips; a thousand ways he seeks
To mend the hurt that his unkindness marred:
   He kisses her; and she, by her good will,
   Will never rise, so he will kiss her still.   480

The night of sorrow now is turned to day:
Her two blue windows faintly she up-heaveth,
Like the fair sun, when in his fresh array
He cheers the morn, and all the earth relieveth:
   And as the bright sun glorifies the sky,
   So is her face illumined with her eye;

Whose beams upon his hairless face are fixed,
As if from thence they borrowed all their shine.
Were never four such lamps together mixed,
Had not his clouded with his brow's repine;*   discontent
   But hers, which through the crystal tears gave light,
   Shone like the moon in water seen by night.

'O, where am I?' quoth she; 'in earth or heaven,
Or in the ocean, drenched,* or in the fire?   drowned
What hour is this? or morn or weary even?
Do I delight to die, or life desire?
   But now I lived, and life was death's annoy;*   affliction
   But now I died, and death was lively joy.

'O, thou didst kill me: kill me once again:
Thy eyes' shrewd* tutor, that hard heart of thine,   artful
Hath taught them scornful tricks, and such disdain,
That they have murdered this poor heart of mine;
   And these mine eyes, true leaders to their queen,
   But for thy piteous lips no more had seen.

'Long may they kiss each other, for this cure!
O, never let their crimson liveries wear!
And as they last, their verdure still endure,
To drive infection from the dangerous year!
    That the star-gazers,* having writ on death,   astrologers
    May say, the plague is banished by thy breath.   510

'Pure lips, sweet seals in my soft lips imprinted,
What bargains may I make, still to be sealing?
To sell myself I can be well contented,
So thou wilt buy, and pay, and use good dealing;
    Which purchase if thou make, for fear of slips*   counterfeit coin
    Set thy seal-manual on my wax-red lips.

'A thousand kisses buys my heart from me;
And pay them at thy leisure, one by one.
What is ten hundred touches unto thee?
Are they not quickly told* and quickly gone?   counted
    Say, for non-payment that the debt should double,
    Is twenty hundred kisses such a trouble?'

'Fair queen,' quoth he, 'if any love you owe me,
Measure my strangeness* with my unripe years: reserve
Before I know myself, seek not to know me;
No fisher but the ungrown fry* forbears: young of a fish
    The mellow plum doth fall, the green sticks fast,
    Or being early plucked is sour to taste.

'Look, the world's comforter, with weary gait,
His day's hot task hath ended in the west;   530
The owl, night's herald, shrieks, 'tis very late;
The sheep are gone to fold, birds to their nest;
    And coal-black clouds that shadow heaven's light
    Do summon us to part, and bid good night.

'Now let me say "Good night," and so say you;
If you will say so, you shall have a kiss.'
'Good night,' quoth she; and, ere he says 'Adieu,'
The honey fee of parting tendered is:
    Her arms do lend his neck a sweet embrace;
    Incorporate then they seem; face grows to face.   540

Till breathless he disjoined, and backward drew
The heavenly moisture, that sweet coral mouth,
Whose precious taste her thirsty lips well knew,
Whereon they surfeit, yet complain on drouth:
    He with her plenty pressed; she faint with dearth,
    Their lips together glued, fall to the earth.

Now quick desire hath caught the yielding prey,
And glutton-like she feeds, yet never filleth;
Her lips are conquerors, his lips obey,
Paying what ransom the insulter willeth;   550
    Whose vulture thought doth pitch the price so high,
    That she will draw his lips' rich treasure dry.

And having felt the sweetness of the spoil,
With blindfold fury she begins to forage;
Her face doth reek and smoke, her blood doth boil,
And careless lust stirs up a desperate courage,
    Planting oblivion,* beating reason back,   *forgetfulness*
    Forgetting shame's pure blush and honour's wrack.*   *ruin*

Hot, faint and weary, with her hard embracing,
Like a wild bird being tamed with too much handling,   560
Or as the fleet-foot roe that's tired with chasing,
Or like the froward* infant stilled with dandling,   *perverse*
    He now obeys, and now no more resisteth,
    While she takes all she can, not all she listeth.

What wax so frozen but dissolves with tempering,
And yields at last to every light impression?
Things out of hope are compassed oft with venturing,
Chiefly in love, whose leave exceeds commission:†
    Affection faints not like a pale-faced coward,
    But then woos best when most his choice is froward.   570

When he did frown, O, had she then gave over,
Such nectar from his lips she had not sucked.
Foul words and frowns must not repel a lover;
What though the rose have prickles, yet 'tis plucked:
    Were beauty under twenty locks kept fast,
    Yet love breaks through, and picks them all at last.

Chiefly in love, whose leave exceeds commission.
Which permits more than any written warrant grants.

For pity now she can no more detain him;
The poor fool prays her that he may depart:
She is resolved no longer to restrain him;
Bids him farewell, and look well to her heart,   580
    The which, by Cupid's bow she doth protest,
    He carries thence incagèd in his breast.

'Sweet boy,' she says, 'this night I'll waste in sorrow,
For my sick heart commands mine eyes to watch.*   stay open
Tell me, love's master, shall we meet to-morrow?
Say, shall we? shall we? wilt thou make the match?'*   agreement
    He tells her, no; to-morrow he intends
    To hunt the boar with certain of his friends.

'The boar!' quoth she; whereat a sudden pale,*   pallor
Like lawn being spread upon the blushing rose,   590
Usurps* her cheeks; she trembles at his tale,   possesses
And on his neck her yoking arms she throws:
    She sinketh down, still hanging by his neck,
    He on her belly falls, she on her back.

Now is she in the very lists* of love,   tournament area
Her champion mounted for the hot encounter:
All is imaginary she doth prove,
He will not manage* her, although he mount her;   break in
    That worse than Tantalus'† is her annoy,
    To clip* Elysium, and to lack her joy.   clasp

Even so poor birds, deceived with painted grapes,
Do surfeit by the eye and pine* the maw,   starve
Even so she languisheth in her mishaps
As those poor birds that helpless* berries saw.   i.e., to feed them
    The warm effects* which she in him finds   consequences
        missing
    She seeks to kindle with continual kissing.

But all in vain; good queen, it will not be:
She hath assayed as much as may be proved;*   experienced
Her pleading hath deserved a greater fee;
She's Love, she loves, and yet she is not loved.   610
    'Fie, fie,' he says, 'you crush me; let me go;
    You have no reason to withhold me so.'

Tantalus. In Greek legend Tantalus, because of his insolence to the gods,
was sent to the Lower World, where he was punished by being placed
in water that receded when he tried to drink it, and surrounded by trees
whose fruit vanished when he tried to pluck it.

'Thou hadst been gone,' quoth she, 'sweet boy, ere this,
But that thou told'st me thou wouldst hunt the boar.
O, be advised:* thou know'st not what it is   take care
With javelin's point a churlish swine to gore,
   Whose tushes* never sheathed he whetteth still,   tusks
   Like to a mortal* butcher, bent to kill.   deadly

'On his bow-back he hath a battle* set   battalion
Of bristly pikes, that ever threat his foes;   620
His eyes, like glow-worms, shine when he doth fret;
His snout digs sepulchres where'er he goes;
   Being moved,* he strikes whate'er is in his way,   enraged
   And whom he strikes his crooked tushes slay.

'His brawny sides, with hairy bristles armed,
Are better proof* than thy spear's point can enter;   armor
His short thick neck cannot be easily harmed;
Being ireful, on the lion he will venture:
   The thorny brambles and embracing bushes,
   As fearful of him, part; through whom he rushes.   630

'Alas, he nought esteems that face of thine,
To which Love's eyes pay tributary gazes;
Nor thy soft hands, sweet lips and crystal eyne,
Whose full perfection all the world amazes;
   But having thee at vantage—wondrous dread!—
   Would root* these beauties as he roots the mead.   uproot

'O, let him keep his loathsome cabin* still;   den
Beauty hath nought to do with such foul fiends:
Come not within his danger* by thy will;   into his power
They that thrive well take counsel of their friends.   640
   When thou didst name the boar, not to dissemble,
   I feared* thy fortune, and my joints did tremble.   feared for

'Didst thou not mark my face? was it not white?
Saw'st thou not signs of fear lurk in mine eye?
Grew I not faint? and fell I not downright?
Within my bosom, whereon thou dost lie,
   My boding* heart pants, beats, and takes no rest,   foreboding
   But, like an earthquake, shakes thee on my breast.

'For where Love reigns, disturbing Jealousy
Doth call himself Affection's sentinel;   650
Gives false alarms, suggesteth mutiny,*   uprising
And in a peaceful hour doth cry "Kill, kill!"†
     Distempering* gentle Love in his desire,   diluting
     As air and water do abate the fire.

'This sour informer, this bate-breeding* spy,   causing contention
This canker* that eats up Love's tender spring,   canker-worm
This carry-tale,* dissentious Jealousy,   telltale
That sometime true news, sometime false doth bring,
     Knocks at my heart, and whispers in mine ear,
     That if I love thee, I thy death should fear: 660

'And more than so, presenteth to mine eye
The picture of an angry-chafing* boar,   chafing with anger
Under whose sharp fangs on his back doth lie
An image like thyself, all stained with gore;
     Whose blood upon the fresh flowers being shed
     Doth make them droop with grief and hang the head.

'What should I do, seeing thee so indeed,
That tremble at the imagination?
The thought of it doth make my faint heart bleed,
And fear doth teach it divination: 670
     I prophesy thy death, my living sorrow,
     If thou encounter with the boar to-morrow.

'But if thou needs wilt hunt, be ruled by me;
Uncouple at the timorous flying hare,
Or at the fox which lives by subtlety,
Or at the roe which no encounter dare:
     Pursue these fearful* creatures o'er the downs,   timid
     And on thy well-breathed horse keep with thy hounds.

'And when thou hast on foot the purblind* hare,   short-sighted
Mark the poor wretch, to overshoot* his troubles,   i.e., escape
How he outruns the wind, and with what care
He cranks* and crosses with a thousand doubles:*   twists / turns
     The many musits* through the which he goes   gaps in a hedge
     Are like a labyrinth to amaze his foes.

"*Kill, kill!*" The cry of soldiers entering a town to sack it.

'Sometime he runs among a flock of sheep,
To make the cunning hounds mistake their smell,
And sometime where earth-delving conies keep,
To stop the loud pursuers in their yell;
    And sometime sorteth* with a herd of deer: *joins*
    Danger deviseth shifts;* wit waits on fear: *expedients*

'For there his smell with others being mingled,
The hot scent-snuffing hounds are driven to doubt,
Ceasing their clamorous cry till they have singled†
With much ado the cold fault* cleanly* out;   *loss of scent /*
                                          completely
    Then do they spend their mouths:* Echo replies,   *i.e., baying*
    As if another chase were in the skies.

'By this, poor Wat, far off upon a hill,
Stands on his hinder legs with listening ear,
To hearken if his foes pursue him still:
Anon their loud alarums he doth hear;   *700*
    And now his grief may be comparèd well
    To one sore sick that hears the passing-bell.*   *funeral bell*

'Then shalt thou see the dew-bedabbled wretch
Turn, and return, indenting* with the way;   *zig-zagging*
Each envious* brier his weary legs doth scratch,   *malicious*
Each shadow makes him stop, each murmur stay:
    For misery is trodden on by many,
    And being low never relieved by any.

'Lie quietly, and hear a little more;
Nay, do not struggle, for thou shalt not rise: *710*
To make thee hate the hunting of the boar,
Unlike myself thou hear'st me moralize,†
    Applying this to that, and so to so;
    For love can comment upon every woe.

Single. To distinguish the scent of the animal pursued from that of
another that has crossed his path.
Moralizing. The practice, widespread in the Middle Ages, of making a
moral application for every sort of treatise or tale; a rhetorical
method convenient for Churchmen, hardly for Venus.

'Where did I leave?'* 'No matter where,' quoth he;　　　stop
'Leave me, and then the story aptly ends:
The night is spent.' 'Why, what of that?' quoth she.
'I am,' quoth he, 'expected of my friends;
　　And now 'tis dark, and going I shall fall.'
　　　'In night,' quoth she, 'desire sees best of all.　　720

'But if thou fall, O, then imagine this,
The earth, in love with thee, thy footing* trips,　　footfall
And all is but to rob thee of a kiss.
Rich preys make true* men thieves; so do thy lips　　honest
　　Make modest Dian† cloudy* and forlorn,　　　sullen
　　　Lest she should steal a kiss, and die forsworn.

'Now of this dark night I perceive the reason:
Cynthia* for shame obscures her silver shine,　　the moon
Till forging Nature be condemned of treason,
For stealing moulds from heaven that were divine;　　730
　　Wherein she framed thee, in high heaven's despite,
　　　To shame the sun by day and her by night.

'And therefore hath she bribed the Destinies
To cross* the curious* workmanship of nature,　　thwart / elaborate
To mingle beauty with infirmities
And pure perfection with impure defeature;*　　disfigurement
　　Making it subject to the tyranny
　　　Of mad mischances and much misery;

'As burning fevers, agues pale and faint,
Life-poisoning pestilence and frenzies wood,*　　mad
The marrow-eating sickness, whose attaint*　　infection
Disorder breeds by heating of the blood:
　　Surfeits, imposthumes,* grief and damned despair,　　abscesses
　　　Swear Nature's death for framing thee so fair.

'And not the least of all these maladies
But in one minute's fight brings beauty under:
Both favour,* savour, hue and qualities,　　beauty
Whereat the impartial gazer late did wonder,
　　Are on the sudden wasted, thawed and done,
　　　As mountain snow melts with the midday sun.　　750

Diana. The goddess of the Moon; Cynthia was a personification of the Moon.

'Therefore, despite of fruitless chastity,
Love-lacking vestals and self-loving nuns,
That on the earth would breed a scarcity
And barren dearth of daughters and of sons,
　　Be prodigal: the lamp that burns by night
　　Dries up his oil to lend the world his light.

'What is thy body but a swallowing grave,
Seeming to bury that posterity
Which by the rights of time thou needs must have,
If thou destroy them not in dark obscurity?　　　　760
　　If so, the world will hold thee in disdain,
　　Sith* in thy pride so fair a hope is slain.　　　since

'So in thyself thyself art made away;
A mischief worse than civil home-bred strife,
Or theirs whose desperate hands themselves do slay
Or butcher-sire that reaves* his son of life.　　　bereaves
　　Foul cankering* rust the hidden treasure frets,*　　corroding /
　　But gold that's put to use more gold begets.'　　devours

'Nay, then,' quoth Adon, 'you will fall again
Into your idle* over-handled theme:　　　　useless
The kiss I gave you is bestowed in vain,
And all in vain you strive against the stream;
　　For, by this black-faced night, desire's foul nurse,
　　Your treatise* makes me like you worse and worse.　　discourse

'If love have lent you twenty thousand tongues,
And every tongue more moving than your own,
Bewitching like the wanton mermaid's songs,
Yet from mine ear the tempting tune is blown;
　　For know, my heart stands armèd in mine ear,
　　And will not let a false sound enter there;　　　780

'Lest the deceiving harmony should run
Into the quiet closure* of my breast;　　　enclosure
And then my little heart were quite undone,
In his bedchamber to be barred of rest.
　　No, lady, no; my heart longs not to groan,
　　But soundly sleeps, while now it sleeps alone.

'What have you urged that I cannot reprove?*   disprove
The path is smooth that leadeth on to danger:
I hate not love, but your device* in love   behavior when
That lends embracements unto every stranger.   790
   You do it for increase: O strange excuse,
   When reason is the bawd to lust's abuse!

'Call it not love, for Love to heaven is fled
Since sweating Lust on earth usurped his name;
Under whose simple semblance he hath fed
Upon fresh beauty, blotting it with blame;
   Which the hot tyrant stains and soon bereaves,
   As caterpillars do the tender leaves.

'Love comforteth like sunshine after rain,
But Lust's effect is tempest after sun;   800
Love's gentle spring doth always fresh remain,
Lust's winter comes ere summer half be done;
   Love surfeits not, Lust like a glutton dies;
   Love is all truth, Lust full of forgèd lies.

'More I could tell, but more I dare not say;
The text is old, the orator too green.*   inexperienced
Therefore, in sadness,* now I will away;   seriously
My face is full of shame, my heart of teen:*   vexation
   Mine ears, that to your wanton talk attended,
   Do burn themselves for having so offended.'   810

With this, he breaketh from the sweet embrace
Of those fair arms which bound him to her breast,
And homeward through the dark lawnd† runs apace;
Leaves Love upon her back deeply distressed.
   Look, how a bright star shooteth from the sky,
   So glides he in the night from Venus' eye:

Which after him she darts, as one on shore
Gazing upon a late-embarkèd friend,
Till the wild waves will have him seen no more,
Whose ridges with the meeting clouds contend: 820
   So did the merciless and pitchy night
   Fold in the object that did feed her sight.

Lawnd. An open space of untilled ground in a wood.

Whereat amazed, as one that unaware
Hath dropped a precious jewel in the flood,
Or 'stonished* as night-wanderers often are,   thunderstruck
Their light blown out in some mistrustful* wood;   causing mistrust
   Even so confounded in the dark she lay,
   Having lost the fair discovery of her way.

And now she beats her heart, whereat it groans,
That all the neighbour caves, as seeming troubled,   830
Make verbal repetition of her moans;
Passion* on passion deeply is redoubled: lament
   'Ay me!' she cries, and twenty times, 'Woe, woe!'
   And twenty echoes twenty times cry so.

She, marking them, begins a wailing note,
And sings extemporally a woeful ditty;
How love makes young men thrall,* and old men dote;   enslaved
How love is wise in folly, foolish-witty:
   Her heavy anthem still concludes in woe,
   And still the choir of echoes answer so.   840

Her song was tedious, and outwore* the night,   outlasted
For lovers' hours are long, though seeming short:
If pleased themselves, others, they think, delight
In such-like circumstance, with such-like sport:
   Their copious stories, oftentimes begun,
   End without audience, and are never done.

For who hath she to spend the night withal,
But idle sounds resembling parasites;
Like shrill-tongued tapsters answering every call,
Soothing the humour of fantastic* wits?   capricious
   She says ' 'Tis so:' they answer all ' 'Tis so;'
   And would say after her, if she said 'No.'

Lo, here the gentle lark, weary of rest,
From his moist cabinet* mounts up on high,   dwelling
And wakes the morning, from whose silver breast
The sun ariseth in his majesty;
   Who doth the world so gloriously behold,
   That cedar-tops and hills seem burnished gold.

Venus salutes him with this fair good-morrow:
'O thou clear* god, and .patron of all light,   unsullied
From whom each lamp and shining star doth borrow
The beauteous influence that makes him bright,
    There lives a son, that sucked an earthly mother,
    May lend thee light, as thou dost lend to other.'

This said, she hasteth to a myrtle grove,
Musing the morning is so much o'erworn,
And yet she hears no tidings of her love:
She hearkens for his hounds and for his horn:
    Anon she hears them chant it lustily,
    And all in haste she coasteth to the cry.*   approaches the baying

And as she runs, the bushes in the way
Some catch her by the neck, some kiss her face,
Some twine about her thigh to make her stay:
She wildly breaketh from their strict embrace,
    Like a milch doe, whose swelling dugs do ache,
    Hasting to feed her fawn hid in some brake.*   thicket

By this she hears the hounds are at a bay;†
Whereat she starts, like one that spies an adder
Wreathed up in fatal folds just in his way,
The fear whereof doth make him shake and shudder;   880
    Even so the timorous yelping of the hounds
    Appals her senses and her spirit cònfounds.*   confuses

For now she knows it is no gentle chase,
But the blunt* boar, rough bear, or lion proud,   rude
Because the cry remaineth in one place,
Where fearfully the dogs exclaim aloud:
    Finding their enemy to be so curst,
    They all strain courtesy† who shall cope* him first   encounter

This dismal cry rings sadly in her ear,
Through which it enters to surprise her heart;   890
Who, overcome by doubt and bloodless fear,
With cold-pale weakness numbs each feeling part:
    Like soldiers, when their captain once doth yield,
    They basely fly, and dare not stay the field.

The hounds are at a bay. The hounds are baying in a circle
round the exhausted boar.
They all strain courtesy. They all were courteous beyond reason.

Thus stands she in a trembling ecstasy;*   mad excitement
Till, cheering up her senses all dismayed,
She tells them 'tis a causeless fantasy,
And childish error, that they are afraid;
 Bids them leave quaking, bids them fear no more:
 And with that word she spied the hunted boar;   900

Whose frothy mouth, bepainted all with red,
Like milk and blood being mingled both together,
A second fear through all her sinews spread,
Which madly hurries her she knows not whither:
 This way she runs, and now she will no further,
 But back retires to rate* the boar for murther.   berate

A thousand spleens* bear her a thousand ways;   passions
She treads the path that she untreads again;
Her more than haste is mated* with delays,   confounded
Like the proceedings of a drunken brain,   910
 Full of respects,* yet nought at all respecting: considerations
 In hand with* all things, nought at all effecting.   busied with

Here kennelled in a brake* she finds a hound,   thicket
And asks the weary caitiff for his master;
And there another licking of his wound,
'Gainst venomed sores the only sovereign plaster;
 And here she meets another sadly scowling,
 To whom she speaks, and he replies with howling.

When he hath ceased his ill-resounding noise,
Another flap-mouthed* mourner, black and grim,   hanging-lipped
Against the welkin volleys out his voice;
Another and another answer him,
 Clapping their proud tails to the ground below,
 Shaking their scratched ears, bleeding as they go.

Look, how the world's poor people are amazed
At apparitions, signs and prodigies,
Whereon with fearful eyes they long have gazed,
Infusing* them with dreadful prophecies;   instilling
 So she at these sad signs draws up her breath,
 And, sighing it again, exclaims on* Death.   upbraids

'Hard-favoured tyrant, ugly, meagre, lean,
Hateful divorce of love,'—thus chides she Death,—
'Grim-grinning ghost, earth's worm,* what dost thou   serpent
   mean
To stifle beauty and to steal his breath,
  Who when he lived, his breath and beauty set
  Gloss on the rose, smell to the violet?

'If he be dead,—O no, it cannot be,
Seeing his beauty, thou shouldst strike at it;—
O yes, it may; thou hast no eyes to see,
But hatefully at random dost thou hit.   940
  Thy mark is feeble age; but thy false dart
  Mistakes that aim, and cleaves an infant's heart.

'Hadst thou but bid beware, then he had spoke,
And, hearing him, thy power had lost his power.
The Destinies will curse thee for this stroke;
They bid thee crop a weed, thou pluck'st a flower:
  Love's golden arrow at him should have fled,
  And not Death's ebon* dart, to strike him dead.   black

'Dost thou drink tears, that thou provokest such weeping?
What may a heavy groan advantage thee?   950
Why hast thou cast into eternal sleeping
Those eyes that taught all other eyes to see?
  Now nature cares not for thy mortal* vigour,   deadly
  Since her best work is ruined with thy rigour.'

Here overcome, as one full of despair,
She vailed* her eyelids, who, like sluices, stopped   let fall
The crystal tide that from her two cheeks fair
In the sweet channel of her bosom dropped;
  But through the flood-gates breaks the silver rain,
  And with his strong course opens them again.   960

O, how her eyes and tears did lend and borrow!
Her eye seen in the tears, tears in her eye;
Both crystals, where they viewed each other's sorrow,†
Sorrow that friendly sighs sought still to dry;
  But like a stormy day, now wind, now rain,
  Sighs dry her cheeks, tears make them wet again.

Both crystals, where they viewed each other's sorrow.
These were magic crystals in which one closely bound emotionally
to another is able to see scenes of his danger or even of his grief.

Variable passions throng her constant woe,
As striving who should best become her grief;
All entertained,* each passion labours so   considered
That every present sorrow seemeth chief,   970
   But none is best: then join they all together,
   Like many clouds consulting for foul weather.

By this, far off she hears some huntsman holloa;
A nurse's song ne'er pleased her babe so well:
The dire imagination she did follow
This sound of hope doth labour to expel;
   For now reviving joy bids her rejoice,
   And flatters her it is Adonis' voice.

Whereat her tears began to turn their tide,
Being prisoned in her eye like pearls in glass: 980
Yet sometimes falls an orient* drop beside,   shining
Which her cheek melts, as scorning it should pass
   To wash the foul face of the sluttish ground,
   Who is but drunken when she seemeth drowned.

O hard-believing love, how strange it seems
Not to believe, and yet too credulous!
Thy weal and woe are both of them extremes;
Despair, and hope, makes thee ridiculous:
   The one doth flatter thee in thoughts unlikely,
   In likely thoughts the other kills thee quickly.   990

Now she unweaves the web that she hath wrought;
Adonis lives, and Death is not to blame;
It was not she that called him all to nought:*   utterly worthless
Now she adds honours to his hateful name;
   She clepes* him king of graves, and grave for kings,   calls
   Imperious* supreme of all mortal things.   imperial

'No, no,' quoth she, 'sweet Death, I did but jest;
Yet pardon me, I felt a kind of fear
When as I met the boar, that bloody beast,
Which knows no pity, but is still severe;   1000
   Then, gentle shadow—truth I must confess—
   I railed on thee, fearing my love's decease.

' 'Tis not my fault: the boar provoked my tongue;
Be wreaked on him, invisible commander;
'Tis he, foul creature, that hath done thee wrong;
I did but act, he's author of thy slander:
    Grief hath two tongues; and never woman yet
    Could rule them both without ten women's wit.'

Thus hoping that Adonis is alive,
Her rash suspect* she doth extenuate;   suspicion
And that his beauty may the better thrive,
With Death she humbly doth insinuate;*   ingratiate herself
    Tells him of trophies,* statues, tombs, and   memorials of victory
        stories
    His victories, his triumphs and his glories.

'O Jove,' quoth she, 'how much a fool was I
To be of such a weak and silly mind
To wail his death who lives and must not die
Till mutual overthrow of mortal kind!
    For he being dead, with him is beauty slain,
    And, beauty dead, black chaos comes again.   1020

'Fie, fie, fond love, thou art so full of fear
As one with treasure laden, hemmed with thieves;
Trifles unwitnessed with eye or ear
Thy coward heart with false bethinking* grieves.'   regretting
    Even at this word she hears a merry horn,
    Whereat she leaps* that was but late forlorn.   i.e., for joy

As falcons to the lure,* away she flies;   i.e., his whistle
The grass stoops not, she treads on it so light;
And in her haste unfortunately spies
The foul boar's conquest on her fair delight;   1030
    Which seen, her eyes, as murdered with the view,
    Like stars ashamed of day, themselves withdrew;

Or, as the snail, whose tender horns being hit,
Shrinks backward in his shelly cave with pain,
And there all smothered up in shade doth sit,
Long after fearing to creep forth again;
    So, at his bloody view, her eyes are fled
    Into the deep-dark cabins of her head:

Where they resign their office and their light
To the disposing of her troubled brain;   1040
Who bids them still consort with ugly night,
And never wound the heart with looks again;
    Who, like a king perplexèd in his throne,
    By their suggestion gives a deadly groan,

Whereat each tributary subject quakes;
As when the wind, imprisoned in the ground,†
Struggling for passage, earth's foundation shakes,
Which with cold terror doth men's minds confound.
    This mutiny* each part doth so surprise,   tumult
    That from their dark beds once more leap her eyes.   1050

And being opened threw unwilling light
Upon the wide wound that the boar had trenched*   cut
In his soft flank; whose wonted lily white
With purple tears, that this wound wept, was drenched:
    No flower was nigh, no grass, herb, leaf or weed,
    But stole his blood and seemed with him to bleed.

This solemn sympathy poor Venus noteth;
Over one shoulder doth she hang her head;
Dumbly she passions,* franticly she doteth;   displays passion
She thinks he could not die, he is not dead: 1060
    Her voice is stopped, her joints forget to bow;
    Her eyes are mad that they have wept till now.

Upon his hurt she looks so steadfastly
That her sight dazzling makes the wound seem three;
And then she reprehends her mangling* eye,   seeing mutilation
That makes more gashes where no breach should be:
    His face seems twain, each several limb is doubled;
    For oft the eye mistakes, the brain being troubled.

'My tongue cannot express my grief for one,
And yet,' quoth she, 'behold two Adons dead!   1070
My sighs are blown away, my salt tears gone,
Mine eyes are turned to fire, my heart to lead:
    Heavy heart's lead, melt at mine eyes' red fire!
    So shall I die by drops of hot desire.

As when the wind, imprisoned in the ground.
A popular notion in Shakespeare's day was that earthquakes were caused
by wind struggling to find egress.

'Alas, poor world, what treasure hast thou lost!
What face remains alive that's worth the viewing?
Whose tongue is music now? what canst thou boast
Of things long since, or any thing ensuing?*   to follow
    The flowers are sweet, their colours fresh and trim;
    But true-sweet beauty lived and died with him.   1080

'Bonnet nor veil henceforth no creature wear!
Nor sun nor wind will ever strive to kiss you:
Having no fair* to lose, you need not fear;   beauty
The sun doth scorn you, and the wind doth hiss you:
    But when Adonis lived, sun and sharp air
    Lurked like two thieves, to rob him of his fair.*   fairness

'And therefore would he put his bonnet* on,   cap
Under whose brim the gaudy sun would peep;
The wind would blow it off, and, being gone,
Play with his locks: then would Adonis weep;   1090
    And straight, in pity of his tender years,
    They both would strive who first should dry his tears.

'To see his face the lion walked along
Behind some hedge, because he would not fear* him;   frighten
To recreate himself when he hath sung,
The tiger would be tame and gently hear him;
    If he had spoke, the wolf would leave his prey,
    And never fright the silly* lamb that day.   helpless

'When he beheld his shadow in the brook,
The fishes spread on it their golden gills;   1100
When he was by, the birds such pleasure took,
That some would sing, some other in their bills
    Would bring him mulberries and ripe-red cherries;
    He fed them with his sight, they him with berries.

'But this foul, grim, and urchin-snouted boar,
Whose downward eye still looketh for a grave,
Ne'er saw the beauteous livery that he wore;
Witness the entertainment* that he gave: reception
    If he did see his face, why then I know
    He thought to kiss him, and hath killed him so.   1110

' 'Tis true, 'tis true; thus was Adonis slain:
He ran upon the boar with his sharp spear,
Who did not whet his teeth at him again,
But by a kiss thought to persuade him there;
    And nuzzling in his flank, the loving swine
    Sheathed unaware the tusk in his soft groin.

'Had I been toothed like him, I must confess,
With kissing him I should have killed him first;
But he is dead, and never did he bless
My youth with his; the more am I accurst.'   1120
    With this, she falleth in the place she stood,
    And stains her face with his congealèd blood.

She looks upon his lips, and they are pale;
She takes him by the hand, and that is cold;
She whispers in his ears a heavy tale,
As if they heard the woeful words she told;
    She lifts the coffer*-lids that close his eyes,   treasure
    Where, lo, two lamps, burnt out, in darkness lies;

Two glasses, where herself herself beheld
A thousand times, and now no more reflect;   1130
Their virtue lost, wherein they late excelled,
And every beauty robbed of his effect:
    'Wonder of time,' quoth she, 'this is my spite,
    That, thou being dead, the day should yet be light.

'Since thou art dead, lo, here I prophesy,
Sorrow on love hereafter shall attend:
It shall be waited on with jealousy,
Find sweet beginning but unsavoury end;
    Ne'er settled equally, but high or low,
    That all love's pleasure shall not match his woe.   1140

'It shall be fickle, false and full of fraud;
Bud, and be blasted, in a breathing-while;*   time
The bottom poison, and the top o'erstrawed*   strewed over
With sweets that shall the truest sight beguile:
    The strongest body shall it make most weak,
    Strike the wise dumb, and teach the fool to speak.

'It shall be sparing and too full of riot,*   disorder
Teaching decrepit age to tread the measures;*   dance
The staring* ruffian shall it keep in quiet,   truculent
Pluck down the rich, enrich the poor with treasures;   1150
  It shall be raging-mad, and silly-mild,
  Make the young old, the old become a child.

'It shall suspect where is no cause of fear;
It shall not fear where it should most mistrust;
It shall be merciful and too severe,
And most deceiving when it seems most just;
  Perverse it shall be where it shows most toward,*   compliant
  Put fear to valour, courage to the coward.

'It shall be cause of war and dire events,
And set dissension 'twixt the son and sire;   1160
Subject and servile to all discontents,
As dry combustious matter is to fire:
  Sith* in his prime* death doth my love destroy,   since / spring
  They that love best their loves shall not enjoy.'

By this, the boy that by her side lay killed
Was melted like a vapour from her sight,
And in his blood, that on the ground lay spilled,
A purple flower sprung up, chequered with white,
  Resembling well his pale cheeks and the blood
  Which in round drops upon their whiteness stood.   1170

She bows her head, the new-sprung flower to smell,
Comparing it to her Adonis' breath;
And says, within her bosom it shall dwell,
Since he himself is reft from her by death:
  She crops* the stalk, and in the breach appears   cuts
  Green-dropping sap, which she compares to tears.

'Poor flower,' quoth she, 'this was thy father's guise—
Sweet issue of a more sweet-smelling sire—
For every little grief to wet his eyes:
To grow unto himself was his desire,   1180
  And so 'tis thine; but know, it is as good
  To wither in my breast as in his blood.

'Here was thy father's bed, here in my breast;
Thou art the next of blood, and 'tis thy right:
Lo, in this hollow cradle take thy rest;
My throbbing heart shall rock thee day and night:
   There shall not be one minute in an hour
   Wherein I will not kiss my sweet love's flower.'

Thus weary of the world, away she hies,
And yokes her silver doves; by whose swift aid   1190
Their mistress, mounted, through the empty skies
In her light chariot quickly is conveyed;
   Holding their course to Paphos,† where their queen
   Means to immure herself and not be seen.

Paphos. The ancient city of Cyprus is the seat of a
temple of Aphrodite (Venus).

THE RAPE OF LUCRECE

Some of Shakespeare's contemporaries took offense at the provocative eroticism of *Venus and Adonis*. The undergraduates who put the poem under their pillows were clearly youthful libertines. John Davies of Herefordshire was one of those who lamented the licentious tendency of the poem.

> Another (Ah Lord help me) vilifies
> With Art of Love, and how to subtilize,
> Making lewd Venus with eternal lines
> To tie Adonis to her love's designs.
> Fine wit is shew'n, but finer twere
> If not attired in such bawdy geare.

Possibly it was criticism of this sort that induced Shakespeare to compose a second poem that would establish the moral soundness of his Muse. To accomplish this result he chose a second story he found in Ovid, which, as he retold it, became an exaltation of chastity and an execration of lust.

Livy had presented the following events as semi-historical. Sextus Tarquinius, son of the King of Rome, having heard Lucrece's husband, Collatinus, boast of his wife's beauty and unassailable chastity, develops a wild passion for her. He leaves a siege at which he and Collatinus were fellow soldiers and goes to visit Lucrece in her palace. She receives him in the hospitable manner that is his due and assigns him a room in a wing of the building as remote as possible from her own quarters. In the dead of night Tarquinius steals along the corridors until he reaches her chamber. Once there, deaf to her appeals, he stifles her cries with the bedclothes and rapes her. The frantic Lucrece at once summons her father and husband, tells them what has happened and then stabs herself to death.

Shakespeare's version of the *Rape* displays the same obsession with rhetorical artifice that he had shown in *Venus and Adonis*. In fact, he devoted his invention much more amply to decoration of the story than to the theme itself. Vestiges of a dramatic structure remain in the poem. It depicts the fall of a prince and the disastrous career of a slave of passion. In some respects it is thus like a Senecan tragedy. To satisfy his lust

Tarquinius risks and loses everything—position, honor, and fame—and gains only disgust and despair. Lucrece is the helpless victim who arouses the same sort of pity and terror as does Desdemona.

Unfortunately Shakespeare's love of rhetoric or a taste for it in his readers buries his dramatic plan. Professor Douglas Bush's trenchant description of this result is: "Declamation roars, while passion sleeps." For example, when Tarquin stands beside Lucrece's bed, she devotes eighty lines to an attempt to dissuade him from his foul deed. After the rape has been committed, the poem becomes Lucrece's long iterative lament, in the course of which she compares her situation with that of Hecuba. This gives her a chance to paint an elaborate picture of Priam's Troy.

> Thus ebbs and flows the current of her sorrow
> And time doth weary time with her complaining.

She expresses her grief and despair not directly but by way of ingenious conceits. Line 1298 of the poem reads, "Conceit and grief an eager combat fight." And conceit is the inevitable victor.

Whatever beauty the modern reader can find in the poem will be in the music of sorrow that rings in many keys and in many modes as the verses accumulate. Lines 1493–4 read

> For sorrow, like a heavy-hanging bell
> Once set on ringing, with his own weight goes.

It is the incessant tolling of the bell behind all the rhetoric and tortured ingenuity of thought and language that gives the poem its occasional power and beauty.

This poem is written in a seven-line stanza called rhyme royal.

THE RAPE OF LUCRECE

From the besieged Ardea all in post,*   haste
Borne by the trustless wings of false desire,
Lust-breathèd Tarquin† leaves the Roman host,
And to Collatium bears the lightless fire,
Which, in pale embers hid, lurks to aspire,*   ascend
   And girdle with embracing flames the waist
   Of Collatine's† fair love, Lucrece the chaste.

Haply that name of 'chaste' unhappily set
This bateless* edge on his keen appetite;   unblunted
When Collatine unwisely did not let*   forbear
To praise the clear unmatchèd red and white
Which triumphed in that sky of his delight,
   Where mortal stars, as bright as heaven's beauties,*   *i.e.*, stars
   With pure aspects did him peculiar duties.

For he the night before, in Tarquin's tent,
Unlocked the treasure of his happy state;
What priceless wealth the heavens had him lent
In the possession of his beauteous mate;
Reckoning his fortune at such high-proud rate,
   That kings might be espousèd to more fame,   20
   But king nor peer to such a peerless dame.

O happiness enjoyed but of a few!
And, if possessed, as soon decayed and done*   consumed
As is the morning's silver-melting dew
Against the golden splendour of the sun!
An éxpired date, cancelled ere well begun:
   Honour and beauty, in the owner's arms,
   Are weakly fortressed from a world of harms.

Lust-breathèd Tarquin. Sextus Tarquinius, son of the King of
Rome, Tarquinius Superbus. He lost his throne in 510 B.C.
Collatine. Collatinus, the noble husband of Lucretia (Lucrece).

Beauty itself doth of itself persuade
The eyes of men without an orator;   30
What needeth then apologies* be made,   defense
To set forth that which is so singular?
Or why is Collatine the publisher*   proclaimer
   Of that rich jewel he should keep unknown
   From thievish ears, because it is his own?

Perchance his boast of Lucrece's sovereignty
Suggested* this proud issue of a king;   tempted
For by our ears our hearts oft tainted be:
Perchance that envy of so rich a thing,
Braving* compare, disdainfully did sting   challenging
   His high-pitched thoughts, that meaner men should
     vaunt*   boast
   That golden hap* which their superiors want.   luck

But some untimely thought did instigate
His all-too-timeless speed, if none of those:
His honour, his affairs, his friends, his state,*   position
Neglected all, with swift intent he goes
To quench the coal which in his liver* glows.   the seat of desire
   O rash-false heat, wrapped in repentant cold,
   Thy hasty spring still blasts,* and ne'er   suffers blight
     grows old!

When at Collatium this false lord arrived,   50
Well was he welcomed by the Roman dame,
Within whose face beauty and virtue strived
Which of them both should underprop her fame:
When virtue bragged, beauty would blush for shame;
   When beauty boasted blushes, in despite
   Virtue would stain that o'er with silver white.

But beauty, in that white intituled,*   blazoned
From Venus' doves doth challenge that fair field:†
Then virtue claims from beauty beauty's red,*   i.e., blushes
Which virtue gave the golden age to gild   60
Their silver cheeks, and called it then their shield;
   Teaching them thus to use it in the fight,
   When shame assailed, the red should fence* the   shield
     white.†

Doth challenge that fair field. Disputes beauty's exclusive right to the field.
The red should fence the white. In heraldry white betokens innocence.
The line means, Beauty should shield innocence.

This heraldry in Lucrece's face was seen,
Argued by beauty's red and virtue's white:
Of either's colour was the other queen,
Proving from world's minority their right:†
Yet their ambition makes them still to fight;
   The sovereignty of either being so great,
   That oft they interchange each other's seat.   70

This silent war of lilies and of roses,
Which Tarquin viewed in her fair face's field,
In their pure ranks his traitor eye encloses;
Where, lest between them both it should be killed,
The coward captive vanquishèd doth yield
   To those two armies, that would let him go
   Rather than triumph in so false a foe.

Now thinks he that her husband's shallow tongue,
The niggard prodigal that praised her so,
In that high task hath done her beauty wrong,   80
Which far exceeds his barren skill to show:
Therefore that praise which Collatine doth owe*   own
   Enchanted Tarquin answers with surmise,
   In silent wonder of still-gazing eyes.

This earthly saint, adorèd by this devil,
Little suspecteth the false worshipper;
For unstained thoughts do seldom dream on evil;
Birds never limed* no secret bushes fear: snared by bird lime
So guiltless she securely* gives good cheer   without anxiety
   And reverend welcome to her princely guest,   90
   Whose inward ill no outward harm expressèd:

For that he coloured with his high estate,
Hiding base sin in plaits* of majesty;   folds (of a robe)
That nothing in him seemed inordinate,
Save sometime too much wonder of his eye,
Which, having all, all could not satisfy;
   But, poorly rich, so wanteth in his store,
   That, cloyed with much, he pineth still for more.

Proving from world's minority their right.
This refers back to the golden age of the world's infancy
when virtue had red to bestow as a gift.

But she, that never coped* with stranger eyes,   encountered
Could pick no meaning from their parling* looks,   speaking
Nor read the subtle-shining secrecies
Writ in the glassy margents* of such books: margins
She touched no unknown baits, nor feared no hooks;
　　Nor could she moralize his wanton sight,†
　　More than his eyes were opened to the light.

He stories to her ears her husband's fame,
Won in the fields of fruitful Italy;
And decks with praises Collatine's high name,
Made glorious by his manly chivalry
With bruisèd arms* and wreaths of victory: dented armor
　　Her joy with heaved-up* hand she doth express,   uplifted
　　And wordless so greets heaven for his success.

Far from the purpose of his coming hither,
He makes excuses for his being there:
No cloudy show of stormy blustering weather
Doth yet in his fair welkin* once appear;   sky
Till sable Night, mother of dread and fear,
　　Upon the world dim darkness doth display,
　　And in her vaulty prison stows* the day.   i.e., hides

For then is Tarquin brought unto his bed.   120
Intending* weariness with heavy spright;*   pretending / spirit
For after supper long he questionèd*   conversed
With modest Lucrece, and wore out the night:
Now leaden slumber with life's strength doth fight;
　　And every one to rest themselves betake,
　　Save thieves and cares and troubled minds that wake.

As one of which doth Tarquin lie revolving
The sundry dangers of his will's* obtaining;   desire's
Yet ever to obtain his will resolving,
Though weak-built hopes persuade him to abstaining: 130
Despair to gain doth traffic oft for gaining,
　　And when great treasure is the meed* proposed,   reward
　　Though death be adjunct,* there's no death   a consequence
　　　supposed.

Nor could she moralize his wanton sight.
Nor could she detect immoral significance in his lewd glances.

Those that much covet are with gain so fond*   foolishly eager
That what they have not, that which they possess,
They scatter and unloose it from their bond,
And so, by hoping more, they have but less;
Or, gaining more, the profit* of excess   advantage
  Is but to surfeit, and such griefs sustain,
    That they prove bankrupt in this poor-rich gain.   140

The aim of all is but to nurse the life
With honour, wealth and ease, in waning age;
And in this aim there is such thwarting strife
That one for all or all for one we gage;*   risk
As life for honour in fell battle's rage;
  Honour for wealth; and oft that wealth doth cost
    The death of all, and all together lost.*   i.e., the loss of all

So that in venturing ill* we leave to be   making a bad
The things we are for that which we expect;   investment
And this ambitious foul infirmity,   150
In having much, torments us with defect
Of that we have: so then we do neglect
  The thing we have, and, all for want of wit,
    Make something nothing by augmenting it.†

Such hazard now must doting Tarquin make,
Pawning his honour to obtain his lust;
And for himself himself he must forsake:
Then where is truth, if there be no self-trust?
When shall he think to find a stranger just,
  When he himself himself confounds,* betrays   destroys
    To slanderous tongues and wretched hateful days?

Now stole upon the time the dead of night,
When heavy sleep had closed up mortal eyes:
No comfortable* star did lend his light,   comforting
No noise but owls' and wolves' death-boding* cries;   foreboding
Now serves the season that they may surprise
  The silly* lambs: pure thoughts are dead and still,   harmless
    While lust and murder wakes to stain and kill.

These three stanzas are typical of the author's method in the poem.
He continually interrupts his narrative with moral reflection.

And now this lustful lord leaped from his bed,
Throwing his mantle rudely o'er his arm;   170
Is madly tossed between desire and dread;
Th' one sweetly flatters, th' other feareth harm;
But honest fear, bewitched with lust's foul charm,
    Doth too too oft betake him to retire,*   retreat
    Beaten away by brain-sick rude desire.

His falchion* on a flint he softly smiteth,   sword
That from the cold stone sparks of fire do fly;
Whereat a waxen torch forthwith he lighteth,
Which must be lode-star* to his lustful eye;   guiding star
And to the flame thus speaks advisedly:*   deliberately
    'As from this cold flint I enforced this fire,
    So Lucrece must I force to my desire.'

Here pale with fear he doth premeditate
The dangers of his loathsome enterprise,
And in his inward mind he doth debate
What following sorrow may on this arise:
Then looking scornfully he doth despise
    His naked armour of still-slaughtered lust,
    And justly thus controls his thoughts unjust:

'Fair torch, burn out thy light, and lend it not   190
To darken her whose light excelleth thine:
And die, unhallowed thoughts, before you blot
With your uncleanness that which is divine:
Offer pure incense to so pure a shrine:
    Let fair humanity abhor the deed
    That spots and stains love's modest snow-white weed.* garment

'O shame to knighthood and to shining arms!
O foul dishonour to my household's grave!†
O impious act, including all foul harms!
A martial man to be soft fancy's* slave!   light love's
True valour still a true respect* should have;   consideration
    Then my digression* is so vile, so base,   offense
    That it will live engraven in my face.

O foul dishonour to my household's grave!
Dishonor to the mortuary chapel of my family, where
the escutcheons of my ancestors are displayed.

'Yea, though I die, the scandal will survive,
And be an eye-sore in my golden coat;
Some loathsome dash* the herald will contrive,   mask of disgrace
To cipher* me how fondly I did dote;   describe
That my posterity, shamed with the note,*   infamy
     Shall curse my bones, and hold it for no sin
     To wish that I their father had not been.   210

'What win I, if I gain the thing I seek?
A dream, a breath, a froth of fleeting joy.
Who buys a minute's mirth to wail a week?
Or sells eternity to get a toy?*   trifle
For one sweet grape who will the vine destroy?
     Or what fond* beggar, but to touch the crown,   foolish
     Would with the sceptre straight be strucken down?

'If Collatinus dream of my intent,
Will he not wake, and in a desperate rage
Post hither, this vile purpose to prevent?   220
This siege that hath engirt his marriage,
This blur to youth, this sorrow to the sage,
     This dying virtue, this surviving shame,
     Whose crime will bear an ever-during* blame.   everlasting

'O what excuse can my invention make,
When thou shalt charge me with so black a deed?
Will not my tongue be mute, my frail joints shake,
Mine eyes forgo their light, my false heart bleed?
The guilt being great, the fear doth still exceed;*   is excessive
     And extreme fear can neither fight nor fly,   230
     But coward-like with trembling terror die.

'Had Collatinus killed my son or sire,
Or lain in ambush to betray my life,
Or were he not my dear friend, this desire
Might have excuse to work upon his wife,
As in revenge or quittal* of such strife: requital
     But as he is my kinsman, my dear friend,
     The shame and fault finds no excuse nor end.

'Shameful it is; ay, if the fact be known:
Hateful it is; there is no hate in loving: 240
I'll beg her love; but she is not her own:
The worst is but denial and reproving:
My will* is strong, past reason's weak removing.   passion
   Who fears a sentence or an old man's saw*   maxim
   Shall by a painted cloth be kept in awe.'†

Thus graceless holds he disputation
'Tween frozen conscience and hot-burning will,*   desire
And with good thoughts makes dispensation,
Urging the worser sense for vantage still;
Which in a moment doth confound* and kill   destroy
   All pure effects, and doth so far proceed
   That what is vile shows like a virtuous deed.

Quoth he, 'She took me kindly by the hand,
And gazed for tidings in my eager eyes,
Fearing some hard news from the warlike band,
Where her belovèd Collatinus lies.
O, how her fear did make her colour rise!
   First red as roses that on lawn* we lay,   fine linen
   Then white as lawn, the roses took* away.   being taken

'And how her hand, in my hand being locked,   260
Forced it to tremble with her loyal fear!
Which struck her sad,† and then it faster rocked,
Until her husband's welfare she did hear;
Whereat she smiled with so sweet a cheer*   expression
   That had Narcissus† seen her as she stood
   Self-love had never drowned him in the flood.

Shall by a painted cloth be kept in awe.
Moral maxims were often wrought into tapestries or painted cloths.
Which struck her sad. "Which," i.e., the fact that Tarquin's
hand trembled like that of a bearer of bad news.
That had Narcissus seen her as she stood.
In Greek myth Narcissus, in seeing his likeness in a pool, fell in love
with it, and, pining away, died for love of himself.

'Why hunt I then for colour* or excuses?   pretexts
All orators are dumb when beauty pleadeth;
Poor wretches have remorse in poor abuses;
Love thrives not in the heart that shadows dreadeth: 270
Affection is my captain, and he leadeth;
   And when his gaudy banner is displayed,
    The coward fights, and will not be dismayed.

'Then, childish fear avaunt! debating die!
Respect and reason wait on wrinkled age!
My heart shall never countermand mine eye:
Sad pause and deep regard beseems the sage;
My part is youth, and beats these from the stage:
   Desire my pilot is, beauty my prize;
    Then who fears sinking where such treasure lies?'   280

As corn* o'ergrown by weeds, so heedful fear   grain
Is almost choked by unresisted lust;
Away he steals with open listening ear,
Full of foul hope and full of fond mistrust;
Both which, as servitors to the unjust,
   So cross him with their opposite persuasion,
    That now he vows a league,† and now invasion.

Within his thought her heavenly image sits,
And in the self-same seat sits Collatine:
That eye which looks on her confounds
    his wits;*   defeats his reason
That eye which him beholds, as more divine,
Unto a view so false will not incline;
   But with a pure appeal seeks to the heart,
    Which once corrupted takes the worser part;

And therein heartens up his servile powers,
Who, flattered by their leader's jocund show,
Stuff up his lust, as minutes fill up hours;
And as their captain,* so their pride doth grow,   i.e., corrupted heart
Paying more slavish tribute than they owe.
   By reprobate desire thus madly led,   300
    The Roman lord marcheth to Lucrece's bed.

That now he vows a league, and now invasion.
League signifies a treaty of peace between hope and mistrust,
which will result in his giving up his enterprise.

The locks between her chamber and his will,
Each one by him enforced,* retires his ward;*   forced / bolt
But, as they open, they all rate* his ill,   chide
Which drives the creeping thief to some regard:
The threshold grates* the door to have him*   rasp /
    heard;   cause him to be
  Night-wandering weasels shriek to see him there;
  They fright him, yet he still pursues his fear.

As each unwilling portal yields him way,
Through little vents and crannies of the place   310
The wind wars with his torch to make him stay,
And blows the smoke of it into his face,
Extinguishing his conduct* in this case;   *i.e.*, torch
  But his hot heart, which fond desire doth scorch,
  Puffs forth another wind that fires the torch:

And being lighted, by the light he spies
Lucretia's glove, wherein her needle sticks:
He takes it from the rushes† where it lies,
And griping* it, the needle his finger pricks;   seizing
As who should say 'This glove to wanton tricks   320
  Is not inured; return again in haste;
  Thou see'st our mistress' ornaments are chaste.'

But all these poor forbiddings could not stay him;
He in the worst sense cònstrues their denial:
The doors, the wind, the glove, that did delay him,
He takes for accidental things of trial;
Or as those bars which stop the hourly dial,*   timepiece
  Who* with a lingering stay his course doth let,*   which (*i.e.*,
  Till every minute pays the hour his debt.   bars) / delay

'So, so,' quoth he, 'these lets attend the time,   330
Like little frosts that sometime threat the spring,
To add a more rejoicing to the prime,*   spring
And give the sneaped* birds more cause to sing.   frostbitten
Pain pays the income of each precious thing;
  Huge rocks, high winds, strong pirates, shelves*   ledges
    and sands,
  The merchant fears, ere rich at home he lands.'

He takes it from the rushes where it lies.
Rushes or sweet-smelling herbs were often substituted
for carpets in Elizabethan houses.

Now is he come unto the chamber door,
That shuts him from the heaven of his thought,
Which with a yielding latch, and with no more,
Hath barred him from the blessèd thing he sought.
So from* himself impiety hath wrought,   340
   That for his prey to pray he doth begin,   unlike
   As if the heavens should countenance his sin.

But in the midst of his unfruitful prayer,
Having solicited the eternal power
That his foul thoughts might compass his fair fair,
And they would stand auspicious to the hour,
Even there he starts:* quoth he, 'I must deflower: shrinks back
   The powers to whom I pray abhor this fact;*   deed
   How can they then assist me in the act?   350

'Then Love and Fortune be my gods, my guide!
My will is backed with resolution:
Thoughts are but dreams till their effects be tried;
The blackest sin is cleared with absolution;
Against love's fire fear's frost hath dissolution.
   The eye of heaven* is out, and misty night   i.e., the sun
   Covers the shame that follows sweet delight.'

This said, his guilty hand plucked up the latch,
And with his knee the door he opens wide.
The dove sleeps fast that this night-owl will catch: 360
Thus treason works ere traitors be espied.
Who sees the lurking serpent steps aside;
   But she, sound sleeping, fearing no such thing,
   Lies at the mercy of his mortal sting.

Into the chamber wickedly he stalks
And gazeth on her yet unstainèd bed.
The curtains being close, about he walks,
Rolling his greedy eyeballs in his head:
By their high treason is his heart misled;
   Which gives the watch-word to his hand full soon   370
   To draw* the cloud that hides the silver moon.   draw aside

Look, as the fair and fiery-pointed sun,
Rushing from forth a cloud, bereaves our sight;
Even so, the curtain drawn, his eyes begun
To wink,* being blinded with a greater light: shut
    Whether it is that she reflects so bright,
      That dazzleth them, or else some shame supposed;
      But blind they are, and keep themselves enclosed.

O, had they in that darksome prison died!
Then had they seen the period* of their ill;   end
Then Collatine again, by Lucrece' side,
In his clear bed might have reposèd still:
    But they must ope, this blessed league to kill;
      And holy-thoughted Lucrece to their sight
      Must sell her joy, her life, her world's delight.

Her lily hand her rosy cheek lies under,
Cozening* the pillow of a lawful kiss;   cheating
Who, therefore angry, seems to part in sunder,
Swelling on either side to want his bliss;
    Between whose hills her head entombèd is: 390
      Where, like a virtuous monument, she lies,
      To be admired of lewd unhallowed eyes.

Without the bed her other fair hand was,
On the green coverlet; whose perfect white
Showed like an April daisy on the grass,
With pearly sweat, resembling dew of night.
    Her eyes, like marigolds, had sheathed their light,
      And canopied in darkness sweetly lay,
      Till they might open to adorn the day.

Her hair, like golden threads, played with her breath;   400
O modest wantons! wanton modesty!
Showing life's triumph in the map* of death,   picture
And death's dim look in life's mortality:
    Each in her sleep themselves so beautify
      As if between them twain there were no strife,
      But that life lived in death and death in life.

Her breasts, like ivory globes circlèd with blue,
A pair of maiden worlds unconquerèd,
Save of their lord no bearing yoke they knew,
And him by oath they truly honourèd.
These worlds in Tarquin new ambition bred;   410
    Who, like a foul usurper, went about*   undertook
    From this fair throne to heave* the owner out.   thrust

What could he see but mightily he noted?
What did he note but strongly he desired?
What he beheld, on that he firmly doted,
And in his will* his wilful eye he tired.   desire
With more than admiration he admired
    Her azure veins, her alabaster skin,
    Her coral lips, her snow-white dimpled chin.   420

As the grim lion fawneth o'er his prey,
Sharp hunger by the conquest satisfied,
So o'er this sleeping soul doth Tarquin stay,
His rage of lust by gazing qualified;*   moderated
Slacked, not suppressed; for standing by her side,
    His eye, which late this mutiny restrains,
    Unto a greater uproar tempts his veins:

And they, like straggling slaves for pillage fighting,
Obdurate vassals fell exploits effecting,
In bloody death and ravishment delighting,   430
Nor children's tears nor mothers' groans respecting,
Swell in their pride, the onset still expecting:
    Anon his beating heart, alarum* striking,   call to arms
    Gives the hot charge, and bids them do their liking.

His drumming heart cheers up his burning eye,
His eye commends* the leading to his hand;   entrusts
His hand, as proud of such a dignity,
Smoking* with pride, marched on to make his stand   observing
On her bare breast, the heart of all her land;   closely
    Whose ranks of blue veins, as his hand did scale,   440
    Left their round turrets destitute and pale.

They, mustering to the quiet cabinet
Where their dear governess and lady lies,
Do tell her she is dreadfully beset,
And fright her with confusion of their cries:
She, much amazed, breaks ope her locked-up eyes,
    Who, peeping forth this tumult to behold,
    Are by his flaming torch dimmed and controlled.

Imagine her as one in dead of night
From forth dull sleep by dreadful fancy waking,   450
That thinks she hath beheld some ghastly sprite,
Whose grim aspèct sets every joint a-shaking;
What terror 'tis! but she, in worser taking,*   plight
    From sleep disturbed, heedfully doth view
    The sight which makes supposed terror true.

Wrapped and confounded in a thousand fears,
Like to a new-killed bird she trembling lies;
She dares not look; yet, winking,* there appears   closing her eyes
Quick-shifting antics,* ugly in her eyes: fantastic shapes
Such shadows* are the weak brain's forgeries;   forms
    Who, angry that the eyes fly from their lights,
    In darkness daunts them with more dreadful sights.

His hand, that yet remains upon her breast,—
Rude ram, to batter such an ivory wall!—
May feel her heart, poor citizen! distressed,
Wounding itself to death, rise up and fall,
Beating her bulk,* that his hand shakes withal.   i.e., body
    This moves in him more rage and lesser pity,
    To make the breech and enter this sweet city.

First, like a trumpet, doth his tongue begin   470
To sound a parley to his heartless* foe;   spiritless
Who o'er the white sheet peers her whiter chin,
The reason of this rash alarm to know,
Which he by dumb demeanour seeks to show;
    But she with vehement prayers urgeth still
    Under what colour* he commits this ill.   pretext

Thus he replies: 'The colour in thy face,
That even for anger makes the lily pale
And the red rose blush at her own disgrace,
Shall plead for me and tell my loving tale: 480
Under that colour am I come to scale
   Thy never-conquered fort: the fault is thine,
   For those thine eyes betray thee unto mine.

'Thus I forestall thee, if thou mean to chide:
Thy beauty hath ensnared thee to this night,
Where thou with patience must my will abide;
My will that marks thee for my earth's delight,
Which I to conquer sought with all my might;
   But as reproof and reason beat it dead,
   By thy bright beauty was it newly bred.   490

'I see what crosses my attempt will bring;
I know what thorns the growing rose defends;
I think the honey guarded with a sting;
All this beforehand counsel comprehends:
But will is deaf and hears no heedful friends;
   Only he hath an eye to gaze on beauty,
   And dotes on what he looks, 'gainst law or duty.

'I have debated, even in my soul,
What wrong, what shame, what sorrow I shall breed;
But nothing can affection's* course control,   desire's
Or stop the headlong fury of his speed.
I know repentant tears ensue the deed,
   Reproach, disdain and deadly enmity;
   Yet strive I to embrace mine infamy.'

This said, he shakes aloft his Roman blade,
Which, like a falcon towering in the skies,
Coucheth* the fowl below with his wings' shade,   makes couch
Whose crooked beak threats if he mount he dies:
So under his insulting falchion lies
   Harmless Lucretia, marking what he tells   510
   With trembling fear, as fowl hear falcon's bells.†

With trembling fear, as fowl hear falcon's bells.
When the trained hawk pounces on its prey, the bells
attached to it sound the approaching danger.

'Lucrece,' quoth he, 'this night I must enjoy thee:
If thou deny, then force must work my way,
For in thy bed I purpose to destroy thee:
That done, some worthless slave of thine I'll slay,
To kill thine honour with thy life's decay;
   And in thy dead arms do I mean to place him,
   Swearing I slew him, seeing thee embrace him.

'So thy surviving husband shall remain
The scornful mark of every open eye;   520
Thy kinsmen hang their heads at this disdain,
Thy issue blurred with nameless bastardy:
And thou, the author of their obloquy,
   Shalt have thy trespass cited up in rhymes
   And sung by children in succeeding times.

'But if thou yield, I rest thy secret friend:
The fault unknown is as a thought unacted;
A little harm done to a great good end
For lawful policy remains enacted.
The poisonous simple* sometime is compacted   medicinal plant
   In a pure compound; being so applied,
   His venom in effect is purified.

'Then, for thy husband and thy children's sake,
Tender* my suit: bequeath not to their lot   deal kindly with
The shame that from them no device can take,
The blemish that will never be forgot;
Worse than a slavish wipe* or birth-hour's blot:*   brand /
   For marks descried in men's nativity   birthmark
   Are nature's faults, not their own infamy.'

Here with a cockatrice' dead-killing eye†   540
He rouseth up himself, and makes a pause;
While she, the picture of true piety,
Like a white hind under the gripe's* sharp claws,†   griffin
Pleads, in a wilderness where are no laws,
   To the rough beast that knows no gentle right,
   Nor aught obeys but his foul appetite.

Here with a cockatrice' dead-killing eye.
A cockatrice was a baselisk, a fabled serpent
whose glance was supposed to kill.

Under the gripe's sharp claws. The griffin here referred to is not the
mythical creature, half eagle and half lion, but a vulture, so named
because of his fancied resemblance to the monster.

But when a black-faced cloud the world doth threat,
In his dim mist the aspiring mountains hiding,
From earth's dark womb some gentle gust doth get,
Which blows these pitchy vapours from their biding,   550
Hindering their present fall by this dividing;
   So his unhallowed haste her words delays,
   And moody Pluto winks* while Orpheus plays.†   shuts his eyes

Yet, foul night-waking cat, he doth but dally,
While in his hold-fast foot the weak mouse panteth:
Her sad behaviour feeds his vulture folly,
A swallowing gulf that even in plenty wanteth:*   is in want
His ear her prayers admits, but his heart granteth
   No penetrable entrance to her plaining:*   complaining
   Tears harden lust, though marble wear with raining.   560

Her pity-pleading eyes are sadly fixed
In the remorseless* wrinkles of his face;   pitiless
Her modest eloquence with sighs is mixed,
Which to her oratory adds more grace.
She puts the period often from his* place,   its
   And midst the sentence so her accent breaks
   That twice she doth begin ere once she speaks.

She conjures him by high almighty Jove,
By knighthood, gentry,* and sweet friendship's oath,   high birth
By her untimely* tears, her husband's love,   inopportune
By holy human law and common troth,
By heaven and earth, and all the power of both,
   That to his borrowed bed he make retire,
   And stoop to honour, not to foul desire.

Quoth she: 'Reward not hospitality
With such black payment as thou hast pretended;*   intended
Mud not the fountain that gave drink to thee;
Mar not the thing that cannot be amended;
End thy ill aim before thy shoot* be ended;   shot
   He is no woodman* that doth bend his bow   sportsman
   To strike a poor unseasonable* doe.   out of season

And moody Pluto winks while Orpheus plays.
Orpheus was a celebrated bard in Greek religion. When his wife
the nymph Eurydice died, he went to Hades in search of her.
Pluto, charmed by his music, returned his wife to him.

'My husband is thy friend; for his sake spare me:
Thyself art mighty; for thine own sake leave me:
Myself a weakling; do not then ensnare me:
Thou look'st not like deceit; do not deceive me.
My sighs, like whirlwinds, labour hence to heave* thee: thrust
     If ever man were moved with woman's moans,
     Be movèd with my tears, my sighs, my groans:

'All which together, like a troubled ocean,
Beat at thy rocky and wreck-threatening heart,   590
To soften it with their continual motion;
For stones dissolved to water do convert.*   change their substance
O, if no harder than a stone thou art,
     Melt at my tears, and be compassionate!
     Soft pity enters at an iron gate.

'In Tarquin's likeness I did entertain thee:
Hast thou put on his shape to do him shame?
To all the host of heaven I complain me,
Thou wrong'st his honour, wound'st his princely name.
Thou art not what thou seem'st; and if the same,   600
     Thou seem'st not what thou art, a god, a king;
     For kings, like gods, should govern* every thing.   control

How will thy shame be seeded in thine age,
When thus thy vices bud before thy spring!
If in thy hope thou darest do such outrage,
What darest thou not when once thou art a king?
O, be remembered,* no outrageous thing   reminded
     From vassal actors* can be wiped away;   subjects who act
     Then kings' misdeeds cannot be hid in clay.

'This deed will make thee only loved for fear;   610
But happy monarchs still are feared for love:
With foul offenders thou perforce must bear,
When they in thee the like offences prove:
If but for fear of this, thy will* remove;   passion
     For princes are the glass, the school, the book,
     Where subjects' eyes do learn, do read, do look.

'And wilt thou be the school where Lust shall learn?
Must he in thee read lectures of such shame?
Wilt thou be glass wherein it shall discern
Authority for sin, warrant for blame,   620
To privilege dishonour in thy name?
    Thou back'st* reproach against long-living laud,*   prefer /
    And makest fair reputation but a bawd.   praise

'Hast thou command? by him that gave it thee,
From a pure heart command thy rebel will:
Draw not thy sword to guard iniquity,
For it was lent thee all that brood to kill.
Thy princely office how canst thou fulfil,
    When, patterned* by thy fault, foul sin may say   using as a
    He learned to sin and thou didst teach the way?   precedent
                                                            630

'Think but how vile a spectacle it were,
To view thy present trespass in another.
Men's faults do seldom to themselves appear;
Their own transgressions partially* they smother: by being partial
This guilt would seem death-worthy in thy brother.
    O, how are they wrapped in with infamies
    That from their own misdeeds askance* their eyes!   turn aside

'To thee, to thee, my heaved-up hands appeal,
Not to seducing lust, thy rash relier:
I sue for exiled majesty's repeal;*   recall
Let him return, and flattering thoughts retire:
His true respect will prison false desire,
    And wipe the dim mist from thy doting eyne,
    That thou shalt see thy state and pity mine.'

'Have done,' quoth he: 'my uncontrollèd tide
Turns not, but swells the higher by this let.
Small lights are soon blown out, huge fires abide,
And with the wind in greater fury fret:
The petty streams that pay a daily debt
    To their salt sovereign, with their fresh falls' haste   650
    Add to his flow, but alter not his taste.'

'Thou art,' quoth she, 'a sea, a sovereign king;
And, lo, there falls into thy boundless flood
Black lust, dishonour, shame, misgoverning,
Who seek to stain the ocean of thy blood.
If all these petty ills shall change thy good,
    Thy sea within a puddle's womb is hearsed,*   coffined
    And not the puddle in thy sea dispersed.

'So shall these slaves be king, and thou their slave;
Thou nobly base, they basely dignified;   660
Thou their fair life, and they thy fouler grave:
Thou loathèd in their shame, they in thy pride:*   lust
The lesser thing should not the greater hide;
    The cedar stoops not to the base shrub's foot,
    But low shrubs wither at the cedar's root.

'So let thy thoughts, low vassals to thy state'—
'No more,' quoth he; 'by heaven, I will not hear thee:
Yield to my love; if not, enforcèd hate,
Instead of love's coy* touch, shall rudely tear thee: caressing
That done, despitefully* I mean to bear thee   maliciously
    Unto the base bed of some rascal groom,*   manservant
    To be thy partner in this shameful doom.'

This said, he sets his foot upon the light,
For light and lust are deadly enemies:
Shame folded up in blind concealing night,
When most unseen, then most doth tyrannize.
The wolf hath seized his prey, the poor lamb cries;
    Till with her own white fleece her voice controlled* restrained
    Entombs her outcry in her lips' sweet fold:

For with the nightly linen that she wears   680
He pens her piteous clamours in her head,
Cooling his hot face in the chastest tears
That ever modest eyes with sorrow shed.
O, that prone* lust should stain so pure a bed!   prostrate
    The spots whereof could weeping purify,
    Her tears should drop on them perpetually.

But she hath lost a dearer thing than life,
And he hath won what he would lose again:
This forcèd league doth force a further strife;
This momentary joy breeds months of pain;   690
This hot desire converts to cold disdain:
   Pure Chastity is rifled of her store,
    And Lust, the thief, far poorer than before.

Look, as the full-fed hound or gorgèd hawk,
Unapt for tender smell or speedy flight,
Make slow pursuit, or altogether balk*   miss
The prey wherein by nature they delight,
So surfeit-taking Tarquin fares this night:
   His taste delicious, in digestion souring,
    Devours his will, that lived by foul devouring.   700

O, deeper sin than bottomless conceit*   imagination
Can comprehend in still imagination!
Drunken Desire must vomit his receipt,*   what he takes in
Ere he can see his own abomination.
While Lust is in his pride,* no exclamation*   in heat / reproach
   Can curb his heat or rein his rash desire,
    Till, like a jade, Self-will himself doth tire.

And then with lank and lean discoloured cheek,
With heavy eye, knit brow, and strengthless pace,
Feeble Desire, all recreant, poor and meek,   710
Like to a bankrupt beggar wails his case:
The flesh being proud,* Desire doth fight with Grace,   passionate
   For there it revels, and when that decays
    The guilty rebel for remission prays.

So fares it with this faultful lord of Rome,
Who this accomplishment* so hotly chased;   fulfillment
For now against himself he sounds this doom,
That through the length of times he stands disgraced:
Besides, his soul's fair temple is defaced,
   To whose weak ruins muster troops of cares,   720
    To ask the spotted princess how she fares.

She says, her subjects with foul insurrection
Have battered down her consecrated wall,
And by their mortal fault brought in subjection
Her immortality, and made her thrall
To living death and pain perpetual:
    Which in her prescience she controllèd still,
    But her foresight could not forestall their will.

Even in this thought through the dark night he stealeth,
A captive victor that hath lost in gain;   730
Bearing away the wound that nothing healeth,
The scar that will, despite of cure, remain;
Leaving his spoil* perplexed in greater pain.   prey
    She bears the load of lust he left behind,
    And he the burthen of a guilty mind.

He like a thievish dog creeps sadly thence;
She like a wearied lamb lies panting there;
He scowls, and hates himself for his offence;
She, desperate, with her nails her flesh doth tear;
He faintly flies, sweating with guilty fear;
    She stays, exclaiming on* the direful night;   denouncing
    He runs, and chides his vanished, loathed delight.

He thence departs a heavy convertite;*   penitent
She there remains a hopeless cast-away;
He in his speed looks for the morning light;
She prays she never may behold the day,
'For day,' quoth she, 'night's 'scapes* doth open lay,   escapades
    And my true eyes have never practised how
    To cloak offences with a cunning* brow.   dissembling

'They think not but that every eye can see   750
The same disgrace which they themselves behold;
And therefore would they still in darkness be,
To have their unseen sin remain untold;
For they their guilt with weeping will unfold,
    And grave,* like water that doth eat in steel,   engrave
    Upon my cheeks what helpless shame I feel.'

Here she exclaims against repose and rest,
And bids her eyes hereafter still be blind.
She wakes her heart by beating on her breast,
And bids it leap from thence, where it may find   760
Some purer chest to close* so pure a mind.   enclose
    Frantic with grief thus breathes she forth her spite
    Against the unseen secrecy of night:

'O comfort-killing Night, image of hell!
Dim register and notary* of shame!   validator
Black stage for tragedies† and murders fell!
Vast sin-concealing chaos! nurse of blame!
Blind muffled bawd! dark harbour for defame!*   disgrace
    Grim cave of death! whispering conspirator
    With close-tongued treason and the ravisher!   770

'O hateful, vaporous and foggy Night!
Since thou art guilty of my cureless crime,
Muster thy mists to meet the eastern light,
Make war against proportioned* course of time;   regulated
Or if thou wilt permit the sun to climb
    His wonted height, yet ere he go to bed,
    Knit poisonous clouds about his golden head.

'With rotten damps ravish the morning air;
Let their exhaled unwholesome breaths make sick
The life of purity, the supreme fair,   780
Ere he arrive* his weary noon-tide prick;*   arrive at /
And let thy misty vapours march so thick   mark (on the dial)
    That in their smoky ranks his smothered light
    May set at noon and make perpetual night.

'Were Tarquin Night, as he is but Night's child,
The silver-shining queen he would distain;*   defile
Her twinkling handmaids* too, by him defiled,   *i.e.*, the stars
Through Night's black bosom should not peep again:
So should I have co-partners in my pain;
    And fellowship in woe doth woe assuage,   790
    As palmers' chat makes short their pilgrimage.

Black stage for tragedies. The Elizabethan stage was hung with black
when tragedies were performed.

'Where* now I have no one to blush with me,   whereas
To cross their arms and hang their heads with mine,
To mask their brows and hide their infamy;
But I alone alone must sit and pine,
Seasoning the earth with showers of silver brine,
    Mingling my talk with tears, my grief with groans,
    Poor wasting monuments of lasting moans.

'O Night, thou furnace of foul-reeking smoke,
Let not the jealous Day behold that face   800
Which underneath thy black all-hiding cloak
Immodestly lies martyred with disgrace!
Keep still possession of thy gloomy place,
    That all the faults which in thy reign are made
    May likewise be sepùlchred in thy shade!

'Make me not object to the tell-tale Day!
The light will show, charàctered* in my brow,   written
The story of sweet chastity's decay,
The impious breach of holy wedlock vow:
Yea, the illiterate, that know not how   810
    To cipher* what is writ in learned books,   decipher
    Will quote* my loathsome trespass in my looks.   portray

'The nurse, to still her child, will tell my story,
And fright her crying babe with Tarquin's name;
The orator, to deck his oratory,
Will couple my reproach to Tarquin's shame;
Feast-finding minstrels, tuning my defame,
    Will tie the hearers to attend each line,
    How Tarquin wronged me, I Collatine.

'Let my good name, that senseless reputation,   820
For Collatine's dear love be kept unspotted:
If that be made a theme for disputation,
The branches of another root are rotted,
And undeserved reproach to him allotted
    That is as clear from this attaint* of mine   dishonor
    As I, ere this, was pure to Collatine.

'O unseen shame! invisible disgrace!
O unfelt sore! crest-wounding, private scar!
Reproach is stamped in Collatinus' face,
And Tarquin's eye may read the mot* afar,   motto
How he in peace is wounded, not in war.
 Alas, how many bear such shameful blows,
 Which not themselves, but he that gives them knows!

'If, Collatine, thine honour lay in me,
From me by strong assault it is bereft.
My honey lost, and I, a drone-like* bee,   *i.e.,* unable to
Have no perfection of my summer left,   collect honey
But robbed and ransacked by injurious theft:
 In thy weak hive a wandering wasp hath crept,
 And suckèd the honey which thy chaste bee kept. 840

'Yet am I guilty of thy honour's wrack;
Yet for thy honour did I entertain him;
Coming from thee, I could not put him back,
For it had been dishonour to disdain him:
Besides, of weariness he did complain him,
 And talked of virtue: O unlooked-for evil,
 When virtue is profanèd in such a devil!

'Why should the worm intrude the maiden bud?
Or hateful cuckoos hatch in sparrows' nests?
Or toads infect fair founts with venom mud?   850
Or tyrant folly lurk in gentle breasts?
Or kings be breakers of their own behests?
 But no perfection is so absolute*   complete
 That some impurity doth not pollute.

'The aged man that coffers up his gold
Is plagued with cramps and gouts and painful fits,
And scarce hath eyes his treasure to behold,
But like still-pining* Tantalus† he sits   forever grieving
And useless barns* the harvest of his wits,   stores
 Having no other pleasure of his gain   860
 But torment that it cannot cure his pain.

.

But like still-pining Tantalus he sits.
For an insolent crime that Tantalus committed, the gods sent him to Tartarus
(hell) where he was placed in water that receded when he tried to drink.

'So then he hath it when he cannot use it,
And leaves it to be mastered by his young;
Who in their pride do presently* abuse it: at once
Their father was too weak, and they too strong,
To hold their cursed-blessed fortune long.
    The sweets we wish for turn to loathèd sours
    Even in the moment that we call them ours.

'Unruly blasts wait on the tender spring;
Unwholesome weeds take root with precious flowers;   870
The adder hisses where the sweet birds sing;
What virtue breeds iniquity devours:
We have no good that we can say is ours
    But ill-annexèd Opportunity
    Or kills his life or else his quality.

'O Opportunity, thy guilt is great!
'Tis thou that executest the traitor's treason;
Thou set'st the wolf where he the lamb may get;
Whoever plots the sin, thou point'st* the season;   appoints
'Tis thou that spurn'st at right, at law, at reason;   880
    And in thy shady cell, where none may spy him,
    Sits Sin, to seize the souls that wander by him.

'Thou makest the vestal violate her oath;†
Thou blow'st the fire when temperance is thawed;
Thou smother'st honesty, thou murder'st troth;
Thou foul abettor! thou notorious bawd!
Thou plantest scandal and displacest laud:*   praise
    Thou ravisher, thou traitor, thou false thief,
    Thy honey turns to gall, thy joy to grief!

'Thy secret pleasure turns to open shame,   890
Thy private feasting to a public fast,
Thy smoothing* titles to a ragged name,   flattering
Thy sugared tongue to bitter wormwood taste:
Thy violent vanities* can never last.   absurdities
    How comes it then, vile Opportunity,
    Being so bad, such numbers seek for thee?

Thou makest the vestal violate her oath.
In Roman religion a vestal was a priestess of Vesta, goddess
of the hearth and home. She was dedicated to the goddess
in childhood and trained in obedience and chastity.

'When wilt thou be the humble suppliant's friend,
And bring him where his suit may be obtained?
When wilt thou sort* an hour great strifes to end?   choose
Or free that soul which wretchedness hath chained?   900
Give physic to the sick, ease to the pained?
   The poor, lame, blind, halt,* creep, cry out for thee;   limp
   But they ne'er meet with Opportunity.

'The patient dies while the physician sleeps;
The orphan pines while the oppressor feeds;
Justice is feasting while the widow weeps;
Advice* is sporting while infection breeds: admonition
Thou grant'st no time for charitable deeds:
   Wrath, envy, treason, rape, and murder's rages,
   Thy heinous hours wait on them as their pages.   910

'When Truth and Virtue have to do with thee,
A thousand crosses keep them from thy aid:
They buy thy help, but Sin ne'er gives a fee;
He gratis comes, and thou art well appaid*   pleased
As well to hear as grant what he hath said.
   My Collatine would else have come to me
   When Tarquin did, but he was stayed by thee.

'Guilty thou art of murder and of theft,
Guilty of perjury and subornation,†
Guilty of treason, forgery and shift,*   swindling
Guilty of incest, that abomination;
An accessary by thine inclination
   To all sins past and all that are to come,
   From the creation to the general doom.

'Mis-shapen Time, copesmate* of ugly Night,   accomplice
Swift subtle post, carrier of grisly care,
Eater of youth, false slave to false delight,
Base watch of woes, sin's pack-horse, virtue's snare;
Thou nursest all and murder'st all that are:
   O, hear me then, injurious, shifting* Time!   crafty
   Be guilty of my death, since of my crime.

Subornation. The act of procuring someone to perform a criminal act.

'Why hath thy servant Opportunity
Betrayed the hours ·thou gavest me to repose,
Cancelled my fortunes and enchainèd me
To endless date of never-ending woes?
Time's office is to fine* the hate of foes,   end
    To eat up errors by opinion bred,
    Not spend the dowry of a lawful bed.

'Time's glory is to calm contending kings,
To unmask falsehood and bring truth to light,   940
To stamp the seal of time in agèd things,
To wake the morn and sentinel the night,
To wrong the wronger till he render right,
    To ruinate proud buildings with thy hours
    And smear with dust their glittering golden towers;

'To fill with worm-holes stately monuments,
To feed oblivion with decay of things,
To blot old books and alter their contènts,
To pluck the quills from ancient ravens' wings,
To dry the old oak's sap and cherish springs,   950
    To spoil antiquities of hammered steel
    And turn the giddy round of Fortune's wheel;

'To show the beldam* daughters of her daughter,   old women
To make the child a man, the man a child,
To slay the tiger that doth live by slaughter,
To tame the unicorn† and lion wild,
To mock the subtle in themselves beguiled,
    To cheer the ploughman with increaseful crops,
    And waste huge stones with little water-drops.

'Why work'st thou mischief in thy pilgrimage,   960
Unless thou couldst return to make amends?
One poor retiring* minute in an age   returning
Would purchase thee a thousand thousand friends,
Lending him wit that to bad debtors lends:
    O, this dread night, wouldst thou one hour come back,
    I could prevent this storm and shun thy wrack!*   ruin

To tame the unicorn. The fabled unicorn (a horselike beast,
equipped with a single horn) was thought to be untamable
unless captured before he was two years old.

'Thou ceaseless lackey* to eternity,   servile attendant
With some mischance cross Tarquin in his flight:
Devise extremes beyond extremity,
To make him curse this cursèd crimeful night: 970
Let ghastly shadows his lewd eyes affright,
    And the dire thought of his committed evil
    Shape every bush a hideous shapeless devil.

'Disturb his hours of rest with restless trances,
Afflict him in his bed with bedrid groans;
Let there bechance him pitiful mischances,
To make him moan; but pity not his moans:
Stone him with hardened hearts, harder than stones;
    And let mild women to him lose their mildness,
    Wilder to him than tigers in their wildness.   980

'Let him have time to tear his curlèd hair,
Let him have time against himself to rave,
Let him have time of time's help to despair,
Let him have time to live a loathèd slave,
Let him have time a beggar's orts* to crave,   scraps
    And time to see one that by alms doth live
    Disdain to him disdainèd scraps to give.

'Let him have time to see his friends his foes,
And merry fools to mock at him resort;
Let him have time to mark how slow time goes   990
In time of sorrow, and how swift and short
His time of folly and his time of sport;
    And ever let his unrecalling* crime   irrevocable
    Have time to wail the abusing of his time.

'O Time, thou tutor both to good and bad,
Teach me to curse him that thou taught'st this ill!
At his own shadow let the thief run mad,
Himself himself seek every hour to kill!
Such wretched hands such wretched blood should spill;
    For who so base would such an office have   1000
    As slanderous* deathsman to so base a slave?   despicable

'The baser is he, coming from a king,
To shame his hope with deeds degenerate:
The mightier man, the mightier is the thing
That makes him honoured or begets him hate;
For greatest scandal waits on greatest state.*   position
    The moon being clouded presently* is missed,   at once
    But little stars may hide them when they list.

'The crow may bathe his coal-black wings in mire,
And unperceivèd fly with the filth away;   1010
But if the like the snow-white swan desire,
The stain upon his silver down will stay.
Poor grooms* are sightless* night, kings   creatures / blind
    glorious day:
    Gnats are unnoted wheresoe'er they fly,
    But eagles gazed upon with every eye.

'Out, idle words, servants to shallow fools!
Unprofitable sounds, weak arbitrators!
Busy yourselves in skill-contending schools;
Debate where leisure serves with dull debaters;
To trembling clients be you mediators: 1020
    For me, I force* not argument a straw,   value
    Since that my case is past the help of law.

'In vain I rail at Opportunity,
At Time, at Tarquin, and uncheerful Night;
In vain I cavil with mine infamy,
In vain I spurn at my confirmed despite:
This helpless smoke of words doth me no right.
    The remedy indeed to do me good
    Is to let forth my foul-defilèd blood.

'Poor hand, why quiver'st thou at this decree?   1030
Honour thyself to rid me of this shame;
For if I die, my honour lives in thee,
But if I live, thou livest in my defame:
Since thou couldst not defend thy loyal dame
    And wast afeard to scratch her wicked foe,
    Kill both thyself and her for yielding so.'

This said, from her be-tumbled couch she starteth,*   springs
To find some desperate instrument of death:
But this no slaughterhouse no tool imparteth
To make more vent for passage of her breath;   1040
Which, thronging through her lips, so vanisheth
  As smoke from Ætna† that in air consumes,
  Or that which from discharged cannon fumes.

'In vain,' quoth she, 'I live, and seek in vain
Some happy mean to end a hapless life.
I feared by Tarquin's falchion to be slain,
Yet for the self-same purpose seek a knife:
But when I feared I was a loyal wife:
  So am I now: O no, that cannot be;
  Of that true type hath Tarquin rifled* me.   robbed

'O, that is gone for which I sought to live,
And therefore now I need not fear to die.
To clear this spot by death, at least I give
A badge of fame to slander's livery,†
A dying life to living infamy:
  Poor helpless help, the treasure stol'n away,
  To burn the guiltless casket where it lay!

'Well, well, dear Collatine, thou shalt not know
The stainèd taste of violated troth;
I will not wrong thy true affection so,   1060
To flatter thee with an infringèd oath;
This bastard graff* shall never come to growth: graft
  He shall not boast who did thy stock pollute
  That thou art doting father of his fruit.

'Nor shall he smile at thee in secret thought,
Nor laugh with his companions at thy state;
But thou shalt know thy interest was not bought
Basely with gold, but stol'n from forth thy gate.
For me, I am the mistress of my fate,
  And with my trespass never will dispense,   1070
  Till life to death acquit my forced offence.

Ætna. A volcano in Sicily.
A badge of fame to slander's livery.
In Shakespeare's day, the servants of nobility
wore silver badges on their livery.

'I will not poison thee with my attaint,*   stain
Nor fold my fault in cleanly-coined excuses;
My sable ground of sin I will not paint,
To hide the truth of this false night's abuses:
My tongue shall utter all; mine eyes, like sluices,
    As from a mountain-spring that feeds a dale,
    Shall gush pure streams to purge my impure tale.'

By this, lamenting Philomel* had ended   the nightingale
The well tuned warble of her nightly sorrow,   1080
And solemn night with slow sad gait descended
To ugly hell; when, lo, the blushing morrow
Lends light to all fair eyes that light will borrow:
    But cloudy Lucrece shames herself to see,
    And therefore still in night would cloistered be.

Revealing day through every cranny spies,
And seems to point her out where she sits weeping;
To whom she sobbing speaks: 'O eye of eyes,
Why pry'st thou through my window? leave thy
        peeping:
Mock with thy tickling beams eyes that are sleeping: 1090
    Brand not my forehead with thy piercing light,
    For day hath nought to do what's done by night.'

Thus cavils she with every thing she sees:
True grief is fond and testy as a child,
Who wayward once, his mood with nought agrees:
Old woes, not infant sorrows, bear them mild;
Continuance tames the one; the other wild,
    Like an unpractised swimmer plunging still
    With too much labour drowns for want of skill.

So she, deep-drenched in a sea of care,   1100
Holds disputation with each thing she views,
And to herself all sorrow doth compare;
No object but her passion's strength renews,
And as one shifts, another straight ensues:
    Sometime her grief is dumb and hath no words;
    Sometime 'tis mad and too much talk affords.

The little birds that tune their morning's joy
Make her moans mad with their sweet melody:
For mirth doth search the bottom of annoy;
Sad souls are slain in merry company;   1110
Grief best is pleased with grief's society:
    True sorrow then is feelingly sufficed
    When with like semblance it is sympathized.

'Tis double death to drown in ken of shore;
He ten times pines* that pines beholding food;   *i.e.,* grieves
To see the salve doth make the wound ache more;
Great grief grieves most at that would do it good;
Deep woes roll forward like a gentle flood,
    Who, being stopped, the bounding banks o'erflows
    Grief dallied* with nor law nor limit knows.   trifled

'You mocking birds,' quoth she, 'your tunes entomb
Within your hollow-swelling feathered breasts,
And in my hearing be you mute and dumb:
My restless discord loves no stops nor rests;
A woeful hostess brooks not merry guests:
    Relish your nimble notes to pleasing ears;
    Distress like dumps* when time is kept with tears.   sad tunes

'Come, Philomel, that sing'st of ravishment,
Make thy sad grove in my dishevelled hair:
As the dank earth weeps at thy languishment,   1130
So I at each sad strain will strain a tear,
And with deep groans the diapason* bear;   concord
    For burden-wise I'll hum on Tarquin still,
    While thou on Tereus descant'st better skill.†

For burden-wise I'll hum on Tarquin still,
While thou on Tereus descant'st better skill.
Like an accompaniment, I'll continue to hum the note Tarquin,
while you more skillfully continue to play variations on the
name and fortunes of Tereus. He, a King of Thrace, married
Procne, daughter of the King of Athens. By her, he had a son,
Itys. Tereus raped his wife's sister, Philomela, and cut out her
tongue. However, Procne managed to release her and then fed Itys
to his father. Procne was changed into a swallow, Philomela into a
nightingale, and Tereus into a lapwing.

'And whiles against a thorn thou bear'st thy part,
To keep thy sharp woes waking, wretched I,
To imitate thee well, against my heart
Will fix a sharp knife, to affright mine eye;
Who, if it wink, shall thereon fall and die.
    These means, as frets upon an instrument,   1140
    Shall tune our heart-strings to true languishment.

'And for, poor bird, thou sing'st not in the day,
As shaming any eye should thee behold,
Some dark deep desert, seated from* the way,   distant from
That knows not parching heat nor freezing cold,
Will we find out; and there we will unfold
    To creatures stern sad tunes, to change their kinds:
    Since men prove beasts, let beasts bear gentle minds.'

As the poor frighted deer, that stands at gaze,
Wildly determining which way to fly,   1150
Or one encompassed with a winding maze,
That cannot tread the way out readily;
So with herself is she in mutiny,
    To live or die, which of the twain were better,
    When life is shamed and death reproach's debtor.

'To kill myself,' quoth she, 'alack, what were it,
But with my body my poor soul's pollution?†
They that lose half with greater patience bear it
Than they whose whole is swallowed in confusion.
That mother tries a merciless conclusion*   cruel experiment
    Who, having two sweet babes, when death
       takes one,
    Will slay the other and be nurse to none.

'My body or my soul, which was the dearer,
When the one pure, the other made divine?
Whose love of either to myself was nearer,
When both were kept for heaven and Collatine?
Ay me! the bark peeled from the lofty pine,
    His leaves will wither and his sap decay;
    So must my soul, her bark* being peeled away.   i.e., her body

---

But with my body my poor soul's pollution.
My suicide will destroy my body and pollute my soul.

'Her house is sacked, her quiet interrupted,   1170
Her mansion battered by the enemy;
Her sacred temple spotted, spoiled,* corrupted,   despoiled
Grossly engirt with daring infamy:
Then let it not be called impiety,
    If in this blemished fort I make some hole
    Through which I may convey this troubled soul.

'Yet die I will not till my Collatine
Have heard the cause of my untimely death;
That he may vow, in that sad hour of mine,
Revenge on him that made me stop my breath.
My stainèd blood to Tarquin I'll bequeath,   1180
    Which by him tainted shall for him be spent,
    And as his due writ in my testament.*   will

'My honour I'll bequeath unto the knife
That wounds my body so dishonourèd.
'Tis honour to deprive dishonoured life;
The one will live, the other being dead:
So of shame's ashes shall my fame be bred;
    For in my death I murder shameful scorn:
    My shame so dead, mine honour is new-born.   1190

'Dear lord of that dear jewel I have lost,
What legacy shall I bequeath to thee?
My resolution, love, shall be thy boast,
By whose example thou revenged mayst be.
How Tarquin must be used, read it in me:
    Myself, thy friend, will kill myself, thy foe,
    And, for my sake, serve thou false Tarquin so.

'This brief abridgement of my will I make:
My soul and body to the skies and ground;
My resolution, husband, do thou take;
Mine honour be the knife's that makes my wound;   1200
My shame be his that did my fame confound;
    And all my fame that lives disbursèd be
    To those that live and think no shame of me.

'Thou, Collatine, shalt oversee* this will;   be executor of
How was I overseen that thou shalt see it!
My blood shall wash the slander of mine ill;
My life's foul deed, my life's fair end shall free it.
Faint not, faint heart, but stoutly say "So be it:"
     Yield to my hand; my hand shall conquer thee: 1210
     Thou dead, both die and both shall victors be.'

This plot* of death when sadly she had laid,*   plan / arranged
And wiped the brinish pearl from her bright eyes,
With untuned tongue she hoarsely calls her maid,
Whose swift obedience to her mistress hies;
For fleet-winged duty with thought's feathers flies.
     Poor Lucrece' cheeks unto her maid seem so
     As winter meads when sun doth melt their snow.

Her mistress she doth give demure good-morrow,
With soft slow tongue, true mark of modesty,   1220
And sorts* a sad look to her lady's sorrow,   adapts
For why her face wore sorrow's livery,
But durst not ask of her audaciously
     Why her two suns were cloud-eclipsèd so,
     Nor why her fair cheeks over-washed with woe.

But as the earth doth weep, the sun being set,
Each flower moistened like a melting eye,
Even so the maid with swelling drops 'gan wet
Her circled eyne, enforced by sympathy
Of those fair suns set in her mistress' sky,   1230
     Who in a salt-waved ocean quench their light,
     Which makes the maid weep like the dewy night.

A pretty while these pretty creatures stand,
Like ivory conduits coral cisterns filling:
One justly weeps; the other takes in hand
No cause, but company, of her drops spilling:
Their gentle sex to weep are often willing,
     Grieving themselves to guess at others' smarts,
     And then they drown their eyes or break their hearts.

For men have marble, women waxen, minds,   1240
And therefore are they formed as marble will;
The weak oppressed, the impression of strange kinds
Is formed in them by force, by fraud, or skill:
Then call them not the authors of their ill,
   No more than wax shall be accounted evil
   Wherein is stamped the semblance of a devil.

Their smoothness, like a goodly champaign* plain,   level
Lays open all the little worms that creep;
In men, as in a rough-grown grove, remain
Cave-keeping evils that obscurely* sleep: hidden
Through crystal walls each little mote will peep:
   Though men can cover crimes with bold stern looks,
   Poor women's faces are their own faults' books.

No man inveigh against the withered flower,
But chide rough winter that the flower hath killed:
Not that devoured, but that which doth devour,
Is worthy blame. O, let it not be hild*   hidden
Poor women's faults, that they are so fulfilled*   filled full
   With men's abuses: those proud lords to blame
   Make weak-made women tenants to their shame.   1260

The precedent* whereof in Lucrece view,   proof
Assailed by night with circumstances strong
Of present death, and shame that might ensue
By that her death, to do her husband wrong:
Such danger to resistance did belong,
   That dying fear through all her body spread;
   And who cannot abuse* a body dead?   maltreat

By this, mild patience bid fair Lucrece speak
To the poor counterfeit* of her complaining: *i.e.,* her maid
'My girl,' quoth she, 'on what occasion break   1270
Those tears from thee, that down thy cheeks are raining?
If thou dost weep for grief of my sustaining,
   Know, gentle wench, it small avails my mood:
   If tears could help, mine own would do me good.

'But tell me, girl, when went'—and there she stayed
Till after a deep groan—'Tarquin from hence?'
'Madam, ere I was up,' replied the maid,
'The more to blame my sluggard negligence:
Yet with the fault I thus far can dispense;
 Myself was stirring ere the break of day,   1280
 And ere I rose was Tarquin gone away.

'But, lady, if your maid may be so bold,
She would request to know your heaviness.'
'O, peace!' quoth Lucrece: 'if it should be told,
The repetition cannot make it less,
For more it is than I can well express:
 And that deep torture may be called a hell
 When more is felt than one hath power to tell.

'Go, get me hither paper, ink and pen:
Yet save that labour, for I have them here.   1290
What should I say? One of my husband's men
Bid thou be ready by and by* to bear   at once
A letter to my lord, my love, my dear:
 Bid him with speed prepare to carry it;
 The cause craves haste and it will soon be writ.'

Her maid is gone, and she prepares to write,
First hovering o'er the paper with her quill:
Conceit* and grief an eager combat fight;   active fancy
What wit sets down is blotted straight with will;
This is too curious-good,* this blunt and ill: contrived
 Much like a press of people at a door,
 Throng her inventions, which shall go before.

At last she thus begins: 'Thou worthy lord
Of that unworthy wife that greeteth thee,
Health to thy person! next vouchsafe t' afford—
If ever, love, thy Lucrece thou wilt see—
Some present speed to come and visit me.
 So, I commend me from our house in grief:
 My woes are tedious, though my words are brief.'

Here folds she up the tenour of her woe,   1310
Her certain sorrow writ uncertainly.
By this short schedule* Collatine may know   document
Her grief, but not her grief's true quality:
She dares not thereof make discovery,
    Lest he should hold it her own gross abuse,*   dishonor
    Ere she with blood had stained her stainèd excuse.

Besides, the life and feeling of her passion
She hoards, to spend when he is by to hear her,
When sighs and groans and tears may grace the fashion
Of her disgrace, the better so to clear her   1320
From that suspicion which the world might bear her.
    To shun this blot, she would not blot the letter
    With words, till action might become them better.

To see sad sights moves more than hear them told;
For then the eye interprets to the ear
The heavy motion* that it doth behold,   grievous action
When every part a part of woe doth bear.
'Tis but a part of sorrow that we hear:
    Deep sounds make lesser noise than shallow fords,*   streams
    And sorrow ebbs, being blown with wind of words.   1330

Her letter now is sealed and on it writ
'At Ardea to my lord with more than haste.'
The post attends,* and she delivers it,   messenger is waiting
Charging the sour-faced groom to hie as fast
As lagging fowls before the northern blast:
    Speed more than speed but dull and slow she
        deems:
    Extremity* still urgeth such extremes.   extreme need

The homely villain* court'sies* to her   household servant / bows
    low,
And blushing on her, with a steadfast eye
Receives the scroll without or yea or no,   1340
And forth with bashful innocence doth hie.
But they whose guilt within their bosoms lie
    Imagine every eye beholds their blame;
    For Lucrece thought he blushed to see her shame:

When, silly groom! God wot, it was defect
Of spirit, life and bold audacity.
Such harmless creatures have a true respect
To talk in deeds, while others saucily
Promise more speed but do it leisurely:
    Even so this pattern* of the worn-out age   model
    Pawned honest looks, but laid no words to gage.*   pledge

His kindled duty kindled her mistrust,
That two red fires in both their faces blazed;
She thought he blushed, as knowing Tarquin's lust,
And blushing with him, wistly* on him gazed;   earnestly
Her earnest eye did make him more amazed:
    The more she saw the blood his cheeks replenish,
    The more she thought he spied in her some blemish.

But long she thinks till he return again,
And yet the duteous vassal scarce is gone.   1360
The weary time she cannot entertain,
For now 'tis stale to sigh, to weep and groan:
So woe hath wearied woe, moan tirèd moan,
    That she her plaints a little while doth stay,
    Pausing for means to mourn some newer way.

At last she calls to mind where hangs a
        piece
Of skilful painting, made for Priam's Troy;
Before the which is drawn* the power of Greece,   drawn up
For Helen's rape the city to destroy,
Threatening cloud-kissing Ilion with annoy;*   injury
    Which the conceited* painter drew so proud,   imaginative
    As heaven, it seemed, to kiss the turrets bowed.

A thousand lamentable objects there,
In scorn of nature, art gave lifeless life:
Many a dry drop seemed a weeping tear,
Shed for the slaughtered husband by the wife:
The red blood reeked, to show the painter's
        strife;*   i.e., to equal nature
    And dying eyes gleamed forth their ashy lights,
    Like dying coals burnt out in tedious nights.

There might you see the labouring pioner†   1380
Begrimed with sweat and smearèd all with dust;
And from the towers of Troy there would appear
The very eyes of men through loop-holes thrust,
Gazing upon the Greeks with little lust:*   pleasure
  Such sweet observance* in this work was had   observation
  That one might see those far-off eyes look sad.

In great commanders grace and majesty
You might behold, triumphing in their faces,
In youth, quick bearing and dexterity;
And here and there the painter interlaces   1390
Pale cowards, marching on with trembling paces;
  Which heartless* peasants did so well resemble   cowardly
  That one might see those far-off eyes look sad.

In Ajax and Ulysses, O, what art
Of physiognomy might one behold!
The face of either ciphered* either's heart;   deciphered
Their face their manners most expressly told:
In Ajax' eyes blunt rage and rigour rolled;
  But the mild glance that sly Ulysses lent
  Showed deep regard and smiling
      government.*   self-control

There pleading might you see grave Nestor stand,
As 'twere encouraging the Greeks to fight,
Making such sober action with his hand
That it beguiled attention, charmed the sight:
In speech, it seemed, his beard all silver white
  Wagged* up and down, and from his lips did fly   moved
  Thin winding breath which purled* up to the sky.   curled

About him were a press of gaping faces,
Which seemed to swallow up his sound advice;
All jointly listening, but with several graces,   1410
As if some mermaid did their ears entice,
Some high, some low, the painter was so nice;*   discriminating
  The scalps of many, almost hid behind,
  To jump up higher seemed, to mock the mind.

Pioner. A member of the engineers who dug excavations in which to
plant explosives to blow up some of the enemies' groundworks.

Here one man's hand leaned on another's head,
His nose being shadowed by his neighbour's ear;
Here one being thronged* bears back, all   pressed by the throng
    boll'n and red;†
Another smothered seems to pelt* and swear;   storm
And in their rage such signs of rage they bear
    As, but for loss of Nestor's golden words,†   1420
    It seemed they would debate* with angry swords.   fight

For much imaginary work was there;
Conceit deceitful,* so compact, so kind,   deceptive fancy
That for Achilles' image stood his spear
Griped in an armed hand; himself behind
Was left unseen, save to the eye of mind:
    A hand, a foot, a face, a leg, a head,
    Stood for the whole to be imaginèd.

And from the walls of strong-besiegèd Troy
When their brave hope, bold Hector, marched to field,   1430
Stood many Trojan mothers sharing joy
To see their youthful sons bright weapons wield;
And to their hope they such odd action yield
    That through their light joy seemed to appear,
    Like bright things stained, a kind of heavy fear.

And from the strand of Dardan,* where they fought,   Troy
To Simois' reedy banks the red blood ran,†
Whose waves to imitate the battle sought
With swelling ridges; and their ranks began
To break upon the gallèd* shore, and than   chafed
    Retire again, till meeting greater ranks
    They join and shoot their foam at Simois' banks.

Here one being thronged bears back, all boll'n and red.
Here is a figure of a man, being pressed upon by the crowd,
with his face all red and swollen, forcing his way back.
As, but for loss of Nestor's golden words.
Nestor was the oldest and wisest warrior in the Greek host,
whose advice was often sought and his restraint obeyed.
To Simois' reedy banks the red blood ran.
The Simois was a small river in the Troad. On its banks
many of the engagements in the Trojan War were fought.

To this well-painted piece is Lucrece come,
To find a face where all distress is stelled.*   delineated
Many she sees where cares have carvèd some,
But none where all distress and dolour dwelled,
Till she despairing Hecuba beheld,
  Staring on Priam's wounds with her old eyes,
  Which bleeding under Pyrrhus' proud foot lies.

In her the painter had anatomized*   dissected
Time's ruin, beauty's wreck, and grim care's reign:
Her cheeks with chaps* and wrinkles were disguised;   lines
Of what she was no semblance did remain:
Her blue blood changed to black in every vein,
  Wanting the spring that those shrunk pipes had fed,
  Showed life imprisoned in a body dead.

On this sad shadow* Lucrece spends her eyes,   painted form
And shapes her sorrow to the beldam's* woes,   old woman's
Who nothing wants to answer her but cries,
And bitter words to ban* her cruel foes: curse
The painter was no god to lend her those;
  And therefore Lucrece swears he did her wrong,
  To give her so much grief and not a tongue.

'Poor instrument,' quoth she, 'without a sound,
I'll tune thy woes with my lamenting tongue,
And drop sweet balm in Priam's† painted wound,
And rail on Pyrrhus that hath done him wrong,
And with my tears quench Troy that burns so long,
  And with my knife scratch out the angry eyes
  Of all the Greeks that are thine enemies.   1470

'Show me the strumpet that began this stir,
That with my nails her beauty I may tear.
Thy heat of lust, fond Paris, did incur
This load of wrath that burning Troy doth bear:
Thy eye kindled the fire that burneth here;
  And here in Troy, for trespass of thine eye,
  The sire, the son, the dame and daughter die.

Priam. The King of ancient Troy; he was slain by Pyrrhus.

'Why should the private pleasure of some one
Become the public plague of many moe?*   more
Let sin, alone committed, light alone   1480
Upon his head that hath transgressèd so;
Let guiltless souls be freed from guilty woe:
    For one's offence why should so many fall,
    To plague a private sin in general?*   upon everyone

'Lo, here weeps Hecuba,* here Priam dies,   Priam's wife
Here manly Hector faints, here Troilus*   a Trojan warrior
    swounds,*   swoons
Here friend by friend in bloody channel lies,
And friend to friend gives unadvisèd* wounds,   accidental
And one man's lust these many lives confounds:
    Had doting Priam checked his son's desire,*   i.e., for Helen
    Troy had been bright with fame and not with fire.'

Here feelingly she weeps Troy's painted woes:
For sorrow, like a heavy-hanging bell
Once set on ringing, with his own weight goes;
Then little strength rings out the doleful knell:
So Lucrece, set a-work, sad tales doth tell
    To pencilled* pensiveness and coloured sorrow;   painted
    She lends them words, and she their looks doth
        borrow.

She throws her eyes about the painting round,
And who she finds forlorn she doth lament.   1500
At last she sees a wretched image bound,
That piteous looks to Phrygian shepherds lent:
His face, though full of cares, yet showed content;
    Onward to Troy with the blunt* swains he goes,   awkward
    So mild that Patience seemed to scorn his woes.

In him the painter laboured with his skill
To hide deceit and give the harmless show
An humble gait, calm looks, eyes wailing still,
A brow unbent, that seemed to welcome woe;
Cheeks neither red nor pale, but mingled so   1510
    That blushing red no guilty instance* gave,   proof of guilt
    Nor ashy pale the fear that false hearts have.

But, like a constant and confirmèd devil,
He entertained a show* so seeming just,   maintained an appearance
And therein so ensconced* his secret evil,   hid
That jealousy* itself could not mistrust   suspicion
False-creeping craft and perjury should thrust
   Into so bright a day such black-faced storms,
   Or blot with hell-born sin such saint-like forms.

The well-skilled workman this mild image drew   1520
For perjured Sinon, whose enchanting story
The credulous old Priam after slew;
Whose words, like wildfire, burnt the shining glory
Of rich-built Ilion, that the skies were sorry,
   And little stars shot from their fixèd places,
   When their glass* fell wherein they viewed   mirrored roof
     their faces.

This picture she advisedly perused,
And chid the painter for his wondrous skill,
Saying, some shape in Sinon's was abused;
So fair a form lodged not a mind so ill: 1530
And still on him she gazed, and gazing still
   Such signs of truth in his plain* face she spied   honest
   That she concludes the picture was belied.

'It cannot be,' quoth she, 'that so much guile'—
She would have said 'can lurk in such a look';
But Tarquin's shape came in her mind the while,
And from her tongue 'can lurk' from 'cannot' took:
'It cannot be' she in that sense forsook,
   And turned it thus, 'It cannot be, I find,
   But such a face should bear a wicked mind: 1540

'For even as subtle Sinon here is painted,
So sober-sad, so weary and so mild,
As if with grief or travail he had fainted,
To me came Tarquin armèd; so beguiled
With outward honesty, but yet defiled
   With inward vice: as Priam him did cherish,
   So did I Tarquin; so my Troy did perish.

'Look, look, how listening Priam wets his eyes,
To see those borrowed* tears that Sinon sheds!   feigned
Priam, why art thou old and yet not wise?   1550
For every tear he falls* a Trojan bleeds: lets fall
His eye drops fire, no water thence proceeds;
   Those round clear pearls of his that move thy pity
   Are balls of quenchless fire to burn thy city.

'Such devils steal effects from lightless hell;
For Sinon in his fire doth quake with cold,
And in that cold hot-burning fire doth dwell;
These contraries such unity do hold,
Only to flatter fools and make them bold:
   So Priam's trust false Sinon's tears doth flatter,   1560
   That he finds means to burn his Troy with water.'

Here, all enraged, such passion her assails,
That patience is quite beaten from her breast.
She tears the senseless Sinon with her nails,
Comparing him to that unhappy guest
Whose deed hath made herself herself detest:
   At last she smilingly with this gives o'er;
   'Fool, fool!' quoth she, 'his wounds will not be sore.'

Thus ebbs and flows the current of her sorrow
And time doth weary time with her complaining.   1570
She looks for night, and then she longs for morrow,
And both she thinks too long with her remaining:
Short time seems long in sorrow's sharp sustaining:
   Though woe be heavy, yet it seldom sleeps,
   And they that watch* see time how slow it creeps.   lie awake

Which all this time hath overslipped her thought,
That she with painted images hath spent;
Being from the feeling of her own grief brought
By deep surmise of others' detriment,
Losing her woes in shows of discontent.   1580
   It easeth some, though none it ever cured,
   To think their dolour others have endured.

But now the mindful messenger come back
Brings home his lord and other company;
Who finds his Lucrece clad in mourning black:
And round about her tear-distainèd eye
Blue circles streamed, like rainbows in the sky:
    These water-galls* in her dim element†   wind galls
    Foretell new storms to those already spent.

Which when her sad-beholding husband saw,   1590
Amazedly in her sad face he stares:
Her eyes, though sod* in tears, looked red and raw,   sodden
Her lively* colour killed with deadly cares.   lifelike
He hath no power to ask her how she fares:
    Both stood, like old acquaintance in a trance,
    Met far from home, wondering each other's chance.

At last he takes her by the bloodless hand,
And thus begins: 'What uncouth ill event
Hath thee befallen, that thou dost trembling stand?
Sweet love, what spite hath thy fair colour spent?   1600
Why art thou thus attired in discontent?
    Unmask, dear dear, this moody heaviness,
    And tell thy grief, that we may give redress.'

Three times with sighs she gives her sorrow fire,
Ere once she can discharge one word of woe:
At length addressed* to answer his desire,   prepared
She modestly prepares to let them know
Her honour is ta'en prisoner by the foe;
    While Collatine and his consorted lords
    With sad attention long to hear her words.   1610

And now this pale swan in her watery nest
Begins the sad dirge of her certain ending:
'Few words,' quoth she, 'shall fit the trespass best,
Where no excuse can give the fault amending:
In me moe woes than words are now depending;
    And my laments would be drawn out too long,
    To tell them all with one poor tired tongue.

These water-galls in her dim element.
A wind gall is a luminous halo on the edge of a
distant cloud, a presage of stormy weather.

'Then be this all the task it hath to say:
Dear husband, in the interest of thy bed
A stranger came, and on that pillow lay   1620
Where thou wast wont to rest thy weary head;
And what wrong else may be imaginèd
  By foul enforcement might be done to me,
  From that, alas, thy Lucrece is not free.

'For in the dreadful dead of dark midnight,
With shining falchion in my chamber came
A creeping creature, with a flaming light,
And softly cried "Awake, thou Roman dame,
And entertain my love; else lasting shame
  On thee and thine this night I will inflict,   1630
  If thou my love's desire do contradict.

' "For some hard-favoured* groom of thine," quoth he,   ugly
"Unless thou yoke thy liking to my will,
I'll murder straight, and then I'll slaughter thee,
And swear I found you where you did fulfil
The loathsome act of lust, and so did kill
  The lechers in their deed: this act will be
  My fame, and thy perpetual infamy."

'With this, I did begin to start* and cry;   shrink away
And then against my heart he set his sword,   1640
Swearing, unless I took all patiently,
I should not live to speak another word;
So should my shame still rest upon record,
  And never be forgot in mighty Rome
  The adulterate* death of Lucrece and her groom.   in adultery

'Mine enemy was strong, my poor self weak,
And far the weaker with so strong a fear:
My bloody judge forbade my tongue to speak;
No rightful plea might plead for justice there:
His scarlet lust came evidence to swear   1650
  That my poor beauty had purloined his eyes;
  And when the judge is robbed, the prisoner dies.

'O, teach me how to make mine own excuse!
Or, at the least, this refuge let me find;
Though my gross blood be stained with this abuse,
Immaculate and spotless is my mind;
That was not forced; that never was inclined
    To accessary yieldings, but still pure†
    Doth in her poisoned closet yet endure.'

Lo, here, the hopeless merchant of this loss,   1660
With head declined, and voice dammed up with woe,
With sad-set eyes and wretched arms across,
From lips new-waxen pale begins to blow
The grief away that stops his answer so:
    But, wretched as he is, he strives in vain;
    What he breathes out his breath drinks up again.

As through an arch the violent roaring tide
Outruns the eye that doth behold his haste,
Yet in the eddy boundeth in his pride
Back to the strait that forced him on so fast,   1670
In rage sent out, recalled in rage, being past:
    Even so his sighs, his sorrows, make a saw,
    To push grief on and back the same grief draw.

Which speechless woe of his poor she attendeth
And his untimely* frenzy thus awaketh: *too late*
'Dear lord, thy sorrow to my sorrow lendeth
Another power; no flood by raining slaketh.
My woe too sensible thy passion maketh
    More feeling-painful: let it then suffice
    To drown one woe, one pair of weeping eyes.   1680

'And for my sake, when I might charm thee so,
For she* that was thy Lucrece, now attend me: *her*
Be suddenly revengèd on my foe,
Thine, mine, his own: suppose thou dost defend me
From what is past: the help that thou shalt lend me
    Comes all too late, yet let the traitor die;
    For sparing justice feeds iniquity.

To accessary yieldings, but still pure.
Accessary yieldings are those that would make her accessory to the rape.

'But ere I name him, you fair lords,' quoth she,
Speaking to those that came with Collatine
'Shall plight your honourable faiths to me,   1690
With swift pursuit to venge this wrong of mine;
For 'tis a meritorious fair design
 To chase injustice with revengeful arms:
 Knights, by their oaths, should right poor ladies'
  harms.'

At this request, with noble disposition
Each present lord began to promise aid,
As bound in knighthood to her imposition,*   charge
Longing to hear the hateful foe bewrayed.*   exposed
But she, that yet her sad task hath not said,
 The protestation stops. 'O, speak,' quoth she,   1700
 'How may this forcèd stain be wiped from me?

'What is the quality of my offence,
Being constrained with dreadful circumstance?
May my pure mind with the foul act dispense,
My low-declinèd honour to advance?
May any terms acquit me from this chance?
 The poisoned fountain clears itself again;
 And why not I from this compellèd stain?'

With this, they all at once began to say,
Her body's stain her mind untainted clears;   1710
While with a joyless smile she turns away
The face, that map which deep impression bears
Of hard misfortune, carved in it with tears.
 'No, no,' quoth she, 'no dame hereafter living
 By my excuse shall claim excuse's giving.'

Here with a sigh, as if her heart would break,
She throws forth Tarquin's name: 'He, he,' she says,
But more than 'he' her poor tongue could not speak;
Till after many accents and delays,
Untimely breathings, sick and short assays,   1720
 She utters this: 'He, he, fair lords, 'tis he,
 That guides this hand to give this wound to me.'

Even here she sheathèd in her harmless breast
A harmful knife, that thence her soul unsheathed:
That blow did bail it from the deep unrest
Of that polluted prison where it breathed:
Her contrite sighs unto the clouds bequeathed
  Her wingèd sprite,* and through her wounds   spirit
    doth fly
  Life's lasting date* from cancelled destiny.   end

Stone-still, astonished* with this deadly deed,   astounded
Stood Collatine and all his lordly crew;
Till Lucrece's father, that beholds her bleed,
Himself on her self-slaughtered body threw;
And from the purple fountain Brutus drew
  The murderous knife, and, as it left the place,
  Her blood, in poor revenge, held it in chase;

And bubbling from her breast, it doth divide
In two slow rivers, that the crimson blood
Circles her body in on every side,
Who, like a late-sacked island, vastly* stood   like a waste
Bare and unpeopled in this fearful flood.
  Some of her blood still pure and red remained,
  And some looked black, and that false Tarquin
    stained.

About the mourning and congealèd face
Of that black blood a watery rigol* goes,   circle
Which seems to weep upon the tainted place:
And ever since, as pitying Lucrece' woes,
Corrupted blood some watery token shows;
  And blood untainted still doth red abide,
  Blushing at that which is so putrified.   1750

'Daughter, dear daughter,' old Lucretius cries,
'That life was mine which thou hast here deprived.
If in the child the father's image lies,
Where shall I live now Lucrece is unlived?
Thou wast not to this end from me derived.
  If children pre-decease progenitors,
  We are their offspring, and they none of ours.

'Poor broken glass, I often did behold
In thy sweet semblance my old age new born;
But now that fair fresh mirror, dim and old,   1760
Shows me a bare-boned death* by time outworn: death's head
O, from thy cheeks my image thou hast torn,
    And shivered all the beauty of my glass,
    That I no more can see what once I was.

'O time, cease thou thy course and last no longer,
If they surcease* to be that should survive.   *i.e.*, cease
Shall rotten death make conquest of the stronger,
And leave the faltering feeble souls alive?
The old bees die, the young possess their hive:
    Then live, sweet Lucrece, live again, and see   1770
    Thy father die, and not thy father thee!'

By this, starts Collatine as from a dream,
And bids Lucretius give his sorrow place;
And then in key-cold Lucrece's bleeding stream
He falls, and bathes the pale fear in his face,
And counterfeits to die with her a space;
    Till manly shame bids him possess his breath,
    And live to be revengèd on her death.

The deep vexation of his inward soul
Hath served a dumb arrest upon his tongue;   1780
Who, mad that sorrow should his use control
Or keep him from heart-easing words so long,
Begins to talk; but through his lips do throng
    Weak words, so thick come in his poor heart's aid
    That no man could distinguish what he said.

Yet sometime 'Tarquin' was pronouncèd plain,
But through his teeth, as if the name he tore.
This windy tempest, till it blow up rain,
Held back his sorrow's tide, to make it more;
At last it rains, and busy winds give o'er:*   cease
    Then son and father weep with equal strife
    Who should weep most, for daughter or for wife.

The one doth call her his, the other his,
Yet neither may possess the claim they lay.
The father says 'She's mine.' 'O, mine she is,'
Replies her husband: 'do not take away
My sorrow's interest; let no mourner say
   He weeps for her, for she was only mine,
    And only must be wailed by Collatine.'

'O,' quoth Lucretius, 'I did give that life   1800
Which she too early and too late hath spilled.'
'Woe, woe,' quoth Collatine, 'she was my wife;
I owed* her, and 'tis mine that she hath killed.'   owned
'My daughter' and 'my wife' with clamours filled
   The dispersed air, who, holding Lucrece' life,
    Answered their cries, 'my daughter' and 'my wife.'

Brutus, who plucked the knife from Lucrece' side,
Seeing such emulation in their woe,
Began to clothe his wit in state and pride,
Burying in Lucrece' wound his folly's show.†   1810
He with the Romans was esteemed so
   As silly-jeering idiots are with kings,
    For sportive words and uttering foolish things:

But now he throws that shallow habit by
Wherein deep policy* did him disguise,   shrewdness
And armed his long-hid wits advisedly*   deliberately
To check the tears in Collatinus' eyes.
'Thou wrongèd lord of Rome,' quoth he, 'arise:
   Let my unsounded* self, supposed a fool,   i.e., deep
    Now set thy long-experienced wit to school.   1820

'Why, Collatine, is woe the cure for woe?
Do wounds help wounds, or grief help grievous deeds?
Is it revenge to give thyself a blow
For his foul act by whom thy fair wife bleeds?
Such childish humour from weak minds proceeds:
   Thy wretched wife mistook the matter so,
    To slay herself, that should have slain her foe.

Burying in Lucrece' wound his folly's show.
Lucius Junius Brutus (510 B.C.) feigned idiocy
in order to escape death by Tarquinius Superbus.

'Courageous Roman, do not steep thy heart
In such relenting dew of lamentations,
But kneel with me and help to bear thy part   1830
To rouse our Roman gods with invocations
That they will suffer these abominations,
   Since Rome herself in them doth stand disgraced,
   By our strong arms from forth her fair streets chased.

'Now, by the Capitol that we adore,
And by this chaste blood so unjustly stained,
By heaven's fair sun that breeds the fat earth's store,
By all our country rights in Rome maintained,
And by chaste Lucrece's soul that late complained
   Her wrongs to us, and by this bloody knife,   1840
   We will revenge the death of this true wife!'

This said, he struck his hand upon his breast,
And kissed the fatal knife, to end his vow,
And to his protestation urged the rest,
Who, wondering at him, did his words allow:*   approve
Then jointly to the ground their knees they bow;
   And that deep vow, which Brutus made before,
   He doth again repeat, and that they swore.

When they had sworn to this advisèd doom,
They did conclude to bear dead Lucrece thence,   1850
To show her bleeding body thorough Rome,
And so to publish Tarquin's foul offence:
Which being done with speedy diligence,
   The Romans plausibly* did give consent   readily
   To Tarquin's everlasting banishment.

THE PHOENIX AND THE TURTLE

The Phoenix and the Turtle was first published in 1601 in a volume containing Robert Chester's *Love's Martyr* and companion pieces by Jonson, Chapman, Marston, and two anonymous writers who sign themselves "Vatum Chuns" and "Ignoto." The subsidiary title of *Love's Martyr* is "Shadowing the Truth of Love in the Constant Fate of the Phoenix and the Turtle." This was the subject of all the authors, including Shakespeare, represented in Chester's quaint collection of allegorical fancies.

The phoenix was a fabulous, unique bird of Egypt. According to the legend, it lived five hundred years in Arabia, then laid an egg in its nest to which it set fire. In the conflagration the bird burned to death, but from its ashes a new phoenix was born. The phoenix became a symbol of the resurrection of the dead.

The general meaning of Shakespeare's poem is clear. It is a celebration of the ideal love of a recently dead married pair under the allegory of the phoenix and the turtledove. It is related to Chaucer's *Parlement of Fowles* and particularly to the abstruse symbolism of emblem literature which flourished during the fifteenth and sixteenth centuries in England and on the Continent. The distinctive characteristic of an emblem, usually an engraved figure, is that it has a meaning more general and abstruse than the representative significance of the drawing. For example, the figure of the turtledove was a time-honored emblem of conjugal love; while the phoenix was the emblem of something unique. Here it stands for the phoenix's absolute and eternal devotion to the turtledove. Like Robert Chester, Shakespeare regards the phoenix as feminine and the dove as masculine. His theme is the mystical union of the two.

The poet's recondite method of celebrating their ideal relationship has always been at least partially understood. The love has so completely merged the two lovers that neither has remained a separate entity. The work thus becomes a "metaphysical" quibbling on the ideas of unity and disunity.

Professor J. V. Cunningham, in a recent article† adopting

† "Essence and the Phoenix," *English Literary History. XIX*, No. 4 (December 1952), pp. 205–296.

the usual interpretation of the poem, finds in it the embodiment of a definite philosophical doctrine. He adopts the idea that the relation of the lovers shadows that of the three persons of the Trinity, as developed by scholastic philosophers, particularly by Saint Thomas Aquinas.

Shakespeare, following the tenets of this philosophy, regards the beloved as the essence of the lover, that is, his intellectual soul, which in turn is the image of God. Yet in the process of becoming one and the same person, neither is annihilated. This mystical relationship is identical with that existing between the three persons of the Trinity as expounded by the scholastics. Father and Son, although distinct persons, are of one and the same "essence."

> So they loved, as love in twain
> Had the essence but in one;
> Two distincts, division none:
> Number there in love was slain.

As for the Holy Ghost, it was conceived to be the mutual love of the Father and Son: a distinct entity but essentially a bond between the two other persons of the Trinity. Since plurality is the consequence of division and the three persons are indivisible, the poet can write, "Number there in love was slain." Shakespeare evidently thought that the most effective way of emphasizing the closeness of the lamented pair, their complete absorption in each other, was to apply to their love the official Catholic doctrine of the mutual relationship of the three persons of the Trinity. In this respect the philosophical content of Shakespeare's poem was completely different from that of the other contributions to Chester's volume.

The lovers represent Sir John Salisbury, a Welsh country gentleman, born in 1566, so two years the poet's junior; and Ursula Stanley, the illegitimate daughter of the Fourth Earl of Derby. They were early married, and separated by untimely death. Sir John was a generous patron of both Welsh and English poets. Chester and the distinguished contributors to his volume were thus paying tribute, probably at Chester's solicitation, to the memory of a minor patron of the arts.

Shakespeare's poem is experimental, not only in its application of a scholastic philosophy to its interpretation, but also in its formal respects. He uses a meter that he nowhere else employs, thirteen four-lined stanzas in trochaics. The "threnos" consists of three-lined stanzas, also in trochaic meter, each stanza having a single rhyme.

The poem also marks Shakespeare's imitation of the technical methods and imaginative resources of the metaphysical poets who were his contemporaries—John Donne, for example. The result is an original and highly effective contribution to the elegiac theme of the collection. More important for our knowledge of Shakespeare, it is a new revelation of the breadth and catholicity of his literary interests.

THE PHOENIX AND THE TURTLE

Let the bird of loudest lay,* *i.e.,* the phoenix
On the sole Arabian tree,
Herald sad and trumpet† be,
To whose sound chaste wings obey.

But thou shrieking harbinger,* *i.e.,* the screech owl
Foul precurrer* of the fiend, forerunner
Augur of the fever's end,* *i.e.,* death
To this troop come thou not near!

From this session interdict
Every fowl of tyrant wing, 10
Save the eagle, feathered king:
Keep the obsequy so strict.

Let the priest in surplice white,
That defunctive music can,†
Be the death-divining swan,
Lest the requiem lack his right.

And thou treble-dated† crow,
That thy sable gender* mak'st black offspring
With the breath thou giv'st and tak'st,
'Mongst our mourners shalt thou go. 20

Here the anthem doth commence:
Love and constancy is dead;
Phœnix and the turtle fled
In a mutual flame from hence.

Trumpet. The trumpeter who summons all well-disposed birds to the funeral.
That defunctive music can.
That knows how to sing the funeral service.
Treble-dated crow. The crow was supposed
to live nine times as long as human beings.

So they loved, as love in twain
Had the essence but in one;
Two distincts, division none:
Number there in love was slain.

Hearts remote, yet not asunder;
Distance, and no space was seen   30
'Twixt this turtle and his queen:
But* in them it were a wonder.   except

So between them love did shine,
That the turtle saw his right
Flaming in the phœnix' sight:
Either was the other's mine.

Property* was thus appalled,   individual possession
That the self was not the same;
Single nature's double name
Neither two nor one was called.†   40

Reason, in itself confounded,
Saw division grow together,
To themselves yet either neither,
Simple were so well compounded;

That it cried, "How true a twain
Seemeth this concordant one!
Love hath reason, reason none,†
If what parts can so remain."

Whereupon it made this threne*   funeral song
To the phœnix and the dove,
Co-supremes and stars of love,   50
As chorus to their tragic scene.

Single nature's double name
Neither two nor one was called.
They could not be called one because their natures were
distinct; nor two, because they were one essence.
Love hath reason, reason none.
Love has its own logic, different from that of reason.

THRENOS*

dirge

Beauty, truth, and rarity,
Grace in all simplicity,
Here enclosed in cinders lie.

Death is now the phœnix' nest;
And the turtle's loyal breast
To eternity doth rest,

Leaving no posterity:
'Twas not their infirmity,
It was married chastity.

60

Truth may seem, but cannot be;
Beauty brag, but 'tis not she:
Truth and beauty buried be.

To this urn let those repair
That are either true or fair;
For these dead birds sigh a prayer.

THE PASSIONATE PILGRIM

In 1599 William Jaggard, a sometimes-dishonest publisher, brought out a small anthology of poetry which he called "*The Passionate Pilgrime* [*i.e.*, lover] By W. Shakespeare." It consisted of twenty lyrics, the last six of which are prefaced by a separate title page reading, "Sonnets To sundry notes of Musicke" (the term "sonnet" in Elizabethan times was applied to any short lyrical poem, usually amatory).

Only five of the twenty poems are definitely by Shakespeare. The first piece in the volume is probably an earlier form of what became sonnet 138 in the entire sequence published in 1609, with some differences in the text. The second selection became sonnet 144, also with a few changes in the reading. The important fact disclosed by this poem is that the little drama of author, friend, and mistress, adumbrated in the sonnets, had by 1599 reached a critical stage.

Three selections were taken from *Love's Labour's Lost*, which had already been published. Number 3 is Longaville's sonnet to Maria (4/3/60–73). Number 5 is Berowne's sonnet to Rosaline in Alexandrines, verses of twelve syllables (4/2/108–122). Number 16 is the ode written by Dumain to Katherine (4/3/101–120).

There are three poems in the volume, numbers 4, 6, and 9, that treat Cytherea's (Venus') wooing of Adonis. The first presents the goddess making love to the youth beside a brook; the second, his escape from her ardor by plunging into the stream; the third, her encounter with Adonis while on his way to the boar hunt. Some critics believe that these verses represent Shakespeare's first exploration of the possibilities of the subject that he treated completely in *Venus and Adonis*.

The other pieces are by Christopher Marlowe, Richard Barnfield, Bartholomew Griffin, and lesser authors, most of whom are unidentified.

The manuscript of this collection was probably the scrapbook of a poetaster's collection of some of his favorite poems, which had found its way into Jaggard's hands.

THE PASSIONATE PILGRIM

I

When my love swears that she is made of truth,
I do believe her, though I know she lies,
That she might think me some untutored youth,
Unskilful in the world's false forgeries.*   deceits
Thus vainly thinking that she thinks me young,
Although I know my years be past the best,
I smiling credit her false-speaking tongue,
Outfacing* faults in love with love's ill rest.*   dissembling (*i.e.*,
                                                    concealing /
But wherefore says my love that she is young?   uneasiness
And wherefore say not I that I am old?   10
O, love's best habit is a soothing tongue,*   *i.e.*, flattery
And age, in love, loves not to have years told.
    Therefore I'll lie with love, and love with me,
    Since that our faults in love thus smothered be.

II

Two loves I have, of comfort and despair,
That like two spirits do suggest me still;
My better angel is a man right fair,
My worser spirit a woman coloured ill.
To win me soon to hell, my female evil
Tempteth my better angel from my side,
And would corrupt my saint to be a devil,
Wooing his purity with her fair pride.
And whether that my angel be turn'd fiend,
Suspect I may, yet not directly* tell: exactly
For being both to me, both to each friend,
I guess one angel in another's hell:
    The truth I shall not know, but live in doubt,
    Till my bad angel fire my good one out.

III

Longaville's sonnet to Maria, *Love's Labour's Lost*, 4/3/60–73.

Did not the heavenly rhetoric of thine eye,
'Gainst whom the world could not hold argument,
Persuade my heart to this false perjury?
Vows for thee broke† deserve not punishment.
A woman I forswore; but I will prove,
Thou being a goddess, I forswore not thee:
My vow was earthly, thou a heavenly love;
Thy grace being gain'd cures all disgrace in me.
My vow was breath,† and breath a vapour is;
Then, thou fair sun, that on this earth doth shine,   10
Exhale this vapour vow; in thee it is:
If broken, then it is no fault of mine.
    If by me broke, what fool is not so wise
    To break an oath,† to win a paradise?

IV

This is the first of three sonnets in this anthology on the subject of Venus and Adonis. They are all possibly by Shakespeare.

Sweet Cytherea, sitting by a brook
With young Adonis, lovely, fresh and green,*   innocent
Did court the lad with many a lovely look,
Such looks as none could look but beauty's queen.
She told him stories to delight his ear,
She showed him favours to allure his eye;
To win his heart, she touched him here and there;
Touches so soft still conquer chastity.
But whether unripe years did want conceit,*   understanding
Or he refused to take her figured proffer,*   inviting gesture
The tender nibbler would not touch the bait,
But smile and jest at every gentle offer:
    Then fell she on her back, fair queen, and toward:
    He rose and ran away; ah, fool too froward.*   perverse

Vows for thee broke. Refers to the oaths sworn by Navarre
and his companions to spend three years in monastic
study segregated from all women.
My vow was breath. The L.L.L. reading is "Vows are but breath."
To break an oath. The L.L.L. text is "to lose an oath."

V

Berowne's sonnet in Alexandrines, from *Love's Labour's Lost*, 4/2/108–122.

If love make me forsworn, how shall I swear to love?
O never faith could hold, if not to beauty vowed:
Though to myself forsworn, to thee I'll constant† prove;
Those thoughts, to me like oaks, to thee like osiers
     bowed.
Study his bias leaves, and makes his book thine eyes,
Where all those pleasures live that art can† comprehend.
If knowledge be the mark, to know thee shall suffice;
Well learned is that tongue that well can thee
     commend:
All ignorant that soul that sees thee without wonder;
Which is to me some praise, that I thy parts admire: 10
Thine eye Jove's lightning seems,† thy voice his
     dreadful thunder,
Which, not to anger bent, is music and sweet fire.
   Celestial as thou art, O do not love that wrong,
   To sing† heaven's praise with such an earthly
     tongue.

VI

This is the second sonnet in the anthology dealing with the story of Venus and Adonis.

Scarce had the sun dried up the dewy morn,
And scarce the herd gone to the hedge for shade,
When Cytherea, all in love forlorn,
A longing tarriance for Adonis made
Under an osier growing by a brook,
A brook where Adon used to cool his spleen:*   heat
Hot was the day; she hotter that did look
For his approach, that often there had been.
Anon he comes, and throws his mantle by,
And stood stark naked on the brook's green brim: 10

Constant. L.L.L. "faithful."
Can. L.L.L. "could."
Seems. L.L.L. "bears."
To sing. L.L.L. "that sings."

The sun look'd on the world with glorious eye,
Yet not so wistly* as this queen on him.   eagerly
   He, spying her, bounced in, whereas he stood:
   'O Jove,' quoth she, 'why was not I a flood!'

VII

   The author of this poem, found only here, is unknown.
Critics find in it no trace of Shakespeare.

Fair is my love, but not so fair as fickle,
Mild as a dove, but neither true nor trusty,
Brighter than glass and yet, as glass is, brittle,
Softer than wax and yet as iron rusty:
   A lily pale, with damask* dye to grace her,   deep red
   None fairer, nor none falser to deface her.

Her lips to mine how often hath she joined,
Between each kiss her oaths of true love swearing;
How many tales to please me hath she coined,
Dreading* my love, the loss thereof still fearing!   doubting
   Yet in the midst of all her pure protestings,
   Her faith, her oaths, her tears, and all were jestings.

She burned with love, as straw with fire flameth;
She burned out love, as soon as straw outburneth;
She framed* the love, and yet she foiled the framing;   roused
She bade love last, and yet she fell a-turning.
   Was this a lover, or a lecher whether?
   Bad in the best, though excellent in neither.

VIII

   This poem is by Richard Barnfield (1574–1627). It had already appeared in *Poems: in Divers Humours,* published in 1598.

If music and sweet poetry agree,
As they must needs, the sister and the brother,
Then must the love be great 'twixt thee and me,
Because thou lovest the one and I the other.
Dowland† to thee is dear, whose heavenly touch

Dowland. John Dowland (1563–1626) was a composer and a famous lutanist.

Upon the lute doth ravish human sense;
Spenser to me, whose deep conceit* is such   thought
As passing all conceit needs no defence.
Thou lovest to hear the sweet melodious sound
That Phœbus' lute, the queen of music, makes;   10
And I in deep delight am chiefly drown'd
When as himself to singing he betakes.
    One god is god of both, as poets feign;
    One knight† loves both, and both in thee remain.

IX

This is the third sonnet in the volume dealing with the story
of Venus and Adonis.

Fair was the morn when the fair queen of love,
. . . .

Paler for sorrow than her milk-white dove,
For Adon's sake, a youngster proud and wild;
Her stand she takes upon a steep-up hill:
And Adonis comes with horn and hounds;
She, silly* queen, with more than love's good will,   simple
Forbade the boy he should not pass those grounds:
'Once,' quoth she, 'did I see a fair sweet youth
Here in these brakes* deep-wounded with a boar,   thickets
Deep in the thigh, a spectacle of ruth!*   cruelty
See, in my thigh,' quoth she, 'here was the sore.'
    She showed hers: he saw more wounds than one,
    And blushing fled, and left her all alone.

X

The author of this poem is unknown. It has been conjec-
tured to be a dirge to be sung by Venus at the death of Adonis.

Sweet rose, fair flower, untimely plucked, soon vaded,*   faded
Plucked in the bud and vaded in the spring!
Bright orient pearl, alack, too timely shaded!
Fair creature, killed too soon by death's sharp sting!
    Like a green plum that hangs upon a tree,
    And falls through wind before the fall should be.

One knight. Sir George Carey. To him Dowland dedicated
his *First book of Songes and Ayres* (1597).

I weep for thee and yet no cause I have;
For why thou left'st me nothing in thy will:
And yet thou left'st me more than I did crave;
For why I craved nothing of thee still: 10
   O yes, dear friend, I pardon crave of thee,
   Thy discontent thou didst bequeath to me.

XI

This poem is probably by Bartholomew Griffin. It was the
third piece in a collection of sixty-two sonnets called *Fidessa,
more chaste than Kind* (1596).

Venus, with young Adonis sitting by her
Under a myrtle shade, began to woo him:
She told the youngling how god Mars did try her,
And as he fell to her, so fell she to him.
'Even thus,' quoth she, 'the warlike god embraced me,'
And then she clipp'd Adonis in her arms;
'Even thus, quoth she, 'the warlike god unlaced me,'
As if the boy should use like loving charms;
'Even thus,' quoth she, 'he seizèd on my lips,'
And with her lips on his did act the seizure: 10
And as she fetchèd breath, away he skips,
And would not take her meaning nor her pleasure.
   Ah, that I had my lady at this bay,*   laurel tree
   To kiss and clip* me till I run away!   clasp

XII

This poem is possibly by Thomas Deloney (1575–1600), a
ballad writer and pamphleteer. Some scholars attribute it to
Shakespeare.

Crabbèd age and youth cannot live together.
Youth is full of pleasance, age is full of care;
Youth like summer morn, age like winter weather;
Youth like summer brave,* age like winter bare.   showy
Youth is full of sport, age's breath is short;
   Youth is nimble, age is lame;
Youth is hot and bold, age is weak and cold;
   Youth is wild, and age is tame.
Age, I do abhor thee; youth, I do adore thee;
   O, my love, my love is young!   10
Age, I do defy thee: O, sweet shepherd, hie thee,
   For methinks thou stay'st too long.

XIII

The author of this poem, which appears only here, is unknown.

Beauty is but a vain and doubtful good;
A shining gloss that vadeth suddenly;
A flower that dies when first it 'gins to bud;
A brittle glass that's broken presently:*   at once
  A doubtful good, a gloss, a glass, a flower,
  Lost, vaded, broken, dead within an hour.

And as goods lost are seld or never found,
As vaded gloss no rubbing will refresh,
As flowers dead lie withered on the ground,
As broken glass no cement can redress,   10
  So beauty blemished once's for ever lost,
  In spite of physic, painting, pain and cost.

XIV

Good night, good rest. Ah, neither be* my share: are
She bade good night that kept my rest away;
And daffed* me to a cabin hanged with care,   sent me off
To descant on* the doubts of my decay.   comment on
  'Farewell,' quoth she, 'and come again tomorrow:
  Fare well I could not, for I supped with sorrow.

Yet at my parting sweetly did she smile,
In scorn or friendship, nill* I construe whether:*   will not / which of the two
'T may be, she joyèd to jest at my exile,
'T may be, again to make me wander thither: 10
  'Wander,' a word for shadows like myself,
  As take the pain, but cannot pluck the pelf.*   gain

Lord, how mine eyes throw gazes to the east!
My heart doth charge the watch; the morning rise
Doth cite* each moving sense from idle rest.   rouse
Not daring trust the office of mine eyes,
  While Philomela* sits and sings, I sit and mark,   the nightingale
  And wish her lays were tunèd like the lark;

For she doth welcome daylight with her ditty,
And drives away dark dreaming night: 20
The night so packed, I post unto my pretty;
Heart hath his hope and eyes their wishèd sight;
   Sorrow changed to solace and solace mixed with sorrow;
   For why, she sighed, and bade me come tomorrow.

Were I with her, the night would post* too soon;   hurry
But now are minutes added to the hours;
To spite me now, each minute seems a moon;
Yet not for me, shine sun to succour flowers!
   Pack* night, peep day; good day, of night now borrow: be off
   Short, night, to-night, and length thyself tomorrow.   30

XV

   Author unknown. The first lines of the poem appeared under the caption "Sonnets To sundry notes of Musicke."

It was a lording's* daughter, the fairest one   gentleman's
   of three,
That likèd of her master* as well as might be,   teacher
Till looking on an Englishman, the fair'st that
   eye could see,
   Her fancy* fell a-turning.   love
Long was the combat doubtful that love with
   love did fight,
To leave the master loveless, or kill the gallant knight:
To put in practice either, alas, it was a spite
   Unto the silly damsel!
But one must be refused; more mickle was the pain
That nothing could be used to turn them both to gain,   10
For of the two the trusty knight was wounded with
   disdain:
   Alas, she could not help it!
Thus art with arms contending was victor of the day,
Which by a gift of learning did bear the maid away:
Then, lullaby, the learned man hath got the lady gay;
   For now my song is ended.

XVI

This is an ode written by Dumain to Katherine in *Love's Labour's Lost*, 4/3/101–120.

On a day, alack the day!
Love, whose month was ever May,
Spied a blossom passing fair,
Playing in the wanton air:
Through the velvet leaves the wind
All unseen 'gan passage find;
That the lover, sick to death,
Wish'd himself the heaven's breath,
'Air,' quoth he, 'thy cheeks may blow;
Air, would I might triumph so!   10
But, alas! my hand hath sworn
Ne'er to pluck thee from thy thorn:
Vow, alack! for youth unmeet:
Youth, so apt to pluck a sweet.
Thou for whom Jove would swear
Juno but an Ethiope were;
And deny himself for Jove,
Turning mortal for thy love.'

XVII

Author unknown. Previously published in a collection of madrigals by Thomas Weelkes (1597).

My flocks feed not,
My ewes breed not,
My rams speed* not;   profit
   All is amiss:
Love's denying,*†   refusal
Faith's defying,*   rejection
Heart's denying,
   Causer of this.
All my merry jigs are quite forgot,
All my lady's love is lost, God wot: 10
Where her faith was firmly fixed in love,
There a nay* is placed without remove.   refusal

Denying. The original "Love is dying" is the better reading.

One silly cross
Wrought all my loss;
   O frowning Fortune, cursèd, fickle dame!
For now I see
Inconstancy
   More in women than in men remain.

In black mourn I,
All fears scorn I,   20
Love hath forlorn me,
   Living in thrall:
Heart is bleeding,
All help needing,
O cruel speeding,
   Fraughted* with gall.   freighted
My shepherd's pipe can sound no deal:
My wether's bell rings doleful knell;
My curtal* dog, that wont to have played,   docked
Plays not at all, but seems afraid;   30
My sighs so deep
Procure* to weep,   cause
   In howling wise, to see my doleful plight.
How sighs resound
Through heartless ground,
   Like a thousand vanquished men in bloody fight!

Clear wells spring not,
Sweet birds sing not,
Green plants bring not
   Forth their dye;   40
Herds stand weeping,
Flocks all sleeping,
Nymphs back peeping
   Fearfully:
All our pleasure known to us poor swains,
All our merry meetings on the plains,
All our evening sport from us is fled,
All our love is lost, for Love is dead.
Farewell, sweet lass,
Thy like ne'er was   50
   For a sweet content, the cause of all my moan.
Poor Corydon
Must live alone;
   Other help for him I see that there is none.

XVIII

Author unknown.

When as thine eye hath chose the dame,
And stalled the deer that thou shouldst strike,
Let reason rule things worthy blame,
As well as fancy,* partial wight: love
    Take counsel of some wiser head,
    Neither too young nor yet unwed.

And when thou comest thy tale to tell,
Smooth not thy tongue with filèd talk,
Lest she some subtle practice* smell,—   deceit
A cripple soon can find a halt;*—   limp
    But plainly say thou lovest her well,
    And set thy person forth to sell.

And to her will frame all thy ways;
Spare not to spend, and chiefly there*   *i.e.*, her maid
Where thy desert may merit praise,
By ringing in thy lady's ear:
    The strongest castle, tower and town,
    The golden bullet beats it down.   30

Serve always with assurèd trust,
And in thy suit be humble true;
Unless thy lady prove unjust,*   unfaithful
Press never thou to choose anew:
    When time shall serve, be thou not slack
    To proffer, though she put thee back.

What though her frowning brows be bent,
Her cloudy looks will calm ere night:
And then too late she will repent
That thus dissembled her delight;
    And twice desire, ere it be day,
    That which with scorn she put away.

What though she strive to try her strength,
And ban* and brawl, and say thee nay,   curse
Her feeble force will yield at length,
When craft hath taught her thus to say;
    'Had women been so strong as men,
    In faith, you had not had it then.'

The wiles and guiles that women work,
Dissembled with an outward show,
The tricks and toys that in them lurk,
The cock that treads them shall not know.   40
   Have you not heard it said full oft,
   A woman's nay doth stand for nought?

Think women still to strive with men,
To sin and never for to saint:
There is no heaven, by holy then,
When time with age shall them attaint.
   Were kisses all the joys in bed,
   One woman would another wed.

But, soft! enough—too much, I fear—
Lest that my mistress hear my song: 50
She will not stick to round* me on th' ear,   whisper
To teach my tongue to be so long:
   Yet will she blush, here be it said,
   To hear her secrets so bewrayed.*   betrayed

XIX

By Marlowe. It appeared in *England's Helicon* (1600) with
the title "The Passionate Shepherd to his Love" with two
additional verses.

Live with me, and be my love,
And we will all the pleasures prove
That hills and valleys, dales and fields,
And all the craggy mountains yields.
There will we sit upon the rocks,
And see the shepherds feed their flocks,
By shallow rivers, by whose falls
Melodious birds sing madrigals.*   love songs
There will I make thee a bed of roses,
With a thousand fragrant posies,   10
A cap of flowers, and a kirtle
Embroidered all with leaves of myrtle.

A belt of straw and ivy buds,
With coral clasps and amber studs;
And if these pleasures may thee move,
Then live with me and be my love.

LOVE'S ANSWER†

If that the world and love were young,
And truth in every shepherd's tongue,
These pretty pleasures might me move
To live with thee and be thy love.   20

XX

By Richard Barnfield.

As it fell upon a day
In the merry month of May,
Sitting in a pleasant shade
Which a grove of myrtles made,
Beasts did leap and birds did sing,
Trees did grow and plants did spring;
Every thing did banish moan,
Save the nightingale alone:
She, poor bird, as all forlorn,
Leaned her breast up-till* a thorn,   up against
And there sung the dolefull'st ditty,
That to hear it was great pity:
'Fie, fie, fie,' now would she cry;
'Tereu, Tereu!† by and by;
That to hear her so complain,
Scarce I could from tears refrain;
For her griefs so lively shown
Made me think upon mine own.
Ah, thought I, thou mourn'st in vain!
None takes pity on thy pain: 20
Senseless trees they cannot hear thee;
Ruthless beasts they will not cheer thee:
King Pandion he is dead;
All thy friends are lapped* in lead;   wrapped
All thy fellow birds do sing,
Careless of thy sorrowing.

"Love's Answer" in *England's Helicon* becomes "The Nymph's reply to the Shepherd."

Tereu. Ovid tells the story of Tereus as follows: He was King of Thrace and married Procne, the daughter of Pandion (see line 23), King of Athens, by whom she had a son, Itys. Tereus raped his wife's sister Philomela and cut out her tongue. Procne released her sister, killed and cooked Itys as a feast for his father. She was changed into a swallow, Philomela into a nightingale, Tereus into a lapwing.

Even so, poor bird, like thee,
None alive will pity me.
Whilst as fickle Fortune smiled,
Thou and I were both beguiled.   30
   Every one that flatters thee
Is no friend in misery.
Words are easy, like the wind;
Faithful friends are hard to find:
Every man will be thy friend
Whilst thou hast wherewith to spend;
But if store of crown be scant,
No man will supply thy want.
If that one be prodigal,
Bountiful they will him call,   40
And with such-like flattering,
'Pity but he were a king';
If he be addict* to vice,   addicted
Quickly him they will entice;
If to women he be bent,
They* have at commandment: *i.e.,* women
   But if Fortune once do frown,
   Then farewell his great renown;
   They that fawned on him before
   Use his company no more.
   He that is thy friend indeed,   50
   He will help thee in thy need:
   If thou sorrow, he will weep;
   If thou wake, he cannot sleep;
   Thus of every grief in heart
   He with thee doth bear a part.
   These are certain signs to know
   Faithful friend from flattering foe.

A LOVER'S COMPLAINT

Thomas Thorpe, the editor of the 1609 volume of Shakespeare's sonnets, appended *A Lover's Complaint* to the sequence. It is a poem of 49 stanzas written in the seven-line stanza—the rhyme royal, which the poet adopted for *The Rape of Lucrece*. The subject is conventional—a girl's lament for her betrayal by an irresistible youth. However, the treatment of the theme is in many respects original. The girl is no lovely young creature but one who is "The carcass of a beauty spent and done."

The setting, too, is somewhat unusual for a pastoral. To be sure, one of the characters is the inevitable old shepherd, "a reverend man that grazed his cattle nigh." It is he who comes upon the faded beauty by the side of a stream, where she is weeping and tearing to shreds love letters, which she first kisses and then throws into the stream. Many "a ring of posied gold" and other gifts meet the same fate. Privileged by his age, the old shepherd asks the girl to tell him the cause of her distress.

Her answer forms the rest of the poem. It is a lament for her lost virtue. Not long ago she fell violently in love with a handsome but unprincipled youth, whom all the girls in the region adored, or as the poet quaintly puts it: "That maidens' eyes stuck over all his face." Knowing full well that he was a gay deceiver, she was careful not to yield at once to his blandishments. "With safest distance I my honour shielded." But at length his arts of seduction, which she describes at length and in detail, prevailed and she fell: "There my white stole of chastity I daffed." Then, like all the other pastoral nymphs in her situation, she was abandoned. This is why the girl is weeping and lamenting by the river's side and bewailing both her folly in yielding and her seducer's irresistible charms.

If this poem is by Shakespeare, it must be an early work, the product of his "prentice hand." Most critics find the language forced and full of awkward verbal inventions. Moreover, the imagery is so far-fetched and infelicitous as often to seem absurd. The general consensus now is that, in spite of the appearance of *A Lover's Complaint* in the same volume with the sonnets, none of it is Shakespeare's work.

A LOVER'S COMPLAINT

From off a hill whose concave womb re-worded
A plaintful story from a sistering vale,
My spirits to attend this double voice accorded,
And·down I laid to list the sad-tuned tale;
Ere long espied a fickle maid full pale,
Tearing of papers, breaking rings a-twain,
Storming her world with sorrow's wind and rain.

Upon her head a platted hive* of straw,   bonnet
Which fortified her visage from the sun,
Whereon the thought might think sometime it saw   10
The carcass of a beauty spent and done:
Time had not scythed all that youth begun,
Nor youth all quit; but, spite of heaven's fell rage,
Some beauty peeped through lattice of seared age.

Oft did she heave her napkin to her eyne,
Which on it had conceited* characters,   quaintly designed
Laundering the silken figures in the brine
That seasoned woe had pelleted in tears,
And often reading what contents it bears;
As often shrieking undistinguished* woe,   humble
In clamours of all size, both high and low.

Sometimes her levelled eyes their carriage ride,†
As they did battery to the spheres intend;
Sometime diverted their poor balls are tied
To the orbed earth; sometimes they do extend
Their view right on; anon their gazes lend
To every place at once, and nowhere fixed
The mind and sight distractedly commixed.

Her hair, nor loose nor tied in formal plat,
Proclaimed in her a careless hand of pride;   30
For some, untucked, descended her sheaved* hat,   straw

Sometimes her levelled eyes their carriage ride.
Sometimes her levelled eyes, as with a gun, carry their load of ammunition.

Hanging her pale and pinèd cheek beside;
Some in her threaden fillet still did bide,
And, true to bondage, would not break from thence,
Though slackly braided in loose negligence.

A thousand favours from a maund* she drew   basket
Of amber, crystal, and of beaded jet,
Which one by one she in a river threw,
Upon whose weeping margent she was set;
Like usury, applying wet to wet,   40
Or monarch's hands that lets not bounty fall
Where want cries* some, but where excess begs all.   cries for

Of folded schedules* had she many a one,   *i.e.*, letters
Which she perused, sighed, tore, and gave the flood;
Cracked many a ring of posied gold and bone,†
Bidding them find their sepulchres in mud;
Found yet moe letters sadly penned in blood,
With sleided* silk feat* and affectedly   untwisted / skillfully
Enswathed, and sealed to curious* secrecy.   fastidious

These often bathed she in her fluxive*. eyes,   weeping
And often kissed, and often 'gan to tear;
Cried 'O false blood, thou register of lies,
What unapprovèd witness dost thou bear!
Ink would have seemed more black and damnèd here!'
This said, in top of rage the lines she rents,
Big discontent so breaking their contents.

A reverend man that grazed his cattle nigh—
Sometime a blusterer,* that the ruffle* knew braggart / excitements
Of court, of city, and had let go by
The swiftest hours, observèd as they flew—   60
Towards this afflicted fancy fastly drew;
And, privileged by age, desires to know
In brief the grounds and motives of her woe.

So slides he down upon his grained bat,*   wooden staff
And comely*-distant sits he by her side;   properly
When he again desires her, being sat,

Cracked many a ring of posied gold and bone.
A posied ring was one with an amorous sentiment
inscribed on the inner side of its band.

Her grievance with his hearing to divide:*   *share*
If that from him there may be aught applied
Which may her suffering ecstasy assuage,
'Tis promised in the charity of age.   70

'Father,' she says, 'though in me you behold
The injury of many a blasting hour,
Let it not tell your judgement I am old;
Not age, but sorrow, over me hath power:
I might as yet have been a spreading flower,
Fresh to myself, if I had self-applied
Love to myself, and to no love beside.

'But, woe is me! too early I attended
A youthful suit—it was to gain my grace—
Of one by nature's outwards so commended,   80
That maidens' eyes stuck over all his face:
Love lacked a dwelling and made him her place;
And when in his fair parts she did abide,
She was new lodged and newly deified.

'His browny locks did hang in crooked curls;
And every light occasion of the wind
Upon his lips their silken parcels hurls.
What's sweet to do, to do will aptly find:
Each eye that saw him did enchant the mind;
For on his visage was in little* drawn   *miniature*
What largeness thinks in Paradise was sawn.*   *sown*

'Small show of man was yet upon his chin;
His phœnix* down began but to appear,   *i.e., matchless*
Like unshorn velvet, on that termless* skin,   *indescribable*
Whose bare* out-bragged the web it seemed to wear: *bareness*
Yet showed his visage by that cost more dear;
And nice* affections wavering stood in doubt   *discriminating*
If best were as it* was, or best without.   *i.e., his beard*

'His qualities were beauteous as his form,
For maiden-tongued he was, and thereof free;*   *i.e., from offense*
Yet, if men moved him, was he such a storm
As oft 'twixt May and April is to see,
When winds breathe sweet, unruly though they be.
His rudeness so with his authòrized youth
Did livery falseness in a pride of truth.

'Well could he ride, and often men would say,
"That horse his mettle from his rider takes:
Proud of subjection, noble by the sway,
What rounds, what bounds, what course, what stop
      he makes!"
And controversy hence a question takes,   110
Whether the horse by him became his deed,
Or he his manage by the well-doing steed.

'But quickly on this side the verdict went:
His real habitude gave life and grace
To appertainings and to ornament,
Accomplished in himself, not in his case:*   situation
All aids, themselves made fairer by their place,
Came for additions; yet their purposed trim
Pieced not his grace, but were all graced by him.

'So on the tip of his subduing tongue   120
All kind of arguments and question deep,
All replication* prompt and reason strong,   rejoinders
For his advantage still did wake and sleep:
To make the weeper laugh, the laugher weep,
He had the dialect* and different skill,   language
Catching all passions in his craft of will;

'That he did in the general bosom reign
Of young, of old, and sexes both enchanted,
To dwell with him in thoughts, or to remain
In personal duty, following where he haunted: 130
Consents bewitched, ere he desire, have granted,
And dialogued for him what he would say,
Asked their own wills and made their wills obey.

'Many there were that did his picture get,
To serve their eyes, and in it put their mind;
Like fools that in the imagination set
The goodly objects which abroad they find
Of lands and mansions, theirs in thought assigned;
And labouring in moe* pleasures to bestow them   more
Than the true gouty landlord which doth owe them: 140

'So many have, that never touched his hand,
Sweetly supposed them mistress of his heart.
My woeful self, that did in freedom stand,

And was my own fee-simple,* not in part,   unrestricted
What with his art in youth and youth in art,
Threw my affections in his charmèd power,
Reserved the stalk and gave him all my flower.

'Yet did I not, as some my equals did,
Demand of him, nor being desired yielded;
Finding myself in honour so forbid,   150
With safest distance I mine honour shielded:
Experience for me many bulwarks builded
Of proofs new-bleeding, which remained the foil
Of this false jewel, and his amorous spoil.

'But, ah, who ever shunned by precedent
The destined ill she must herself assay?
Or forced examples, 'gainst her own content,
To put the by-past perils in her way?
Counsel may stop awhile what will not stay;
For when we rage, advice is often seen   160
By blunting us to make our wits more keen.

'Nor gives it satisfaction to our blood,*   passion
That we must curb it upon others' proof;*   tests
To be forbod* the sweets that seem so good,   forbidden
For fear of harms that preach in our behoof.
O appetite, from judgement stand aloof!
The one a palate hath that needs will taste,
Though Reason weep, and cry "It is thy last."

'For further I could say "This man's untrue,"
And knew the patterns of his foul beguiling;   170
Heard where his plants in others' orchards grew,
Saw how deceits were gilded in his smiling;
Knew vows were ever brokers* to defiling;   peddlers
Thought characters and words merely but art,
And bastards of his foul adulterate heart.

'And long upon these terms I held my city,
Till thus he 'gan besiege me: "Gentle maid,
Have of my suffering youth some feeling pity,
And be not of my holy vows afraid:
That's to ye sworn to none was ever said;   180
For feasts of love I have been called unto,
Till now did ne'er invite, nor never woo.

' "All my offences that abroad you see
Are errors of the blood, none of the mind;
Love made them not: with acture* they may be,   action
Where neither party is nor true nor kind:
They sought their shame that so their shame did find:
And so much less of shame in me remains
By how much of me their reproach contains.

' "Among the many that mine eyes have seen,   190
Not one whose flame my heart so much as warmed,
Or my affection put to the smallest teen,
Or any of my leisures* ever charmed: leisure hours
Harm have I done to them, but ne'er was harmed;
Kept hearts in liveries,* but mine own was free,   i.e., my service
And reigned commanding in his monarchy.

' "Look here, what tributes wounded fancies sent me,
Of palèd pearls and rubies red as blood;
Figuring that they their passions likewise lent me
Of grief and blushes, aptly understood   200
In bloodless white and the encrimsoned mood;
Effects of terror and dear modesty,
Encamped in hearts, but fighting outwardly.

' "And, lo, behold these talents* of their hair,   riches
With twisted metal amorously impleached,*   entwined
I have received from many a several fair,
Their kind acceptance weepingly beseeched,
With the annexions of fair gems enriched,
And deep-brained sonnets that did amplify
Each stone's dear nature, worth and quality.   210

' "The diamond, why, 'twas beautiful and hard,
Whereto his invised* properties did tend;   invisible
The deep-green emerald, in whose fresh regard
Weak sights their sickly radiance do amend;
The heaven-hued sapphire and the opal blend
With objects manifold: each several stone,
With wit well blazoned,* smiled or made some moan.   interpreted

' "Lo, all these trophies of affections hot,
Of pensived* and subdued desires the tender,   pensive
Nature hath charged me that I hoard them not,   220

But yield them up where I myself must render,
That is, to you, my origin and ender;
For these, of force, must your oblations be,
Since I their altar, you enpatron me.

' "O, then, advance of yours that phraseless* hand,   baffling
Whose white weighs down the airy scale of praise;   description
Take all these similes to your own command,
Hallowed with sighs that burning lungs did raise;
What me your minister, for you obeys,
Works under you; and to your audit comes   230
Their distract* parcels in combinèd sums.   disjoined

' "Lo, this device was sent me from a nun,
Or sister sanctified, of holiest note;
Which late her noble suit in court did shun,
Whose rarest havings* made the blossoms dote;   talents
For she was sought by spirits of richest coat,
But kept cold distance, and did thence remove,
To spend her living in eternal love.

' "But, O my sweet, what labour is 't to leave
The thing we have not, mastering what not strives,   240
Playing the place which did no form receive,
Playing patient sports in unconstrained gyves?*   shackles
She that her fame so to herself contrives,
The scars of battle 'scapeth by the flight,
And makes her absence valiant, not her might.

' "O, pardon me, in that my boast is true:
The accident which brought me to her eye
Upon the moment did her force subdue,
And now she would the cagèd cloister fly:
Religious love put out Religion's eye: 250
Not to be tempted, would she be immured,
And now, to tempt all, liberty procured.

' "How mighty then you are, O, hear me tell!
The broken bosoms that to me belong
Have emptied all their fountains in my well,
And mine I pour your ocean all among:
I strong o'er them, and you o'er me being strong,
Must for your victory us all congest,*   gather in one
As compound love to physic your cold breast.

' "My parts had power to charm a sacred nun,   260
Who disciplined, ay, dieted in grace,
Believed her eyes when they to assail begun,
All vows and consecrations giving place:
O most potential love! vow, bond, nor space,
In thee hath neither sting, knot, nor confine,
For thou art all, and all things else are thine.

' "When thou impressest, what are precepts worth
Of stale example? When thou wilt inflame,
How coldly those impediments stand forth
Of wealth, of filial fear, law, kindred, fame!   270
Love's arms are peace, 'gainst rule, 'gainst sense,
       'gainst shame;
And sweetens, in the suffering pangs it bears,
The aloes* of all forces, shocks and fears.   bitterness

' "Now all these hearts that do on mine depend,
Feeling it break, with bleeding groans they pine;
And supplicant their sighs to you extend,
To leave the battery that you make 'gainst mine,
Lending soft audience to my sweet design,
And credent soul to that strong-bonded oath
That shall prefer and undertake my troth."   280

'This said, his watery eyes he did dismount,*   lower
Whose sights till then were levelled on my face;
Each cheek a river running from a fount
With brinish current downward flowed apace:
O, how the channel to the stream gave grace!
Who glazed with crystal gate the glowing roses
That flame through water which their hue encloses.

'O father, what a hell of witchcraft lies
In the small orb of one particular tear!
But with the inundation of the eyes   290
What rocky heart to water will not wear?
What breast so cold that is not warmèd here?
O cleft effect! cold modesty, hot wrath,
Both fire from hence and chill extincture* hath.   extinction

'For, lo, his passion, but an art of craft,
Even there resolved my reason into tears;
There my white stole of chastity I daffed,*   doffed

Shook off my sober guards and civil* fears;   decorous
Appear to him, as he to me appears,
All melting; though our drops this difference bore,   300
His poisoned me, and mine did him restore.

'In him a plentitude of subtle matter,*   tricks
Applied to cautels,* all strange forms receives,   deceits
Of burning blushes, or of weeping water,
Or swounding paleness; and he takes and leaves,
In either's aptness, as it best deceives,
To blush at speeches rank,* to weep at woes,   excessive
Or to turn white and swound at tragic shows:

'That not a heart which in his level came
Could 'scape the hail of his all-hurting aim   310
Showing fair nature is both kind and tame
And, veiled in them, did win whom he would maim:
Against the thing he sought he would exclaim;
When he most burned in heart-wished luxury,*   lust
He preached pure maid and praised cold chastity.

'Thus merely with the garment of a Grace
The naked and concealèd fiend he covered;
That the unexperient gave the tempter place,
Which, like a cherubin, above them hovered.
Who, young and simple, would not be so lovered?   320
Ay me! I fell, and yet do question make
What I should do again for such a sake.

'O, that infected moisture of his eye,
O, that false fire which in his cheek so glowed,
O, that forced thunder from his heart did fly,
O, that sad breath his spongy lungs bestowed,
O, all that borrowed motion seeming owed,
Would yet again betray the fore-betrayed,
And new pervert a reconcilèd maid!'

Chronology of Shakespeare's Life

HISTORIC AND LITERARY EVENTS   SHAKESPEARE AND HIS FAMILY

1558
Elizabeth I crowned Queen.
Thomas Kyd born.
Robert Greene born.

1561
Francis Bacon born.

John Shakespeare elected
  Chamberlain of Stratford.

1564
Christopher Marlowe born.
Galileo Galilei born.

Shakespeare born, April 23;
  baptized April 26.

1566

Gilbert, Shakespeare's brother,
  born; died 1612.

1567
Mary, Queen of Scots,
  dethroned. James VI (later
  James I of England) crowned.

1572
Massacre of St. Bartholomew.
Ben Jonson born. •

1573
John Donne born.

1575
Earl of Leicester's entertainment
  of the Queen at Kenilworth.

1576
Burbage builds the first public
  playhouse, The Theatre.

1577
Drake begins circumnavigation
  of the earth; finished 1580.
Holinshed's *Chronicles of
  England, Scotland and
  Ireland.*

1579
John Lyly's *Euphues: The
    Anatomy of Wit.*

1581
Tenne Tragedies of Seneca.

1582
                                    Shakespeare's marriage.

1583
Philip Massinger born.   Shakespeare's daughter,
The Queen's company formed.   Susanna, born.

1584
Reginald Scot's *The
    Discovery of Witchcraft.*

1585   Shakespeare's twins,
                                      Hamnet and Judith, born.

1586
Sir Philip Sidney killed at
    Zutphen.
John Ford born.

1587
Mary, Queen of Scots, beheaded.
Marlowe's *Tamburlaine, I.*
Kyd's *Spanish Tragedy.*

1588
Defeat of the Spanish Armada.
Principal actors of Lord
    Leicester's Company join
    Lord Strange's Men.
Marlowe's *Tamburlaine, II.*
Lyly's *Endimion.*

1589
Henry of Navarre crowned   *Comedy of Errors.*
    King of France as Henry IV.
Greene's *Friar Bacon and
    Friar Bungay.*
Marlowe's *Jew of Malta.*

1590
Sidney's *Arcadia* published.   *Titus Andronicus.*
Spenser's *Faerie Queene (I-III).* *Henry VI, I.*

1591   *Henry VI, II.*
                                 Henry VI, III.

1592

Death of Greene.
Marlowe's *Doctor Faustus* and
   Edward II.

Two Gentlemen of Verona.

1593

Theatres closed by plague.
Death of Marlowe.

Venus and Adonis.
Sonnets begun.
Richard III.

1594

Shakespeare's company becomes
   the Lord Chamberlain's Men.
Death of Kyd.

Rape of Lucrece.
Love's Labour's Lost.
Taming of the Shrew.
King John.

1595

Raleigh's first expedition to
   Guiana.
Spenser's *Amoretti,*
   Epithalamium.
Sidney's *Defense of Poesy*
   published.

Richard II.
A Midsummer Night's Dream.
Merchant of Venice.

1596

Spenser's *The Faerie Queene,*
   Books IV-VI, *Four Hymns,*
   and *Prothalamium.*

Romeo and Juliet.
Hamnet Shakespeare dies.

1597

Bacon's *Essays* (first edition).
King James's *Demonologie.*

Henry IV, I.
Merry Wives of Windsor.
Shakespeare buys and renovates
   New Place in Stratford.

1598

Edict of Nantes issued by
   Henry IV, giving Huguenots
   political rights.
Jonson's *Every Man in His*
   Humour acted.
Seven books of Chapman's
   translation of the *Iliad.*

Henry IV, II.
Much Ado About Nothing.

1599

Death of Spenser.
Globe Theatre built.
Essex' expedition to Ireland.
Jonson's *Every Man out of His*
   Humour acted.
Dekker's *Shoemaker's Holiday.*

Henry V.
Julius Caesar.

1600

Fortune Theatre built.
East India Company founded.
Children of The Chapel acquire
  a hall in Blackfriars'
  Monastery.

As You Like It.
Twelfth Night.

1601

Insurrection and execution of
  Essex.

Hamlet.
Troilus and Cressida.

1602

Sir Thos. Bodley's Library at
  Oxford opened.

All's Well That Ends Well.

1603

Death of Queen Elizabeth I.
Accession of James I.
Shakespeare's company
  becomes the King's Men.
Heywood's *A Woman Killed
  with Kindness.*
Jonson's *Sejanus His Fall.*
Florio's translation of
  Montaigne's *Essays.*

1604

Treaty of Peace with Spain.

Measure for Measure.
Othello.

1605

The Gunpowder Plot.
Middleton's *A Trick to Catch
  the Old One.*

King Lear.

1606

Jonson's *Volpone.*

Macbeth.

1607

Settlement of Jamestown,
  Virginia.
Beaumont's *The Knight of the
  Burning Pestle.*

Antony and Cleopatra.
Timon of Athens.
Shakespeare's daughter Susanna
  married to Dr. John Hall.

1608

Burbage leases Blackfriars'
  Theatre for Shakespeare's
  company.
John Milton born.

Coriolanus.
Pericles, Prince of Tyre.

1609

Beaumont and Fletcher's
  Philaster.

Shakespeare's *Sonnets* published.

1610

Beaumont and Fletcher's
  Maid's Tragedy.

Cymbeline.

1611

Chapman completes translation
  of the *Iliad*.
Authorized version of
  the Bible.

The Winter's Tale.
The Tempest.

1612

Death of Prince Henry.
Beaumont retires from the
  theatre.
Webster's *The White Devil*.
Shelton's translation of
  Don Quixote, Part I.

1613

Globe Theatre burns.
Marriage of Princess Elizabeth
  to the Elector Palatine.

Henry VIII (with Fletcher).
The Two Noble Kinsmen (with
  Fletcher).
Buys a house in Blackfriars.

1614

Globe Theatre rebuilt.
Jonson's *Bartholomew Fair*.
Webster's *The Duchess of Malfi*.

1616

Death of Beaumont and
  Cervantes.
Jonson publishes his plays in a
  single volume entitled
  The Works of Ben Jonson.

Marriage of Judith Shakespeare
  to Thomas Quiney.
Death of Shakespeare, April 23.

1623

Publication of the Folio edition
  of Shakespeare's plays.

Death of Ann Hathaway.

Bibliography

I. REFERENCE

BROOKE, C. F. TUCKER, Ed. *Shakespeare of Stratford.* New Haven: Yale University Press, 1926. This volume, a handbook for students, gives the reader a brief, scholarly survey of the essential facts about the dramatist and his work.

KÖKERITZ, HELGE. *Shakespeare's Pronunciation.* New Haven: Yale University Press, 1953. The latest authoritative work on this important subject.

II. SHAKESPEARE'S LIFE

ALEXANDER, PETER. *Shakespeare's Life and Art.* London: James Nisbet, 1939. Many important and new insights into the relation of Shakespeare's life to his art.

BRANDES, GEORG M. C. *William Shakespeare: A Critical Study.* Translated by William Archer. London: William Heinemann, 1902. A "life" by one of the most famous literary critics of the nineteenth century.

CHAMBERS, SIR EDMUND K. *William Shakespeare: A Study of Facts and Problems.* 2 vols. New York: Oxford University Press, 1930. A thorough assemblage of all the important facts of Shakespeare's life by the most rigorous scholar in the field.

CHUTE, MARCHETTE. *Shakespeare of London.* New York: E. P. Dutton, 1949. An excellent biography of Shakespeare. It contains a bibliography.

LEE, SIR SIDNEY. *A Life of William Shakespeare.* 4th ed. New York: The Macmillan Co., 1929. For years the most authoritative account of the Poet's life.

VAN DOREN, MARK. *Shakespeare.* New York: Doubleday, 1953. This is an appreciation by a sensitive critic who is himself a poet.

III. SHAKESPEARE'S TIMES

JENKINS, ELIZABETH. *Elizabeth the Great.* New York: Coward-McCann, 1959. The most recent American biography, a distinguished piece of scholarship and literary skill.

NEALE, JOHN E. *Queen Elizabeth.* New York: Harcourt, Brace, 1934. The authoritative biography.

RALEIGH, SIR WALTER. *Shakespeare's England: An Account of the Life and Manners of His Age.* 2 vols. Oxford: Oxford University Press, 1917. A complete account of the habits, interests and activities of the people during Shakespeare's lifetime.

STEEHOLM, CLARA and HARDY. *James I of England*. New York: Crown Publishers, 1938. A lively and acute account of James's personal life and kingship.

TILLYARD, E. M. W. *The Elizabethan World Picture*. New York: The Macmillan Co., 1944. The authoritative account of the geography—celestial and earthly—and the organization of the world as the Elizabethan pictured it.

IV. THE SONNETS

ACHESON, ARTHUR. *Shakespeare's Sonnet Story*. London: B. Quaritch, 1933. A confident assertion that George Chapman is the rival Poet, and Mrs. Anne Davenant (who never existed) the Dark Lady.

ARCHER, WILLIAM. "Shakespeare's Sonnets: The Case Against Southampton," *Fortnightly Review*, 1897. LXVIII, 817-834.

DOUGLAS, LORD ALFRED. *The True History of Shakespeare's Sonnets*. London: M. Secker, 1933. Lord Alfred defends Shakespeare against the charge of homosexuality.

FURNIVALL, F. J. "Shakespeare and Mary Fitton," *Theatre*, 1897. XXX, 293-298. An examination of the belief that Mary Fitton is the Dark Lady of the sonnets.

HUBLER, EDWARD. *The Sense of Shakespeare's Sonnets*. Princeton: Princeton University Press, 1952. This study is concerned with the Poet's "lyric preceptions" of controlling ideas in the sonnets.

LEE, SIR SIDNEY (Introduction by). *Elizabethan Sonnets*. 2 vols. Westminster: A. Constable, 1904. A collection of the sonnets of Sir Philip Sidney, Samuel Daniel, Henry Constable, Thomas Lodge, Barnabe Barnes, Giles Fletcher, Machael Drayton, Edmund Spenser, William Percy, and some lesser writers—"Poetae Minimi."

———. "Shakespeare and the Earl of Pembroke," *Fortnightly Review*, 1898. LXIX, 210-223.

———. "Shakespeare and the Earl of Southampton," *Cornhill Magazine*, 1898. LXXVII, N. S. IV, 482-495.

LEISHMAN, JAMES BLAIR. *Themes and Variations on Shakespeare's Sonnets*. New York: Hilary House, 1962. An illustration of the parallels to Shakespeare's sonnets in the poems and sonnets of his predecessors, including Horace, Ovid, and Tasso.

PALMER, GEORGE HERBERT. *Intimations of Immortality in the Sonnets of Shakespeare*. Boston: Houghton, Mifflin, 1912. "A small band of readers addicted to the sonnets make a hushed company of almost religious devotees."

ROBERTSON, JOHN MACKINNON. *The Problems of Shakespeare's Sonnets*. London: G. Routledge, 1926. Expressions of doubt of the genuineness of many of the sonnets, on the grounds of inferior style.

———. *Shakespeare and Chapman*. London: T. F. Unwin, 1917.

ROLLINS, HYDER E., Ed. *A Variorum Edition of Shakespeare: The Sonnets*. 2 vols. Philadelphia: Lippincott, 1944.

XROWSE, A. L. *William Shakespeare, A Biography*. New York: Harper & Row, 1964. An ardent advocate of Southampton as the Friend, Rowse finds the Earl's influence in many of Shakespeare's early plays.

TYLER, THOMAS. *The Herbert-Fitton Theory of Shakespeare's Sonnets; A Reply*. London: D. Nutt, 1898. Extended "proof" that the Earl of Pembroke was the Friend of the sonnets, and Mary Fitton the Dark Lady.

WELLS, H. W. "A New Preface to Shakespeare's Sonnets," *The* (New York) *Shakespeare Association Bulletin*, 1937. XII, 128 ff.

XWILSON, JOHN DOVER. *An Introduction to the Sonnets of Shakespeare*. New York: Cambridge University Press, 1964. A reasoned advocacy of Pembroke's candidacy for the friend.

PATIENTIA EST ORNAMENTVM CVSTO DIA ET PROTECTIO VITAE.